Praise for *Transforming Supply Ch*

'One of the most insightful books in supply chain management this decade. From providing a deep understanding of the new drivers that shape value chains and entirely new perspectives on market research and segmentation, to new concepts in overarching business strategy development. The way in which these forces shape business and supply chain strategy is brilliantly explained. The book covers all these concepts with a fresh perspective on customer-centric behavior, channels to market, and how to align internal culture to outside realities. It is also probably one of the first books to cover the new world of Industry 4.0 and its impact on supply chains in great detail, as well as giving us a view of how this will shape supply chains in the future.'
Dr Jan Havenga, Professor, Logistics; Director, SCM Centre, Stellenbosch University, Cape Town, South Africa

'*Transforming Supply Chains* causes one to think comprehensively in aligning data-driven supply chains and related technology to meet the increasing demands of the segmented customer base in an ever-changing and increasingly efficient and service-oriented environment.'
Gregory J. Owens, Former Global Head of SCM, Accenture; CEO, Manugistics; Chairman and CEO, Iron Planet, Senoia, Georgia, USA

'Since enterprises have complex goals they are likely to have complex challenges. *Transforming Supply Chains* gives you fresh insights on how to optimize the complexity of large enterprises. Gattorna and Ellis have anchored their perspectives on optimization in the customer/market, rather than in efficiency and cost. This book helps you identify how your company's supply chains can drive better digital and physical customer experiences. A key message is – if you want to get some control over disruption – then it's best to disrupt your own organization and do it by bringing the voice of the customer into supply chain decision making. This belongs in the library of any business executive.'
Dr Lloyd Vogelman, CEO Corteks Company, Sydney, Australia

'Customer expectations and business dynamics are changing on almost every level – if you agree and are looking for a playbook for kick starting your supply chain transformation, look no further, this is it. Backed by real-world case studies, time-tested research, and thought-provoking insights, this is a one-of-a-kind guide you simply must read – and then share with your team!'
Bill Marrin, Director, World 50, Inc., Atlanta, Georgia, USA

'The authors set the scene for this book very well, referencing topical events that are currently interrupting global supply chains, i.e. the potential trade war between the US and China; unpredictable decisions by the Trump Administration; and Brexit. Then follows a sequence of suggested methodologies to counter the disruptive effects of these and other events, e.g. "outside-in" thinking and the Dynamic Alignment™ model; AI, digitization, IoT, Blockchain, all of which are designed to assist us to cope with the new era of volatility. The authors are genuine SC "thought leaders" for this contribution.'
Christina Huang, GM, Bright Blue Sea Global Supply Chain Management Co., Shenzhen, China

'*Transforming Supply Chains* will provide useful frameworks to kickstart practitioner thinking around end-to-end supply chains for years to come. With over 100 helpful pictorial summaries or concept visualizations, this book provides a high-level map of the transformation

process and detailed trail guides (to use a mountaineering metaphor) to help prepare you and your teams for the challenge ahead.'
Mary Long, former VP Logistics and Network Planning, Domino's;
Managing Director, Global Supply Chain Forum,
The Haslam College of Business, University of Tennessee, Knoxville, Tennessee,
USA

'Does your supply chain efficiently, effectively, and in real time meet the heterogeneous customer and consumer demand for personalization and seamless experience, on-line and off-line?
If your answer is NO, you should consider adopting the author's Dynamic Alignment™ model and genuinely transforming your strategy and organization. To guide you in your transformation journey, reading this book should be on the top of your "to do" list.'
Dr Jerry Wind, The Lauder Professor Emeritus and Professor of Marketing at the
Wharton School,
University of Pennsylvania, Philadelphia, USA

'The authors correctly point out that supply chains cannot continue to operate in isolation – ignoring geopolitics, climate change, social media and fragmenting consumer behaviors. The book defines new ways of incorporating these factors into supply chain design and daily operations. An important read for any supply chain professional and C-level executive who wants to understand how supply chains can create competitive advantage in a fast-changing world.'
Dave Anderson, Managing General Partner, Supply Chain Ventures,
Biddeford, Maine, USA

'With tried and tested frameworks, Dr Gattorna and Deborah Ellis provide a solid basis to move forward to embrace digital supply chains and face the future bravely. Comprehensive, generous and up-to-date with the latest thinking, their book and its points of learning give confidence to those embarking on a transformational journey. I particularly like the visual aids to "Kick-start your thinking" at the end of each chapter as they bring clarity on what to do next through prompting self-reflection and discovery.'
Dr Ivana Crestani, Director, The Ryder Self Group,
Sydney, Australia

'*Transforming Supply Chains* is a *must read* for executives seeking to better navigate and adapt to the digital world we are living in. Relevant and timely insights from two highly respected thought leaders in the global supply chain domain.'
Richard H. Thompson, International Director,
Supply Chain & Logistics Solutions, JLL, Chicago, USA

'Business success in today's volatile and uncertain world is increasingly dependent upon supply chains that are capable of adapting to rapidly changing conditions. As John Gattorna and Deborah Ellis point out in this insightful book few companies are equipped to respond to the challenges presented by the dawning of the digital age.
This is a book with great relevance to all business leaders who are seeking to find practical ways to future-proof their supply chains.'
Dr Martin Christopher, Emeritus Professor of Marketing and Logistics,
Cranfield School of Management, Cranfield University, Bedford, UK

Transforming Supply Chains

Pearson

Transforming
Supply Chains

**REALIGN YOUR BUSINESS TO BETTER SERVE
CUSTOMERS IN A DISRUPTIVE WORLD**

John Gattorna and Deborah Ellis

Pearson

Harlow, England • London • New York • Boston • San Francisco • Toronto • Sydney • Dubai • Singapore • Hong Kong
Tokyo • Seoul • Taipei • New Delhi • Cape Town • São Paulo • Mexico City • Madrid • Amsterdam • Munich • Paris • Milan

PEARSON EDUCATION LIMITED
KAO Two
KAO Park
Harlow
CM17 9SR
United Kingdom
Tel: +44 (0)1279 623623
Web: www.pearson.com/uk

First edition published 2020 (print and electronic)

© Pearson Education Limited 2020 (print and electronic)

The rights of John Gattorna and Deborah Ellis to be identified as authors of this work have been asserted by them in accordance with the Copyright, Designs and Patents Act 1988.

ISBN: 978-1-292-28684-6 (print)
   978-1-292-28685-3 (PDF)
   978-1-292-28686-0 (ePub)

British Library Cataloguing-in-Publication Data
A catalogue record for the print edition is available from the British Library

Library of Congress Cataloging-in-Publication Data
A catalog record for the print edition is available from the Library of Congress
10 9 8 7 6 5 4 3 2 1
23 22 21 20 19

Cover image © Miemo Penttinen – miemo.net/Moment/Getty Image

Print edition typeset in 10/14 and Plantin MT Pro by SPi Global
Printed by Ashford Colour Press Ltd, Gosport

NOTE THAT ANY PAGE CROSS REFERENCES REFER TO THE PRINT EDITION

To Ella, Charlotte, Jake and Johnny, our family's next generation of digital natives.
JG

To Peter and Team Ellis, my steadfast supporters.
DE

Contents

CONTENTS

About the authors

Dr John Gattorna

John Gattorna has been working in and around enterprise supply chains since 1975. In the intervening four decades he has been focused on giving the study and practice of supply chain management some badly needed conceptual depth in order to made it a more predictive field of endeavor rather than just operations-focused.

Once he and his co-workers, including Deborah Ellis, had developed the whole-of-enterprise Dynamic Alignment™ concept, he set about to test this model at every opportunity inside global companies in order to make it more granular, and therefore usable. The current model is very refined, and is being applied by some of the best global companies with significant success.

John's 'outside-in' philosophy is now being adopted by many of those who have followed his work over the years. He has written several books and plans to write more as the currently emerging digital world unfolds before our eyes. He lives in Sydney, Australia, is married to Lea, and has two sons, two daughters-in-law, two granddaughters and two grandsons.

John can be reached at john@gattornaalignment.com.

Deborah Ellis

For more than twenty years Deborah Ellis has consulted with companies aiming to lift their supply chain and logistics performance. She has led projects in Europe, USA, China, India and South America, as well as in her home base of Australia, for leading companies including Schneider Electric, Cochlear, Shell, Ralph Lauren, DHL and Unilever. She has also been engaged in industry-level supply chain projects in agriculture, mining, cash distribution and fashion.

Deborah has contributed chapters and articles on supply chain topics including network design, humanitarian logistics, blockchain, reverse logistics, and the future role of the supply chain, and has presented at international conferences on a range of supply chain–related subjects.

Earlier in her career Deborah held operational roles in logistics with the Swire Group and Mars. Her academic background is in Economics. She lives in Sydney, Australia, with her patient husband, and has three wonderful sons.

Deborah can be reached at debellis@gattornaalignment.com.

Authors' acknowledgments

When conducting 'thought leadership' research in the supply chain domain you need 'laboratories' to work in, and these laboratories have been provided by the wonderful clients we have been fortunate enough to work with over the years. Clients such as Annette Clayton (CSCO and President NAM) and Stuart Whiting (SVP Logistics & Data) at Schneider Electric; Dr Kirsten Molloy (CEO), Jenny Francis and Chad Moffiet (Capacity Planning) at the Hunter Valley Coal Chain Co-ordinator (HVCCC), to mention just a few. We thank our visionary clients for engaging with us on the task of evolving future designs in the supply chain.

Likewise, with our global series of Supply Chain Retreats, conducted annually across the world in Sydney, Singapore, Amsterdam, and in 2019 in Cape Town and Hamburg as well, these small-group invited audiences provide us with direct feedback on our new developments, as well as provide the inspiration to continue, sometimes down different pathways. Thank you to the hundreds of top executives who have attended these pivotal events over the years.

Closer to home there is our own team to thank for their great work in preparing this book for publication – Anja Wolf, who leads much of our research, and Jacqui Turner, who covers all the administrative aspects – we thank you both very sincerely. You are both irreplaceable. And thanks also to Jodie Warters at Joco Design for your help with the associated design work.

At Pearson, Eloise Cook, Publisher, Trade, Consumer and Professional Business, worked on the concept of a short, easy-to-read supply chain book on the transformation topic from the start, supported by her colleagues who have joined the team as the process continued through to publication date – thank you for your combined time and effort on our behalf to produce this book as the very best it could be.

John Gattorna
Deborah Ellis

Publisher's acknowledgments

Text credits

1 Pearson Education, Inc: Gattorna, John, Dynamic Supply Chains, 3rd edn., FT Publishing, Harlow, 2015. **2 Pearson Education, Inc:** Gattorna, John, Dynamic Supply Chains, 3rd edn., FT Publishing, Harlow, 2015. **3 Pearson Education, Inc:** Gattorna, John, Dynamic Supply Chains, 3rd edn., FT Publishing, Harlow, 2015. **5 Pearson Education, Inc:** Gattorna, John, Dynamic Supply Chains, 3rd edn., FT Publishing, Harlow, 2015. **6 Pearson Education, Inc:** Gattorna, John, Dynamic Supply Chains, 3rd edn., FT Publishing, Harlow, 2015. **8 Pearson Education, Inc:** Gattorna, John, Dynamic Supply Chains, 3rd edn., FT Publishing, Harlow, 2015. **12 Pearson Education, Inc:** Adapted from Gattorna, John, Dynamic Supply Chains, 3rd edn., FT Publishing, Harlow, 2015, p.25. **15 Pearson Education, Inc:** Adapted from Gattorna, John, Dynamic Supply Chains, 3rd edn., FT Publishing, Harlow, 2015, p.29. **16 Pearson Education, Inc:** Adapted from Gattorna, John, Dynamic Supply Chains, 3rd edn., FT Publishing, Harlow, 2015, p.47. **17 Pearson Education, Inc:** Gattorna, John, Dynamic Supply Chains, 3rd edn., FT Publishing, Harlow, 2015. **20 Pearson Education, Inc:** Adapted from Figure 2.4 in Gattorna, John, Dynamic Supply Chains, 3rd edn., FT Publishing, Harlow, 2015, p.58. **24 Pearson Education, Inc:** Gattorna, John, Dynamic Supply Chains, 3rd edn., FT Publishing, Harlow, 2015. **27 Pearson Education, Inc:** This is an updated version of the methodology first published in Gattorna, John, Dynamic Supply Chains, 3rd edn., FT Publishing, Harlow, 2015, Figure 2.14, p.78. **29 Pearson Education, Inc:** Adapted from Christopher, Martin, Logistics and Supply Chain Management, 5th edn., FT Prentice Hall, Harlow, 2016, p.37. **31 Pearson Education, Inc:** Adapted from Gattorna, John, Dynamic Supply Chains, 3rd edn., FT Publishing, Harlow, 2015, p.64. **35 Pearson Education, Inc:** Adapted from Gattorna, John, Dynamic Supply Chains, 3rd edn., FT Publishing, Harlow, 2015, p.58. **37 Pearson Education, Inc:** Gattorna, John, Dynamic Supply Chains, 3rd edn., FT Publishing, Harlow,

2015. **42 Pearson Education, Inc:** Adapted from Gattorna, John, Dynamic Supply Chains, 3rd edn., FT Publishing, Harlow, 2015, p.381. **43 Pearson Education, Inc:** Adapted from Gattorna, John, Dynamic Supply Chains, 3rd edn., FT Publishing, Harlow, 2015, p.381. **43 Pearson Education, Inc:** Gattorna, John, Dynamic Supply Chains, 3rd edn., FT Publishing, Harlow, 2015. **51 Pearson Education, Inc:** Adapted from Gattorna, John, Dynamic Supply Chains, 3rd edn., FT Publishing, Harlow, 2015, p.202. **56 Pearson Education, Inc:** Adapted from Gattorna, John, Dynamic Supply Chains, 3rd edn., FT Publishing, Harlow, 2015, p.242. **57 Pearson Education, Inc:** Adapted from Gattorna, John, Dynamic Supply Chains, 3rd edn., FT Publishing, Harlow, 2015, p.282. **60 Pearson Education, Inc:** Gattorna, John, Dynamic Supply Chains, 3rd edn., FT Publishing, Harlow, 2015. **71 Pearson Education, Inc:** Gattorna, John, Dynamic Supply Chains, 3rd edn., FT Publishing, Harlow, 2015, p.404. **80 Pearson Education, Inc:** Gattorna, John, Dynamic Supply Chains, 3rd edn., FT Publishing, Harlow, 2015. **86 Pearson Education, Inc:** Adapted from Gattorna, John, Dynamic Supply Chains, 3rd edn., FT Publishing, Harlow, 2015, p.64. **100 Pearson Education, Inc:** Gattorna, John, Dynamic Supply Chains, 3rd edn., FT Publishing, Harlow, 2015. **106 Iyad Mourtada:** Based on Iyad Mourtada, "Omni Channel Retail: The future of retail", https://www.shopify.com.au/retail/119924675-10-slideshare-presentations-on-the-future-of-omni-channel-retail. **111 Pearson Education, Inc:** Gattorna, John, Dynamic Supply Chains, 3rd edn., FT Publishing, Harlow, 2015. **117 Pearson Education, Inc:** Adapted from Gattorna, John, Dynamic Supply Chains, 3rd edn., FT Publishing, Harlow, 2015, p.111. **118 Pearson Education, Inc:** Gattorna, John, Dynamic Supply Chains, 3rd edn., FT Publishing, Harlow, 2015. **122 Pearson Education, Inc:** Adapted from Gattorna, John, Dynamic Supply Chains, 3rd edn., FT Publishing, Harlow, 2015, p.206. **124 Pearson Education, Inc:** Adapted from Gattorna, John, Dynamic Supply Chains, 3rd edn., FT Publishing, Harlow, 2015, p.245. **125 Pearson Education, Inc:** Adapted from Gattorna, John, Dynamic Supply Chains, 3rd edn., FT Publishing, Harlow, 2015, p.245. **127 Pearson Education, Inc:** Adapted from Gattorna, John, Dynamic Supply Chains, 3rd edn., FT Publishing, Harlow, 2015, p.327. **128 Pearson Education, Inc:** Adapted from Gattorna, John, Dynamic Supply Chains, 3rd edn., FT Publishing, Harlow, 2015, p.360. **130**

Pearson Education, Inc: Adapted from Gattorna, John, Dynamic Supply Chains, 3rd edn., FT Publishing, Harlow, 2015, p.149. **131 Pearson Education, Inc:** Gattorna, John, Dynamic Supply Chains, 3rd edn., FT Publishing, Harlow, 2015. **132 Pearson Education, Inc:** Gattorna, John, Dynamic Supply Chains, 3rd edn., FT Publishing, Harlow, 2015. **133 Pearson Education, Inc:** Gattorna, John, Dynamic Supply Chains, 3rd edn., FT Publishing, Harlow, 2015. **134 Pearson Education, Inc:** Gattorna, John, Dynamic Supply Chains, 3rd edn., FT Publishing, Harlow, 2015. **134 Harvard Business Publishing:** Based on Managing your innovations portfolio, Harvard Business Review p.69, May 2012. **136 Harvard Business Publishing:** Based on The Design of Business by Roger Martin (Harvard Business Press, 2009), Figure 2.1, page 54. **137 Pearson Education, Inc:** Gattorna, John, Dynamic Supply Chains, 3rd edn., FT Publishing, Harlow, 2015. **138 DHL International GmbH:** DHL Trend Research (2018), Logistics Trend Radar, p.15. http://www.dhl.com/en/about_us/logistics_insights/dhl_trend_research/trendradar.html#.W5d3IgzY2w. **139 Pearson Education, Inc:** Gattorna, John, Dynamic Supply Chains, 3rd edn., FT Publishing, Harlow, 2015. **140 Pearson Education, Inc:** Gattorna, John, Dynamic Supply Chains, 3rd edn., FT Publishing, Harlow, 2015. **142 Pearson Education, Inc:** Gattorna, John, Dynamic Supply Chains, 3rd edn., FT Publishing, Harlow, 2015. **145 Pearson Education, Inc:** Gattorna, John, Dynamic Supply Chains, 3rd edn., FT Publishing, Harlow, 2015. **149 Pearson Education, Inc:** Gattorna, John, Dynamic Supply Chains, 3rd edn., FT Publishing, Harlow, 2015. **150 KNEX, Inc:** Reproduced with Permission, KNEX, Inc, 2018. **153 Cryptonomos:** https://ins.world/INS-ICO-Whitepaper.pdf. **156 Pearson Education, Inc:** Gattorna, John, Dynamic Supply Chains, 3rd edn., FT Publishing, Harlow, 2015. **156 Pearson Education, Inc:** Gattorna, John, Dynamic Supply Chains, 3rd edn., FT Publishing, Harlow, 2015. **157 Pearson Education, Inc:** Gattorna, John, Dynamic Supply Chains, 3rd edn., FT Publishing, Harlow, 2015. **158 Pearson Education, Inc:** Gattorna, John, Dynamic Supply Chains, 3rd edn., FT Publishing, Harlow, 2015. **162 Penguin Random House:** Friedman, Thomas L., in conversation with Teller, Eric, Thank you for being late, Allen Lane, Penguin Random House, UK, 2016, p.35. **162 Penguin Random House:** Friedman, T., Thank you for being late, Allen Lane – Penguin Random House,

UK, 2016, p.36. **165 Kogan Page Ltd:** Khan, Omera, Product design and the supply chain: competing through design, Kogan Page, Gt. Britain, 2019, p.31. **165 Hachette Book Group:** Adapted from Fine, C. H. (1998). Clock Speed: Winning Industry Control in the Age of Temporary Advantage, Basic Books, p. 146. **166 California Management Review:** Based on Blackburn, J. D., Guide, D. R. Jr., Souza, G. C., Van Wassenhove, L. N. (2004). Reverse Supply Chains for Commercial Returns. California Management Review, Berkeley 46.2, p. 6-22. **167 Pearson Education, Inc:** Adapted from Christopher, M. (2011). Logistics & Supply Chain Management. Fourth Edition. Prentice Hall, p.132-133. **169 Pearson Education, Inc:** Christopher, M. (2011). Logistics & Supply Chain Management, 4th edn., Prentice Hall, p.126. **171 Hachette Book Group:** Adapted from Fine, C.H., (1998), Clock Speed: Winning Industry Control in the Age of Temporary Advantage, Basic Books, Cambridge, MA, p.71. **173 Pearson Education, Inc:** Adapted from Figure 1.1, Gattorna, John, Dynamic Supply Chains, 3rd edn., FT Publishing, Harlow, 2015. **176 Harvard Business School Publishing:** Rigby, Darrell K., Sutherland, Jeff, and Noble, Andy, 'Agile Scale: how to go from a few teams to hundreds', Harvard Business Review, May-June, 2018, pps. 88-96. **177 Pearson Education, Inc:** Adapted from Figure 1.1, Gattorna, John, Dynamic Supply Chains, 3rd edn., FT Publishing, Harlow, 2015. **178 Siemens AG:** Press Release, Siemens AG website, 1 August, 2018. **178 Pearson Education, Inc:** Sourced from Gattorna, John, Dynamic Supply Chains, 3rd edn., FT Publishing, Harlow, 2015, pps., 426-431 following an earlier site visit to Inditex in La Coruna. **184 Pearson Education, Inc:** Gattorna, John, Dynamic Supply Chains, 3rd edn., FT Publishing, Harlow, 2015. **187 Massachusetts Institute of Technology:** Based on Clayton M. Christensen, Thomas Bartman, and Derek van Bever, MIT Sloan Magazine, 'The Hard Truth About Business Model Innovation', Fall 2016 Issue. **193 Pearson Education, Inc:** Gattorna, John, Dynamic Supply Chains, 3rd edn., FT Publishing, Harlow, 2015. **195 Pearson Education, Inc:** Gattorna, John, Dynamic Supply Chains, 3rd edn., FT Publishing, Harlow, 2015. **196 Pearson Education, Inc:** Gattorna, John, Dynamic Supply Chains, 3rd edn., FT Publishing, Harlow, 2015. **197 Pearson Education, Inc:** Gattorna, John, Dynamic Supply Chains, 3rd edn., FT Publishing, Harlow, 2015. **198 Pearson Education, Inc:** Gattorna, John, Dynamic Supply

Chains, 3rd edn., FT Publishing, Harlow, 2015. **205 Fortune Media IP Limited:** Thomas Friedman: We're in the Middle of 3 Climate Changes, Not Just 1 By ARIC JENKINS July 18, 2018

Photo credits
148 123RF: Scott Betts/123RF. **149 Shutterstock:** Leightonoc/Shutterstock

A word about the title

Time to stop, rethink and transform

During the conduct of our 2017 and 2018 Global Supply Chain 'thought leadership' Retreat Series in Sydney, Singapore, Hong Kong and Amsterdam, the one topic that kept coming up in conversation was '*transformation*'. It seemed as though all the senior executives attending these various locations had '*transformation*' on their minds, as they became increasingly aware of the growing volatility in their respective markets.

For some, they were just beginning to think about how to redesign their legacy supply chain networks. For others, they were already well into the journey, some as much as seven years, and they were the ones who knew how hard the transition was. Those who hadn't started had no idea of what was ahead of them. No pain, no gain as they say!

So, this got our attention. Maybe we should write a book entirely focused on how to design and execute the transformation of enterprise supply chains. Of course, we already knew from experience with some of our global clients, who had been on this journey for a number of years, that when you set out to transform your supply chains, in effect you are transforming the entire enterprise. It is as all-encompassing as that. So, it's not something for the faint-hearted to undertake. You have to go in with your eyes wide open and be prepared to demonstrate relentless leadership.

The previous book by one of our co-authors (Gattorna, 2015) described in great detail how to design and manage people-centric value networks.[1] It introduced several frameworks to guide executives in this task, including our proprietary Dynamic Alignment™ model, supported by Design Thinking. And it set out what the configuration of the five major types of supply chain configurations might look like. But it didn't focus down on the specific task of reinventing and transforming the current supply chain capability.

Given the rapid increase in volatility in the operating environment in most markets in the intervening four years, and the direct feedback from attendees at our global Retreats, we saw a distinct gap. What executives needed was a short, succinct guide on how they might go about re-designing their supply chain networks and, just as importantly, how to get these designs fully implemented in quick time. Time is the enemy in these days of increasing digitization.

Hence, the idea for this book rapidly grew in our minds, enthusiastically supported by Eloise Cook, Publisher at Pearson. The exact title took some time to agree, but emerged as: *Transforming supply chains: realign your business to better serve customers in a disruptive world.*

Admittedly, this is a bit of a mouthful, but it says it all. That's what this book is trying to do for our reader community and followers in the supply chain domain, everywhere. And we think it is very timely because nothing comparable exists in print at this time. A genuine guide book of sorts, written in plain language, as free as possible of jargon. We hope you enjoy reading it as much as we have enjoyed writing it.

John Gattorna & Deborah Ellis
Sydney
1 January 2019

Foreword

first met Dr John Gattorna and his colleague, Deborah Ellis, at the inaugural LLamasoft Summer Conference on Supply Chain Design in 2011, Ann Arbor, Michigan. It was to become a momentous occasion, but I had no reason to know that at the time.

It was a beautiful blue-sky Michigan morning. The late spring sun was shining brightly but hadn't yet cooked off the residual chill of the early morning mist. A few summer school students were coolly ambling along the sidewalks of the University of Michigan campus, but I was already sweating as I pinged along the sidewalks towards my destination.

Over the previous 10-plus years, I had watched the company I started in my apartment, grow from an implausible infant idea to a tight toddling team, entering an adolescent arrogance that we might, just maybe, be on to something new and important. Like any lanky teen, we thought we could change the world, and we were the only ones who knew it. Naturally, it was time to throw a party and tell everyone else about it.

We believed that we had stumbled across an amazing new discovery: the application of *Design* with a capital-D to the supply chain management task. While the rest of the supply chain field was on their hands and knees searching for pennies, pennies falling out of one lame-assed copycat continuous improvement effort after another, LLamasoft was about to ring in the revolution of 'design'. We knew that supply chain executives were desperate for big ideas, hungry for big changes, but they were trapped under the oppressive weight of incremental improvements, suffocating in stifling corporate boardrooms, gazing out their windows waiting for someone to save them with one big idea: supply chain performance was imprisoned by the original configurations that had grown up over time. This was the era of 'one-size-fits-all'. But to save the trees, you have to see the forest. Great supply chain planning could not move beyond the boundaries of current mediocre supply chain designs.

To fix the supply chain, you start with design.

We were on a mission, no doubt, as I powered to my destination to give my first keynote at LLamasoft's first conference on that June morning in 2011. Wiping the moisture from my brow, I felt we were about to change our corner of the world. As time would tell, I was wildly right and profoundly wrong at the same time.

My speech went well enough, the room was packed with our customers, and almost nobody fell asleep. I remember the thrill and awe of introducing Apollo 11 Astronaut Buzz Aldrin to the room, and the immense pride I felt at hearing him validate the importance of simulation modeling and analysis to designing supply chains.

A short time later, while decompressing, one of our executives introduced Dr John Gattorna to the stage. He was a 'well known thought leader in the supply chain space'. He had founded and grown a supply chain consulting company and subsequently started Accenture's supply chain practice in Asia; he had written several books and papers, and he was from Australia. Cool!

As John began to talk, I hadn't planned to pay much attention. I had customers and employees on my mind, and my CEO to-do list needed revising. After a few minutes, I happened to glance up from my laptop and saw four different time series shapes on the projected screen. I remember the heading as 'Demand Flow' types, and I immediately recognized these patterns. LLamasoft had worked on hundreds of supply chain design and optimization projects, across multiple industries, with companies around the world. These were the patterns we were starting to recognize, but hadn't even thought about grouping, much less classifying them.

I tuned in. John was talking about these demand patterns as an estab-lished fact. Different products in different industries tended to generate these demand behaviors. Some were highly variable; some were predictable; some lumpy; some were spikes out of nowhere. John was on slide 3, I believe, as he explained how he had already spent decades studying these behaviors, and their impact on supply chains. What I didn't know at the time was that his colleague and co-author of this book had been on most of the journey with him.

I wondered how far he would go, and as I thought about how far one might take this understanding of buyer behavior and its implications for supply chains, John was a mile ahead. He was already identifying how supply chain organizations evolve; how certain organization designs are better fits for certain segments. John profiled companies that had mismatched supply chain strategies and customer buying patterns, and had spent years slogging through the holy work of transforming supply chains from poor performers to examples of excellence. John studied leadership; he dug up details on IT systems and decision making. Most importantly, John and his close-knit team of co-workers didn't sit on the sidelines. They worked alongside leaders shoulder-to-shoulder, helping them get better, and documenting everything as they went, eventually publishing most of the insights gained.

John Gattorna grabbed my attention in 2011 and has never given it up. So few people in any professional field are capable of working hands-on in the trenches to change things, while simultaneously keeping their vision on the distant horizon. John combines thinking and doing, and his many decades of deep thinking and first-person experience have provided him with a perspective that I now clearly can name as wisdom.

LLamasoft went on to change the world, just as I had thought it might, though not always the way I thought it would. Supply Chain Design is not a new concept now; it wasn't a new concept then either. John was already living there, doing his best to tell anyone who would listen that long-term survival doesn't happen by accident. It happens by design. I'd like to think that LLamasoft was a good steward at carrying that message forward with tools and technology. We didn't invent supply chain design. But I hope we gave it a boost, and that that boost has helped highlight the need for executives to read, think and seek out wisdom from every available and respectable source.

If you want your organization to survive, you'll need to design it properly, and keep re-designing it, continuously as the operating environment changes before your eyes. Design is a journey that always moves you forward, to a goal you'll never reach; it's like a mirage, but you have to keep after it and not stand still. Reaching the end isn't the point. Designing means seeing the forest for the trees, envisioning the supply chain you must have instead of being imprisoned by the one you do have.

It's on this note that the latest work by John and his long-term collaborator, Deb Ellis (a deep thinker in her own right) is a welcome, indeed, necessary addition to the canon. The pace of transformation continues to shock and surprise us all. Transformation in the Digital Era means Continuous Transformation. John and Deb have offered this latest book, packed with wisdom, as a user's manual for executives with big minds and little time. I hope you'll see the ideas, practices and points-of-view that follow as a concentrated dose of answers for the current time. I hope you'll go on to take a deep dive into *Dynamic Supply Chains* and *Dynamic Supply Chain Alignment,* earlier books by John. I recommend that you make the time to do so, but if you don't, *Transforming Supply Chains* will change your thinking regardless.

The great system thinker Herbert Simon once wrote 'Everyone designs who devises courses of action aimed at changing existing situations into preferred ones.' Today's supply chains won't fix themselves, any more than today's problems will solve themselves.

Solve problems. See the big picture. Design a better future for your enterprise, its incumbent supply chains and the customers they serve.

Donald A. Hicks
Founder and Chairman of the Board
LLamasoft, Inc
Ann Arbor, Michigan
3 March, 2019

Preface

The value of 'thought leadership' in a supply chain context

'Thought leadership' in a supply chain context means making a conscious effort to advance the thinking, and seek new and innovative ideas, in what is a relatively young field of management science. The emphasis here is on 'the science'. In its short 50-year history, there have been periods in which development has been slow, usually coinciding with times of rapid growth in demand, where the natural reaction is simply to fulfil the sales coming towards the business, by any means possible. More recently volatility has become the major distraction. Unfortunately, in this hectic environment, few, if any, lessons are learnt for future application.

But, among all this noise surely there will be gems that can have a potentially major impact on the way we do business. Our job as 'thought leaders' is to find and apply these gems in the big haystack of global business and to suggest new ways to design and operate supply chains that are able to deal effectively with issues as they arise.

Business executives in industry and commerce rarely get an opportunity to stop, take stock and do some serious thinking about how they are approaching their role in the company. 'Thinking time' and the associated 'curiosity' is like gold to them. That is why we started our global series of Supply Chain 'thought leadership' Retreats in 2017 and have kept them going by popular acclaim. They now cover three main regions of the world, i.e. Asia Pacific (Sydney and Singapore), sub-Saharan Africa (Cape Town) and Europe (Amsterdam and Hamburg). Our specific intention is to do some of the heavy lifting on behalf of these busy executives, think about and test new ideas and methodologies, and present these in a concentrated format each year for an invited audience to reflect on and discuss with us and their peers. This is the way to learn, fast.

Consistent with this *'pushing the edge of the envelope'* philosophy, the reader will find that this book contains some strong *points of view* regarding future developments in the supply chain domain. One of these perspectives is the critical necessity to rise above the 'functional' thinking that has pervaded the domain since inception, epitomized by the one-size-fits-all configuration of yesteryear, and replace it with a cross-functional, multi-disciplinary mindset that requires the commitment of everyone in the enterprise. In effect, we are suggesting that enterprises embrace a genuine end-to-end (E2E) supply chain *philosophy*, for the sake of all stakeholders, and especially for the satisfaction of customers and consumers alike. They are, after all, the sole focus of our combined efforts.

As advisors and researchers, we have worked in this subject matter area for the last four decades and we see our role as one of breaking existing paradigms, formed in a different era, under very different operating conditions, and replacing them with new paradigms more relevant to the increasingly turbulent operating environments now being experienced. This is the 'new normal' of volatility as Christopher and Holweg describe it.[1]

We have set ourselves to go back to the fundamentals in the marketplace and surface the deep-rooted underlying expectations of customers, consumers and suppliers in an effort to develop heuristics that will, more precisely, guide future development of supply chain designs and operations and, coincidentally, offset the rapid onset of complexity. Complexity hampers progress! In the process, we have fully engaged with the idea of a E2E digitized supply chain in order to deliver the required visibility, transparency and provenance demanded by today's relentless consumers.

Furthermore, we contend that senior leaders working in the supply chain domain, everywhere, should take on the mantle of 'thought leaders' in their respective businesses, each seeking the *best solutions* for their unique situation. Remaining ever-curious is an important ingredient to future success in today's and tomorrow's world. We are not avid supporters of so-called 'best practice' because it can mean very different things in different operating environments, such that direct comparability remains an issue.

Through our applied research in the field, working with collaborative clients, supplemented by our annual global Supply Chain 'thought leadership' Retreats, we aim to help senior supply chain leaders reflect on where they sit along the development cycle and, just as importantly, where they should be aiming to get. Going from one state to the other is what we call 'transformation'.

Unfortunately, supply chain practitioners don't engage in enough research, primary or secondary, buried as they are in 'business-as-usual' activity. But with the urgent push now evident for more innovation in the way we design and operate our supply chains, senior leaders need to pay much more attention to this strategic imperative. It is an activity that should run in parallel with business-as-usual, and inform the latter from time to time.

Our work in this space is designed to accelerate the innovation adoption process and raise the performance of supply chains everywhere, for the benefit of the companies involved and for society at large. After all, supply chains are all-pervasive and omni-present in that they support the very existence of our modern lifestyle.

John Gattorna & Deborah Ellis
Sydney
1 January, 2019

Introduction

ince the turn of the century, everything in life has seemingly acceler-
ated. Customers going online have become increasingly demanding
and the operating environment has become progressively more complex.
Indeed, traditional supply chains don't work any more or have problems that
negatively impact customers down the chain. This means that companies
wishing to survive and thrive in the coming decades must *transform* themselves, continuously, in order to become more agile and market responsive.

The problem is: where to start this transformation journey? We all pay
lip service to being *customer-centric*, but the reality is that most of the world's
large corporations have built up their logistics networks (and, by extension,
their enterprise supply chains) over many years of sunk investment, pursuing
the flawed philosophy of 'one-size-fits-all'.

For a while, and particularly during periods of high growth, this approach
seemed to work. But we are now seeing and experiencing increasing turbulence in practically all our major industries, which is leading to costly mis-
alignments between suppliers and their customers/end users. The world is
no longer as forgiving as it was just a few decades ago.

The solution to this dilemma is twofold: 1. adopt an *'outside-in'* perspective of your market by seeing the world through the lens of your customers;
and 2. using the insights gained in this way, reverse engineer the capabilities
inside your enterprise to align more precisely with customers' expectations
in your target markets. This sounds easy on the surface, but it is actually
quite difficult to do because it requires a 180° mindset shift.

Through several decades of research in the field, we have developed a
solution to the above stated problem; we call it Dynamic Alignment™. This
is our proprietary framework, which *directly* links the target market, bridging
operational strategies, internal cultural capability and the leadership styles
inside the enterprise.

The model starts by examining the structure of the market and segmenting customers' expectations into not one, but several dominant buying behaviors. These are a manifestation of the unchanging expectations that customers develop over time. Once we have identified how the target market is structured in terms of the different groups of behaviors present, we can develop matching *value propositions* and corresponding operational strategies for each behavioral segment.

Again, using the behavioral segments as a *frame-of-reference*, we are able to work back inside the business, developing the appropriate set of internal capabilities and corresponding subcultures for the customer set identified in the external market, i.e. a 'mirroring' effect. All this activity is driven and, ultimately, shaped by the leadership team, with one eye on the external market. That's why we think leadership is so pivotal to success in business and commerce today and going forward.

In effect, we are hardwiring the enterprise to address up to five dominant buying behaviors (instead of one under the current regime), with the embedded *flex* to handle those customers who change their primary buying behaviors under changed operating conditions or have several different buying behaviors according to the different product/service categories being purchased at the time. Hence the need for a *dynamic* solution. Static, set-and-forget solutions are totally ineffective in the 'new normal' of volatility. We must match *volatility* with faster internal rhythms – we call these faster rhythms *clockspeed*.

For those that follow this prescription, the rewards are significant. It allows us to escape from the twin evils of over- and under-servicing, which we were exposed to in the one-size-fits-all approach and, instead, reallocate our limited resources according to the actual customer expectations in front of us. This leads directly to greater customer satisfaction and a corresponding lift in revenue as a result of the greater attention paid to our best customers and a reduction in cost-to-serve as we withdraw service from those customers who have hitherto been over-serviced, and generally unappreciative of this extra effort on our behalf. The word to describe this much sought-after condition is *precision*!

In cases where we have implemented this genuinely customer-centric design, it has been possible to increase margins appreciably in a relatively short time and, in one case, to double margins within a year.

But this requires a concerted effort, at all levels of the enterprise. On the outside, we have to get closer to our customers (and suppliers) and, using the data obtained through field research and/or analytics, begin the process of reshaping our internal capabilities, i.e. organization design; processes; technology mix; KPIs; talent selection; etc. In other words, the enterprise must inject itself with the virus of *change* as the antidote to the *status quo* and go much further, actively embracing continuous innovation as a way to offset the potential negative impact of increased disruptions in the marketplace.

Consistent with the roadmap laid out above, Chapter 1 is a call to action in a world some would say has gone mad.

In Chapter 2, we offer a suggested solution that, in effect, becomes our compass as we set out to navigate the choppy seas constantly shifting before our eyes. We must find *heuristics* through which to filter the way we see the world and, in the process, find patterns that will, in turn, help us reduce the mounting complexity.

In Chapter 3, drawing on the work of Roger Martin and the development of 'design thinking', we propose one such heuristic (or filter) in the form of our own proprietary Dynamic Alignment™ framework – three decades in the making – to help us navigate through the maze separating us from our customers.

Through use of this heuristic, we discovered the five archetypal supply chain types and each of these is described in detail in Chapter 4. Together, they provide the *flex* we need to service the ever-moving customer and end consumer.

Chapters 5–8 describe the additional dimensions necessary to make these supply chain types function at a faster *clockspeed*, i.e. data analytics and faster decision making (Chapter 5); proactive responses to the new omni-channel world (Chapter 6); shaping of critical internal capabilities and the role of leadership (Chapter 7); and digitization in all its forms (Chapter 8). We now live in a digital world and, if you are not digitizing your E2E supply chain, you are fast becoming irrelevant.

Chapter 9 attacks the difficult task of convincing the C-level that nothing good will happen unless they adopt a fully end-to-end supply chain *philosophy* that is shared and contributed to by all functions in the business. This is what will drive the horizontal flow of products and services across the entire organization to meet the full spectrum of customers' expectations, day-to-day.

Chapter 10 sets out a vision of future go-to-market business models, where traditional rivalries are subjugated to the desire for scale and increased competitiveness. Getting into bed with strange bedfellows is to be expected in this future world.

On that note, we end with Chapter 11 by outlining exactly what the '*as is*' and '*to be*' conditions look like in an enterprise undergoing genuine, as distinct from superficial, *transformation*. All the moving parts must be in synch and, overall, the organization has to find a balance between 'business as usual' and the 'innovation initiatives' that will secure the business into the foreseeable future.

So, the suggested mantra going forward should be: *Think customer; act digital!*

CHAPTER 1

Adapt or die – the problems facing traditional supply chains

Surviving in today's fast-moving topsy-turvy world

Introduction

As we approach the end of the second decade of the 21st century, the words of Bob Dylan in his album of the same name, *The World Gone Wrong*,[1] are ringing in our ears.

The impact of political instability around the world is impeding the efforts of global companies to efficiently drive cross-border trade. It will also disrupt global sourcing strategies designed to make in-bound supply chains leaner through accessibility to a greater diversity of sources. Indeed, 'political risk is the new normal, as regulatory changes, both foreign and domestic, challenge global supply chains'.[2] To this we would add another source of disruption that is not so evident – the increasing administrative burden of monitoring and complying to constantly shifting government policies at the micro level.[3]

Donald Trump's years in the White House have led to the undoing of long-standing multi-lateral trade agreements and, worse, US-led trade wars with China and other major trading countries. 'Left unchecked, these . . . could threaten the global trade order, leaving casualties in disrupted supply chains that will hurt US companies . . .'[4]

The automotive industry is a prime example of how trade wars can disrupt global supply chains. For example, a car assembled in the US might have its engine manufactured in Germany, its transmission system from Mexico and its GPS from South Korea.[5] Such a sophisticated supply chain network, formed over many years of globalization, is difficult to unwind quickly. One large multinational industrial company, which manufactures in the US for the domestic market and imports some componentry from outside sources, has seen its costs jump by $100 million per annum because of the new raft of tariffs introduced in 2018. Surely this is an example of the dysfunctional impact of such policies, which in turn lead to higher prices for the US user/consumer.

On top of trade wars, the UK decision to leave the EU (Brexit) has only compounded matters. 'Supply chains across Britain and the EU appear to be splitting apart, with companies betting that trade barriers will materialise after Brexit.'[6] 'Splitting existing supply chains on both sides of the channel is likely to raise costs and reduce efficiency, and will be particularly important in complicated manufacturing sectors such as the automotive sector.[7] All this uncertainty is the enemy of efficient supply chains! Supply chains work best in a predictable operating environment, a condition that is becoming increasingly rare these days.

All the above concerns are well summed up by Michael Lewis in his book, *The Fifth Risk*.[8] He is interviewing John MacWilliams, a US Department of Energy (DOE) employee, and asks him about the risks the world faces in this dangerous period that we live in. John MacWilliams gives him a long list of risks that we face, but, in particular, he specifies the *fifth risk*, i.e. 'the risk a society runs when it falls into the habit of responding to long-term risks, with short-term solutions'. How true that is, and how well this description fits the world we live in right now, with governments everywhere failing the 'leadership test'. This leaves a big vacuum, which in turn must be filled as best as possible by leaders in the industrial world, outside of government.

Lewis goes on to say that '. . . it is the innovation that never occurs, and the knowledge that was never created, because you have ceased to lay the groundwork for it. It is what you never learned that might have saved you'.[9] His words apply across the full spectrum of society, but here we would like to apply them to global supply chains, because they are so pervasive in our lives, and pose an existential risk if not developed sufficiently in order to stay ahead of the demands of our current standard of living.

Globalization as we know it also is under threat through the rapid rise of *nationalism* and, as a result, supply chain networks are threatened with fragmentation, everywhere. Indeed, it appears that the global elite have been caught out completely by developments such as Brexit and the rise of Donald Trump, largely '. . . because these events simply did not fit the mental model of the world so many of us have worked with for the past several decades'.[10] So is it likely that the same elites are in danger of missing the possible *deglobalization* movement that is building in countries across the world and, in the process, not making appropriate plans?[11]

The effects of climate change on corporate supply chains

As the physical effects of climate change worsen, particularly changes in weather and water patterns, many industries are exposed to high risks. Food and agribusinesses are particularly vulnerable.[12] Some companies are acting now rather than waiting until things worsen beyond the point of recovery. For example, IKEA, the world's largest furniture manufacturer/retailer has '. . . pledged to use renewable and recycled materials in products as part of a plan to have a positive impact on the world's climate by the end of the next decade'.[13]

Likewise, Apple, Google, Microsoft and Amazon have committed to continue to fight climate change.[14] And German sportswear company, Adidas, has specific plans to cut waste in its manufacturing processes.[15]

This is very good news because the leadership shown by these big brands surely will influence others to follow suit in their respective industries. Interestingly, it appears to be the big corporates showing the way in lieu of the distinct inaction on the part of governments. This trend appears to signal renewed interest by corporates in 'sustainability'. According to Robert Eccles, *et al.,* '. . . companies that adopted environmental, social and governance policies in the 1990s have outperformed those that didn't'.[16] Who would have thought!

More recently, the wildfires in Southern California have severely disrupted logistics in that State by closing down goods' movements. And these types of unplanned events are likely to continue, albeit at an increasing rate. Those in charge of supply chain design and operations everywhere must, therefore, rethink how to operate in the immediate and longer-term futures.

Technology as a disrupter and solution provider

In terms of a disrupter, you don't have to look any further than the Apple iPhone, born in 2007. This one device single-handedly upended several industries, i.e. the PC market; telecoms; entertainment; gaming; and healthcare with, most probably, more to follow. So, technology as a 'disrupter' is not a bad thing, but it does mean big adjustments have to be made by the affected parties.

In his book, *Thank You For Being Late*,[17] Thomas Friedman charts the path of technological change against human adaptability, and finds that we are badly lagging behind.[18] His solution is to 'learn faster and govern smarter' to get back on the [technology] curve. In many ways, this is a great demonstration of Ashby's Law of Requisite Variety,[19] where the forces of complexity and sophistication fight it out to establish dominance over the other, albeit for only short time intervals. In the current situation, therefore, technology can be viewed both as a disrupter and a potential solution to disruption of all kinds. Later in the book, we will see evidence of how technology can be our friend in bringing sophisticated solutions to the fore and helping us to run our supply chains at a faster tempo.

Nonetheless, it is amazing how far we have come in a few short years. One of the co-authors of this book met Buzz Aldrin at the first Llamasoft SummerCon in Ann Arbor in 2011, and he related the story of how the Apple iPhone, as we know it today, has many times the computing power of the Eagle landing craft that landed on the Moon in 1969!

The task before us, therefore, is to successfully apply as much of this computing power as possible to designing and operating contemporary supply chains for the common good of mankind!

Uberization of the supply chain[20]

With the dawn of the digital age comes the possibility of Uberizing the supply chain, where assets are shared, pushing utilization rates up and accompanying transaction costs down. We are just at the bottom of this learning curve, so there is a long way to go, but the learning curve surely will be steep and fast. It is another example of a disrupter that can be harnessed for the greater good if we think deeply about how to do this.

Another dimension of this trend is the fragmentation of work. According to Guy Ryder, director general of the United Nations International Labour Organization (ILO), 'Uberisation of work has begun,'[21] and there is '. . . increasing atomisation in the way in which work is organised. This puts us on the cusp of yet another technological revolution.'[22]

The unanswered question is: what impact will this and other similar developments have on the number of available jobs? The popular consensus is that job opportunities will decrease as automation increases. But David Bozeman, VP, Amazon Transportation begs to differ.[23] He says that his company is employing more people at the same time as it increases automation. And the shortage of drivers in the Western economies points to structural shifts that increasing automation may help address. So there is still much to discover about the net impacts of these converging trends.

Social media and the social licence

Unthought of just a few years ago, customers are now embracing social media as a way to exert pressure on companies to respond quickly to their demands. But according to Keith Quesenberry,[24] '. . . most companies aren't set up to do that'. He argues that '. . . companies need a cross-functional social media team . . . ' working together to build and sustain effective relationships with online consumers.

Companies must also increasingly take into account the 'social licence to operate' notion, where support for projects must be won from key stakeholders, including consumers, to avoid subsequent fallout and reputational risk.

Volatility – the 'new normal' for the foreseeable future

In 2017, Martin Christopher and Matthias Holweg called volatility the 'new normal',[25] and how events have proved them right. Indeed, in earlier work, they introduced a statistical tool to track global volatility, the Supply Chain Volatility Index (SCVI), which confirmed that since the Global Financial Crisis (GFC) we have continued to experience an 'era of turbulence', indicated by an increased rate of change in key variables that negatively impact supply chain performance.[26]

They go on to say that '. . . because the likelihood is that the centre-of-gravity of a supply chain is going to change frequently in the future, given the volatility of the business environment, the need for *flexibility* in the supply/demand network increases'.[27] Their solution to creating the necessary flexibility is a combination of a change mindset, access to capacity as required and access to knowledge and talent. 'Either way it should be recognised that resilience comes at a cost and thus the question arises as to the cost/benefit of an investment in improved resilience.'[28] They conclude by saying that '. . . building structural flexibility will not be free, yet a conscious decision about what level of flexibility to provide will enable Firms to navigate the uncertain waters that are yet to come'.[29]

Indeed, responding to this challenge is what this book is all about. Our entire approach is aimed at finding new and innovative ways to embed the structural flexibility required to service each and every product-market combination, but in a sustainable way. And no one said this would be easy. In the words of Paul Michelman,[30] we must '. . . have the courage to accept a more difficult reality: the only way we can protect what we love is by actively pursuing a stable, just, and sustainable world. Every action has a consequence. Every inaction perhaps even more so.' We have been warned. Now we must act and ensure that the world is a better place for the next generation. The forces of darkness arraigned against us must be fought and subdued.

An example of technology as a positive disrupter

In a keynote session at the 2018 Council of Supply Chain Management Professional's Edge Conference in Nashville on 2 October 2018, Keller Rinaudo, founder and CEO of robotics start-up Zipline, described how they had developed aerial drones to deliver blood and other medical supplies to remote areas of Rwanda, in a world first.[31] One of the authors was present at this presentation and was amazed at what Zipline had achieved by combining technology and ingenuity, overcoming many obstacles to deliver a first world healthcare system to Rwanda on a national basis, for less than the current cost of their hitherto third world system! This is exactly what we were referring to above.

Rinaudo's driving passion is explained by his quote: 'There is a moral imperative to make supply chains work for everyone, not just the 10 percent of people who live in the right countries.'[32]

Zipline's work in Rwanda is a 'disrupter' that went through many stages of experimentation, starting with a blank piece of paper. This is a key point and, in Rinaudo's view, 'the service doesn't have to be perfect from Day 1 – just get started and learn by doing. Then scale.' And that is exactly what they did, leading ultimately to a major breakthrough in the way healthcare is delivered in this landlocked country.

Zipline 'uses 40-pound autonomous aircraft to deliver blood to hospitals (and health clinics) across Rwanda, bypassing the country's poor road system. The drones are launched from a catapult-like structure at the Zipline distribution center (DC) . . . and then fly at 30 feet across a varied landscape and through all types of weather before dropping paper parachutes carrying the much needed blood. The aircraft then returns to the DC, retrieved by a guide-wire system and quickly readied for re-use.'[33]

The cost for each delivery varies from US$5–50 depending on distance traveled by the drone, which is less than the current cost by surface transport! But the real zinger is that the blood is delivered within an hour of being ordered by the doctor, which is an astounding service response given the conditions in the country. And the wastage of the product has reduced to zero because of the expedited handling. All the metrics are going in the right direction.

Zipline are planning to extend their operations to Ghana and are also exploring bringing the system to US hospitals. This is a wonderful story born out of a vision by an exceptional individual, to bring healthcare services to everyone on the planet at an affordable cost. It is science fiction turned into practical delivery, and there are surely more cases like this ready to roll. We live in exciting times.

The secret sauce

As a starting point, the *secret sauce,* in the face of all the current turmoil, is to focus on finding ways to make and maintain 'direct' linkages with end users/consumers who, in effect, are the lowest common denominator of success. Zipline is a powerful example of this very point. Don't listen to the experts and naysayers who say it can't be done. Listen to the end user/consumers, interpret what they are trying to say and work back from there.

Without a direct line of sight on the end user/consumer, noise gets in the way and we lose sight of the real messages being conveyed. Remember, *supply chains are driven by people*. People on the outside called consumers, customers and suppliers; serviced by people on the inside of businesses called staff and management. These people are making thousands of decisions every day, supported by time-saving technology. And we need to understand how these consumers and customers think in order to anticipate the demands they will place on us, and prepare accordingly. It is no longer appropriate or indeed possible to react faster and faster to satisfy their demands. New more cost-effective ways must be found, as a matter of urgency.

Supply chains are a pervasive influence on the lives of everyone on planet Earth and we must preserve their integrity if they are to deliver the required services for humanity, day-by-day, without fail. According to Jay Samit, '. . . nearly everything we eat, wear and buy – from cranberries to crankshafts – moves through a supply chain'.[34] Let's not forget that.

So, at this point, the challenge we leave you with is this: how do we design, build and operate contemporary supply chains that will allow us to grow the top and bottom lines of our businesses, on a sustainable basis, into the foreseeable future? That is what this book is about.

Points of view

1 We live in a world where the 'new normal' is increased instability, brought about by a multitude of causes – political uncertainty combined with a leadership vacuum among governments everywhere; technology disrupters; emerging new business models; and the shift away from globalization back to economic nationalism. These and other factors are contributing to the fragmentation of established supply chain networks.

2 Climate change, as it impacts the environment, weather and water patterns, is bringing higher risks to food and beverage supply chains in particular.

3 Some big global brands are taking a stand and fighting back. They are leading a renewed focus on sustainability – and, in so doing, are filling the gaps left by the inaction of governments around the world.

4 Technology is proving to be both a disrupter and solution provider as companies race to solve the mounting problems caused by the factors listed in 1, above.

5 Uberization is one of the biggest and highest impact disrupters, affecting whole industries and potentially changing the way work is structured in the future.

6 Social media, unknown just a few short years ago, is now so pervasive it has the potential to influence the ethics of powerful corporates.

7 All the above points are summed up well by Christopher and Holweg[35] when they refer to *volatility* as the 'new normal' in our lives. So, let's get used to it and get on the front foot. To survive, we must inoculate ourselves with the change serum.

8 Fortunately, we have examples like Zipline's work in the healthcare system in Rwanda to encourage us to keep going in search of that magical combination of understanding consumer expectations (implicit or explicit), and the technological know-how that will bring innovative new ideas to life.

9 In short, we are in the midst of a life and death struggle by commercial organizations to overcome the negative impact of all the veritable Exocets coming towards them and, at the same time, keeping all their stakeholders onside. This will require nothing short of a *dynamic transformation,* led by a courageous leadership team that is relentless in its execution, and always mindful of the consequences of their decisions. Nothing short of this will bring the desired long-term success. The rest of the book provides a blueprint for the leadership of our enterprises to follow.

CHAPTER 2

Dynamic alignment – a heuristic to cut through complexity

High performance supply chains do not just evolve

Introduction

In Chapter 3, we make a strong case for kick-starting any design or redesign of your enterprise supply chains, by first interpreting customer expectations and then using the insights gained to guide the corresponding internal re-engineering work.

In fact, we will go further than that and contend that, for successful transformation of your enterprise supply chains, you must consciously *design* all your internal activity and external interactions with customers and suppliers in mind. The days of just letting supply chains evolve are gone forever.

For that reason, we are introducing *in this chapter,* two frameworks that will become vital filters in support of the transformation process.

Our Dynamic Alignment™ model is a core filter, or heuristic, because it provides a method by which we are able to keep the enterprise aligned with the ever-shifting marketplace. This important property is reinforced by Roger Martin and others with their notion of 'design thinking'.[1] Essentially, heuristics cut through complexity; and this is key to guiding substantial change in the supply chain.

Introducing Dynamic Alignment™

The Dynamic Alignment™ model was born as a concept in 1989 and has been developed and refined continuously since then. It was the joint effort of John Gattorna and Norman Chorn.[2] The first public paper on this new notion (originally called Strategic Alignment) was presented at the International Conference of the Strategic Management Society, Stockholm, in 1990.[3]

In conceptual terms, it represented the bringing together of the external marketplace with the internal culture and leadership of the enterprise, linked by operational strategy. The four discrete levels of this model are depicted in Figure 2.1.

The model developed out of frustration with the lack of any robust theory at the time to explain the role of logistics operations (later to evolve into supply chain operations) and how these should be designed and managed to most cost-effectively support the organization's business strategy. The combination of academic insights from across several management disciplines, plus work with diverse clients, was distilled to the four core elements that need to be aligned in order for an enterprise to perform well. Interestingly, this four-level model was later found by our clients to be relevant for all aspects of enterprise performance, not just the supply chain.

The core concept represented by Dynamic Alignment™ is that organizational performance is optimized when the strategy and internal capability of the organization are 'aligned' with the marketplace in which it operates. The more precise the alignment is, the better. Essentially, this 'outside-in'

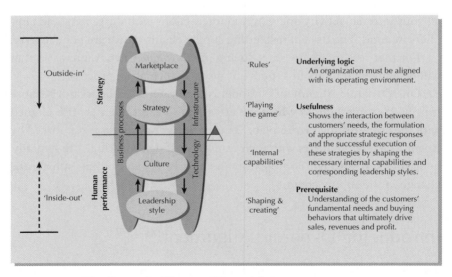

FIGURE 2.1 ◆ The Dynamic Alignment™ model

Source: Adapted from Gattorna (2015) p. 25

approach argues (backed by research) that a firm's 'fit' with the market and the corresponding operating environment is the key to sustainable performance.

Dynamic Alignment™ assumes that there is no universally 'good' strategy, 'right' culture or leadership style – everything is situational. This assumption is supported in academic research and in our own practical experience with multiple clients. Different marketplaces require different strategies and corresponding internal capabilities.

Since the early days of its introduction as a concept, fieldwork has continued for over three decades, at every level of the model, in an effort to fill in the gaps and get it to a more granular level.

A behavioral metric

An important breakthrough in the practical application of the Dynamic Alignment™ model came via our early focus on level 4, *leadership style*. This had been a shared interest and we had a hunch that, in the end, the leadership and leadership style of an enterprise would prove pivotal to the success of that enterprise. And so it proved to be!

We studied the original work of Jung,[4] and later efforts by Adizes[5] and Faust[6] to interpret Jung's work into a more pragmatic, usable framework to describe the styles of individual executives and the forces that shaped their behavior as leaders. For this purpose, Adizes[7] had resolved all the psychological forces identified by Jung into two pairs of countervailing forces, i.e. Entrepreneurial (E), opposed by Administration (A); and Producer (P), opposed by Integration (I), as shown in Figure 2.2.

At about the same time, academics and consultants were starting to use methods based on the same Jungian underpinnings to interpret the differences they saw in *groups* of people, especially to analyze organizational cultures. If you look at what has become known as the Competing Values Framework[8] developed by Cameron and Quinn in the 1980s, you will see that the four forces or dimensions that it uses equate closely to those used to define leadership by Adizes.

Our important breakthrough idea was to realize that these methods of classifying human behavior at the individual and group levels (that were being used to understand more about leadership and corporate culture) could also be used to classify customer behavior – whether they be individual consumers or business customers involving a number of executives involved in decision-making units.

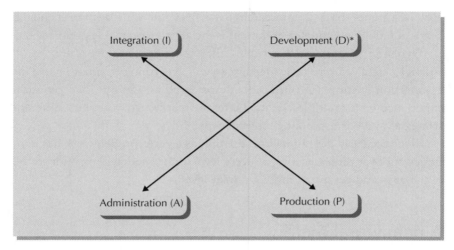

FIGURE 2.2 ◆ **Countervailing forces**

(*Adizes used Entrepreneurial (E) for this force)

This insight gave us a common metric to describe activity at three levels of the Dynamic Alignment™ model, and it was not difficult to modify the method to describe the inanimate second level – *operational strategy* – using the same behavioral metric.

After substituting Development (D) for Adizes' Entrepreneurial (E), the *P-A-D-I Logics coding system,* that could be applied at all four levels of the Dynamic Alignment™ model, was born. The generalized version of the P-A-D-I metric is shown in Figure 2.3.

The *universality* of the metric for describing how both individuals and groups of individuals behave can be seen in a few examples:

◆ Customers who are loyal, want a long-term relationship, like the reassurance of brand and are not overly price-sensitive, could be described as *'I' customers.*

◆ If we were running an operation that was very focused on maintaining controls, security, tight systems, accuracy and avoiding risk – the old-fashioned model of a bank – we would have an *'A' subculture.*

◆ A highly creative manager, who is always pursuing new ideas and the latest R&D, with little interest in maintaining the status quo, might be described as a *'D' leader.*

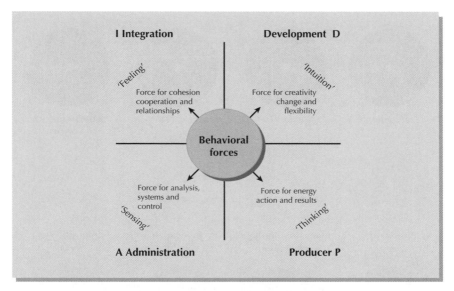

FIGURE 2.3 ◆ **Behavioral forces at play in individuals and groups**

Source: Adapted from Gattorna (2015) p. 29

Inherent in the Dynamic Alignment™ model is the concept that supply chains are driven by people. The archetypes that emerge using the P-A-D-I behavioral metric, provide a way to categorize what different customers value most, the response strategies that are appropriate, the internal capabilities and subcultures that must be in place to deliver these strategies, and the leadership styles that work in different situations. Taken together, these enable us to define the types of tailored supply chains that are required to deliver value to different segments of customers.

Sixteen archetypes

When looking at a marketplace, the classification scheme that results from applying the P-A-D-I metric to markets enables 16 archetypal groupings (or segments) of customers to be identified; these are depicted in Figure 2.4. We have labeled them with a summary descriptor to capture the essence of each segment. A more detailed list of attributes are listed for five of these

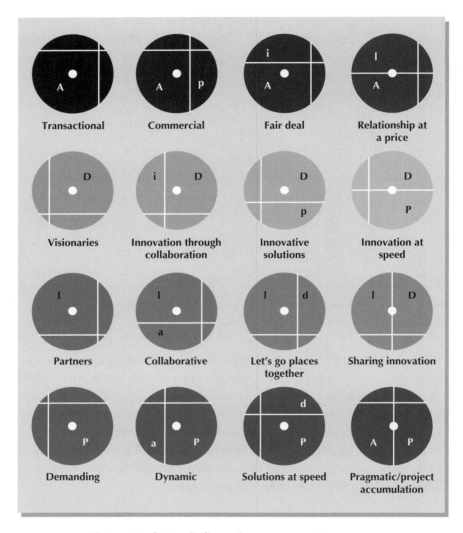

FIGURE 2.4 ◆ Sixteen 'archetypal' dimensions or segments

Source: Adapted from Gattorna (2015) p. 47

segments in Figure 2.6 in the following pages. You will note that the method we have developed to depict the segments draws on a summary position in the P-A-D-I matrix, and the position of the *center of gravity* indicates the bias in each of these 16 'logics'.

The significance of the behavioral metric described above cannot be under-estimated because it overcame a major impediment to progress: the ability to describe and compare the four key performance elements at play in any enterprise. As engineers well know, you can't compare apples, oranges, pears and bananas; you have to reduce everything to equivalent apples for comparison purposes.

This codification of each layer in the Dynamic Alignment™ model allows us to directly link and compare what is in the customer's mind and, therefore, how we should design the appropriate responses. The *direct* connection is critical and is, in fact, what has been missing in all attempts to develop viable operational strategies to date.

The understanding of how to describe all four levels in the same behavioral metric is akin to discovering something that has been there all the time, but is, as yet, unseen. It is like 'hiding something in plain sight'! At last we have the common language we have been searching for.

We see this problem before our eyes, acting out every day inside the business, between the functions, where different language, terminology and metrics are used, thus making it near impossible to communicate effectively *across* the business. If we have a problem as fundamental as this inside the enterprise, it's not surprising that we have an even bigger problem truly understanding the mindset of our external stakeholders, especially our customers and suppliers.

Nelson Mandela captured the essence of the problem very succinctly in another context when he commented that '. . . without language, one cannot talk to people and understand them; one cannot share their hopes and aspirations, grasp their history, appreciate their poetry or savour their songs. I again realized that we were not different people with separate languages; we were one people, with different tongues'.[9] It's the different tongues that are the real problem.

Design Thinking

The Design Thinking concept, as articulated by Roger Martin,[10] sits well with our Dynamic Alignment™ model, even though it came some two decades later.

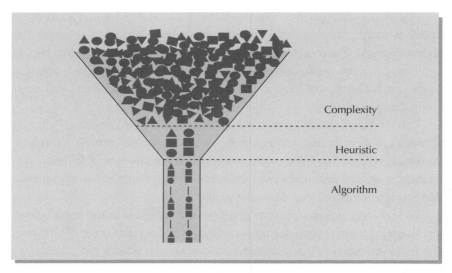

FIGURE 2.5 ◆ **The Knowledge Funnel in Design Thinking**

Martin introduces the notion of a '*knowledge funnel*'. He refers to the open end of the funnel as where all the mystery and complexities reside, as in our increasingly complex operating environment.

He speaks of the need for a 'heuristic' through which we filter these mysteries and complexities to reveal patterns that can be acted upon. We see our Dynamic Alignment™ model as one such heuristic, because it helps to reveal patterns of behavior in the marketplace which require different responses. We call these patterns customer behavior *segments*.

Once we can see the patterns (or segments in this case), it is possible to design specific, repeatable processes to drive the efficiency at scale that we all so desire. This industrialization of the solution identified in the heuristic is what Martin refers to as the 'Algorithm'. The idea of filtering complexity through a heuristic to reach this outcome is depicted in Figure 2.5.

The Design Thinking concept has transferred the designer's mindset to the business world; and it has been very influential in how large and small companies now approach innovation. In this context we argue that innovation does not only refer to new products, new customers or new technologies – it is also a mindset that is needed to continually improve performance with our current products and customers.

Multiple segments in most markets

The next critical stage of the heuristic that developed from our ongoing work with clients was the recognition that most organizations were not serving one segment but were facing an array of behavioral segments with different needs and expectations. Thus, they could have strategies and a supply chain that were well-aligned with one segment, but could be missing the mark with a large part of the residual market because they had not recognized the diversity they faced. And this is a very common scenario – 'one-size-fits-all' supply chain strategies.

Over time, it also became apparent that there was some pattern even to the range of segments. Across diverse industries we found that the five customer segments, shown in Figure 2.6, were the most common, or the most significant, in terms of impact.

The most frequently seen segments were *collaborative, transactional* and *dynamic,* which reflected familiar ways in which individuals and businesses thought about buying particular categories. We have also seen that the structure of buying for *projects* is so influential in terms of different expectations that it can override all other influences and, hence, we have learnt to define it as a different segment. And, finally, there are occasions where the needs of the situation are so outside the norm that conventional ways of operating are not appropriate and *innovative solutions* are required. Thus, of the 16 archetypal options implied by our coding method mentioned earlier, five in particular were most often required.

Dynamic Alignment™ implies that each of these segments requires specific *strategies* and underpinning *capabilities.* We will explore these segments and the appropriate supply chain responses in more detail in Chapters 3 and 4.

We have also seen, however, that customers change their behavior from time to time. Under duress, or for short periods, they may shift their priorities – and move, for example from being primarily price-buyers (transactional) wanting a solution at any cost (innovative solutions). This is why we have used the term '*Dynamic*' Alignment for our model.

Very large organizations can also exhibit a range of buying behaviors within the same organization. A large retailer, for example, can be buying from the same supplier several home-brand ranges in *transactional* mode; one-off promotional ranges in *dynamic* mode; and they may also have a team working with a supplier in *innovation* mode, on completely new product categories. All at the same time!

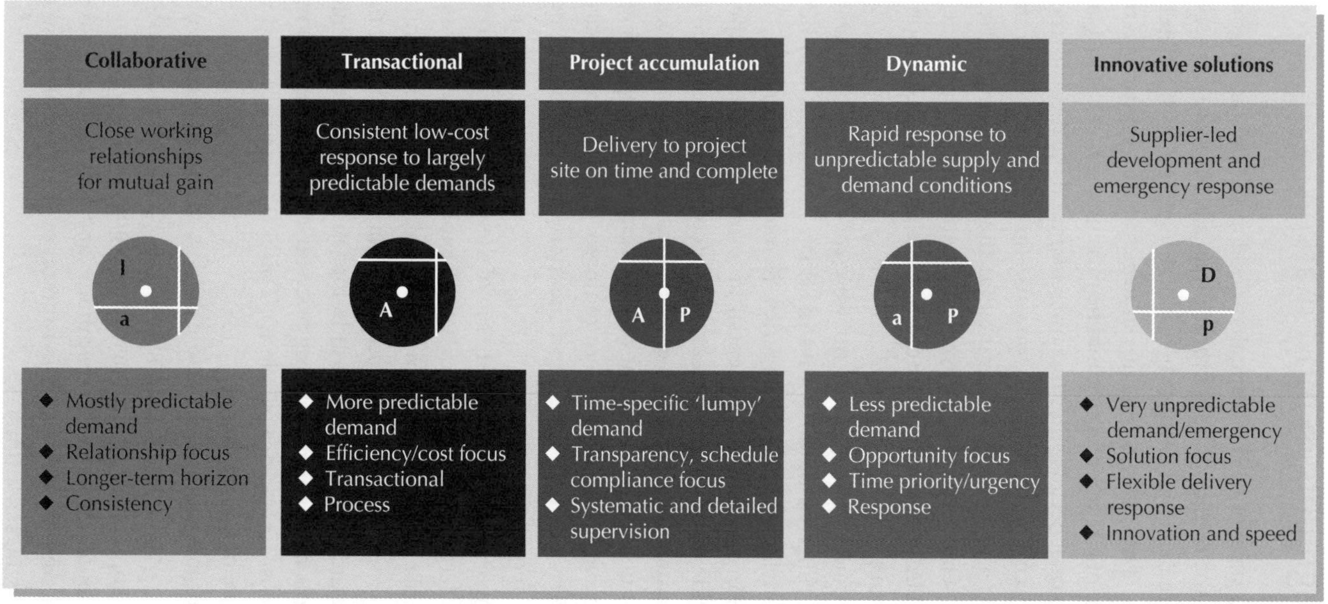

FIGURE 2.6 ◆ **The five most common behavioral segments**

Source: Adapted from Figure 2.4 in Gattorna (2015), p. 58

From static to dynamic design

With the help of 'outside-in' thinking, as espoused in Design Thinking and our proprietary Dynamic Alignment™ model, we chart a path to more dynamic supply chains that have the capability to serve an array of different needs in the market without constant adjustment and customization. This conscious linkage between a customer's buying behaviors and internal strategy and capabilities is the starting point for more effective supply chains. We will explore what these supply chains look like in the next few chapters.

CASE STUDY: Teys Australia

A highly successful joint venture built on proactive leadership and a market-focused guiding framework

Situation

Australia is a major producer and exporter of beef to world markets. In 2011, the second and third largest beef processing and exporting businesses merged. One was a private company, Teys Bros, built by two generations of the Teys family; the other was owned by one of the largest food companies in the world, Cargill. The new business was called Teys Australia.

This is the story of how this unlikely pairing resulted in a highly successful joint venture (JV) that created value for both sets of owners and for many of the customers they served.

The complexity

Teys Bros and Cargill were very different enterprises: one a large corporate, with a multinational perspective. The other an entrepreneurial, centrally managed, family business.

They both sold in domestic and international markets to a range of overlapping customers. And they both struggled with servicing customers reliably in a supply-constrained industry.

A common focus

Prior to the decision to merge, Teys Bros had been working on its market-facing strategy. It had initiated some early work to segment customers using the Dynamic Alignment™ framework and was exploring if the approach could help to prioritize focus and allocate supply.

Cargill had been using a similar approach to better understand its own customer base.

When the pre-JV discussions turned to the impact in the market, the two businesses found they potentially had a common approach and a common language. Immediately after the merger, a new piece of research was commissioned to segment the combined customer base using Dynamic Alignment™ methods.

The senior leadership team were very conscious that many mergers fail to create value and that customer resistance and internal integration are key challenges.

Results

The market segmentation enabled Teys Australia to kick off the JV with a cohesive, fresh approach to the (rather concerned) market. The segmentation also highlighted a large, potentially collaborative group of customers that neither company had fully recognized nor responded to previously because of the constrained supply situation. The new strategy focused on growing the share of wallet with this segment particularly, and differentiated strategies for each other group to align with what they valued most.

Beyond the external benefits, though, were the internal spin-off benefits of focusing the new business on market alignment. Rather than a battle of cultures, the new strategy heralded a different approach which made sense to both teams and their energy was channeled into ensuring its success. Thus, in focusing on external alignment, the by-product was internal cohesion.

This was not just a transition strategy. The common language and segmentation-driven approach persists seven years on.

And the financial results tell the rest of the story – Teys Australia continues to grow strongly year-on-year and has cemented its targeted place as a collaborative and reliable supplier in both local and global markets.

What can we learn?

1 Proactive leadership: the Teys Australia senior team describe themselves as custodians of the market and custodians of the culture. This is a simplifying and unifying mindset in a period of intense change.

2 Differentiated market and supply chain strategies can improve market alignment and financial performance, even when supply is constrained.

3 The galvanizing effect of having a clear line of sight to the market right across the business.

4 A large percentage of mergers do not achieve their goals – recognizing and preparing for the impact in the market is a key element.

Teys Australia is now turning its attention to end-to-end alignment, with a segmentation of supply base and strategies to connect supply more directly to customer demand. This is a natural extension of its market-facing strategy, and this cohesive long-term approach is in stark contrast to the stop-start strategies of many businesses driven by shorter-term goals.

Points of view

1 High-performance supply chains do not just evolve; they have to be consciously *designed* to fit specific product-market combinations.

2 The design or redesign process must work from '*outside-in*'; not the other way around. The field of Design Thinking supports this view.

3 Dynamic Alignment™ is our proprietary filter or heuristic – it enables us to see patterns in the market and the demand data, and respond with precision.

4 The *secret sauce* in the Dynamic Alignment™ model is its ability to describe every level in the same way, using a *coding method* that involves a common *behavioral metric*. The metric is akin to having a common language to use in communicating inside and outside the enterprise.

5 We identified 16 possible archetypal groupings of customers present in any marketplace. Of these, any five dominant groupings can account for upwards of 80 per cent coverage of a target market.

6 It is clear from experience across industries that many organizations potentially face more than one buyer behavior segment within a single customer, and up to five behavioral segments in their target market.

Kick-start your thinking[11]

In this and following chapters we will include a short exercise to challenge the thinking of readers after they have absorbed the content of each chapter.

YOUR SEGMENTS AT A GLANCE

Review the typical expectations of customers in each of the five segments below and consider if you have customers that fit the profile.

Collaborative	Transactional	Dynamic	Project accumulation	Innovative solutions
What do they value?				
◆ Relationships	◆ Low cost	◆ Speed	◆ Schedule compliance	◆ Innovation
◆ Trust	◆ Efficiency	◆ Flexibility	◆ On time	◆ Speed
◆ Stability	◆ Structure	◆ Ease	◆ On budget	◆ Creative solutions
◆ Reliability	◆ Reliability	◆ Winning	◆ Expedite for exceptions	◆ Flexibility
What don't they value?				
◆ Lack of acknowledgment	◆ Relationships	◆ Indecision	◆ Ambiguity	◆ Process
◆ Risk	◆ Creativity	◆ Relationships	◆ Uncertainty	◆ Rules
			◆ Delay	
Your customers				

CHAPTER 3

'Outside-in' design for supply chains

Seeing the world through the eyes of your customers and other key stakeholders

Introduction

S upply chains first became a formal field of management study in the 1960s, with the publication of seminal articles on distribution management by Neuschel[1] and Stolle.[2] But the surrounding thinking developed relatively slowly for several decades after that pivotal turning point.

Given the growth in many markets around the world in the last two decades of the twentieth century, the main preoccupation of commercial enterprises seems to have been solely about fulfilling the sometimes rapid growth in demand at practically any cost, and finding a 'one-size-fits-all' design to do the job.

Unfortunately, unmitigated growth hides a multitude of sins and fosters development of poor practices. Such is the case in supply chain development, where little or no finesse was applied to the task, which in turn led to the proliferation of supply chain networks firmly rooted in 'inside-out' thinking. The actual expectations of customers (or suppliers) was not factored into the equation.

This, we believe, is the fatal flaw in many operations in a more volatile and service sensitive environment. It is why they fail to contribute to growth and why there is an opportunity for new business models to capture, even formerly loyal, customers' attention and change their buying routines.

Seeking to be genuinely 'customer-centric'

In the last chapter, we introduced a 'Design Thinking' approach and a heuristic that enables supply chains to be more directly linked to the markets they serve – Dynamic Alignment™. We emphasized that understanding customers' behavioral drivers provides insight into the types of supply chains that are effective for different customers and situations. In this chapter, we look at the 'design' element in more detail – what do we need to know and how do we go about structuring our supply chains to more precisely align with customers' expectations.

Many organizations aim to be 'customer-centric', but, without practical methods to bring the 'voice of the customer' to life in an orderly way, this is purely aspirational. This chapter aims to address this gap, at least at the strategic level.

A methodology to kick-off 'outside-in' design for current businesses

The methodology we use in the field to identify the customer behavioral segments present and to 'kick-off' the design of service offers and supply chains is depicted in Figure 3.1.

It brings together four inputs that are essential to guide design: primary customer research; demand pattern analysis; a conscious triangulation with the broader business strategy to decide the focus segments; and network modeling to shape the major infrastructure and flow decisions.

The output is differentiated service offers and a strategic design of the supply chain needed to deliver them. It *is not* the detailed definition of process, which IT system to employ or how to implement the sales and operations planning process. But it will create a boundary and vision for what these will need to deliver for each supply chain required.

But, before we get to the outputs, let's look at the various inputs, starting with customer research.

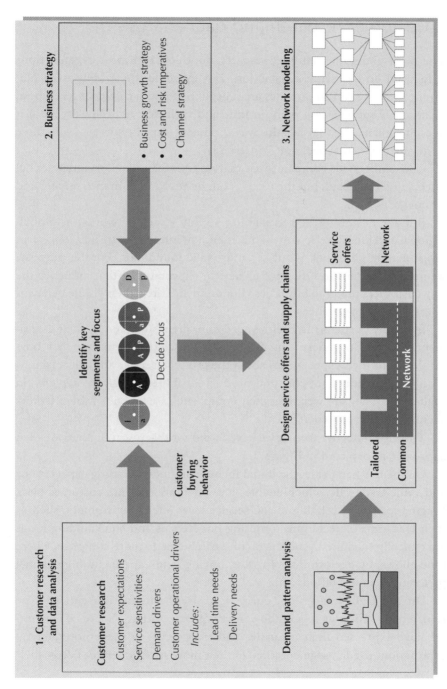

FIGURE 3.1 ◆ **Research inputs to dynamic supply chain design**

Source: Adapted from Gattorna (2015) p. 78

1 Customer research and data analysis

The most common customer research conducted in most organizations is focused on assessing satisfaction. For example, the widely used Net Promoter Score (NPS) provides an indication of how a customer feels about a particular supplier at a point in time and their degree of 'loyalty'. But it doesn't explain why they feel this way. And next time the survey is run, these same customers may feel quite differently!

Consumer goods companies use market research to understand potential buyers in more detail, but the focus is on the reaction to brand, pricing and competitors.

But for designing or redesigning supply chain networks, at global, regional and local levels, with all the attendant infrastructure and long-term investment implications, we need a more solid foundation. For this purpose, we need to understand the base values (or expectations) that influence the way customers prefer to buy. These underpin and drive their visible behavior in the form of preferences.

In supply chain terms, their expectations are also driven by their assessment of value. Customers consciously or unconsciously factor into their buying decisions their expectations about the product, service and, increasingly, a wider spectrum of supplier and product attributes. These are depicted in Figure 3.2. They are weighing their composite assessment of these factors against the cost of ownership.

The most effective format we have found for this research is a two-sided approach, as depicted in Figure 3.3.

On the left-hand side, the initial focus is on understanding expectations and value trade-offs, which enables a segmentation of the customer base. Pragmatic aspects relating to the service level offer to customers, such as their lead-time expectations, ordering preferences and stockholding levels are typically examined. And the picture can be made more complete, where time allows, by exploring the broader buying landscape including channel preferences, brand affinity, etc.

On the right-hand side, current levels of satisfaction can also be researched – but now it is in the context of expectations. So, once customers have expressed their priorities, either in terms of their more general expectations used in segmentation, or their more specific service needs, their

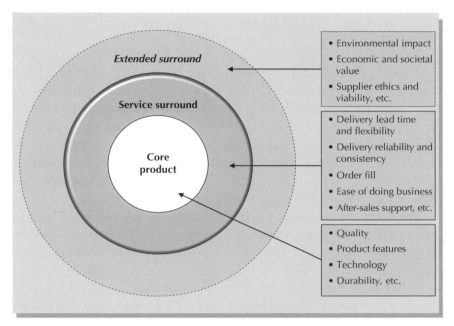

FIGURE 3.2 ◆ The (extended) range of product features and benefits that represent 'value' to customers

Source: Adapted from Christopher, M. (2016) *Logistics and Supply Chain Management*. 5th edn, p. 37. Harlow: FT Prentice Hall

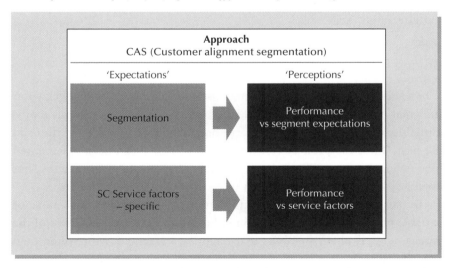

FIGURE 3.3 ◆ Customer research for supply chain design – expectations vs perceptions

perceptions (opinions) of current supplier performance (and potentially even competitor performance) can be measured.

To measure customer *expectations,* we use a variation of the Conjoint Analysis method of market research, which aims to understand the 'trade-offs' or choices that customers are prepared to make when they are deciding on the purchase of a particular product or service category. And buried in the bundle of attributes surrounding a purchase are several that have key implications for the supply chain itself and, usually, these are explored in more depth. The coding mechanism introduced in Chapter 2 is, of course, the key to interpreting, and creating meaning from, the vast range of expectations that could be expressed.

This form of research is used by marketing at the consumer level to understand product attributes and pricing trade-offs. We have extended its application considerably and have found it equally valuable for use in understanding business-to-business purchasing. Essentially, the same principles apply. Key individuals, or groups of executives, interact as a decision-making unit (DMU) and make choices for the business. The preferences they exhibit have been forged from a more complex interplay of organizational culture, their own market situation, the position of the category they are purchasing (strategic, commodity, etc.) and their own history and bias – but, in practical terms, they make decisions that add up to our sales – so we need to understand them.

Buying behavior manifests as demand patterns

When seeking to understand existing customers and their buying behavior, the great advantage that we have is the history of their transactions that is available, which enables us to observe how they have interacted with us in the past. Thus the primary research descibed above can be supplemented by demand analytics. We are then not only considering what they say, but how they have behaved along the way.

In particular, we look at demand patterns to understand how stable or variable past demand from a customer has been. This is an indicator of the types of supply chain solutions that might be warranted. More often than not, the very stable, predictable patterns are likely to be associated with *collaborative* or *transactional* customers; and these are important because

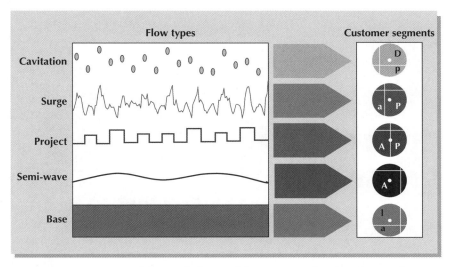

FIGURE 3.4 ◆ Patterns of demand observed in many product/service markets

Source: Adapted from Gattorna (2015) p. 64

they can become the *baseload* of an operation. See Figure 3.4, which demonstrates what the different order-driven patterns might look like when customer segments are separated out into a laminar flow format.

Of course, in practice, this is difficult to do, but not impossible with the help of advanced techniques such as the Coefficient of Variation (CoV).[3] In our experience, we have found at least 40 per cent of total demand for particular product/service categories can often be explained by the combined base and semi-wave patterns. This type of insight is gold because it allows the designer to separate baseload activity from the rest and, in the process, reduce costs overall, as well as reduce any additional complexity introduced through mixing volatile and stable behaviors together.

Customer vs product driven

Earlier commentators such as Fisher[4] and Lee[5] tended to confuse the issue of segmentation methodology by placing undue emphasis on products and product characteristics. In fact, a given product can be demanded by customers with dissimilar expectations and service priorities – and the best supply chain to deliver them will thus be different.

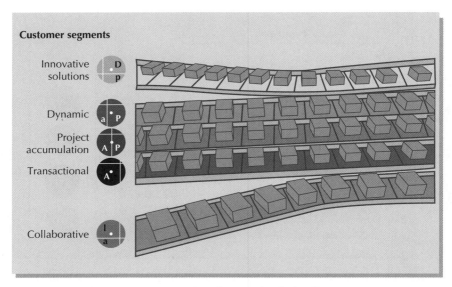

Customer segments

Innovative solutions

Dynamic

Project accumulation

Transactional

Collaborative

FIGURE 3.5 ◆ **The conveyor metaphor for supply chain alignment**

The logic for thinking 'customer' first, rather than 'product' is illustrated by the conveyor metaphor depicted in Figure 3.5. The supply chain servicing each segment will have different operating characteristics, such that the customer at the receiving end gets exactly what they are expecting in terms of the channel they buy from, packaging, pricing, delivery lead-time, etc.

And, should market conditions, or the customer's situation, change at any time that same customer may opt to temporarily change their buying behavior on the next purchase occasion, in which case the same product could well travel down an alternative conveyor/supply chain pathway to meet his/her revised expectations. That's why we need an embedded 'dynamic' capability in our enterprise supply chain networks. This ability to flex, within a static configuration, is far more effective than chasing the customer's new expectations through customization, which creates costly exceptions in the process.

Having said that, there is clearly some linkage between products and their characteristics and their corresponding demand patterns. An understanding of this relationship is critical to supply chain design on the ground.

Referring to Figure 3.6, in our work with clients, we found that the relationship between demand patterns on the left (created by customers' buying

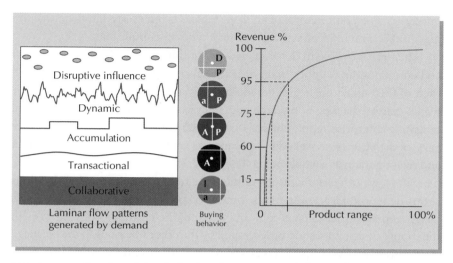

FIGURE 3.6 ◆ **Synchronizing behavioral segments and the product Pareto**

behaviors) and the product Pareto on the right held on most occasions. Slow-selling products (the 'long tail') are very often also volatile and difficult to forecast; even when they are being purchased by generally predictable customers. There are typically, also, customers that come in and out and one-off customers for these often more specialized products.

This knowledge plays a role in determining which part of the product range will be stocked where. More stable products may need to be close to customers to facilitate convenient, regular offtake where lead-time expectations are short, while volatile products may be centralized to reduce inventory cost with express transport used to 'catch up' lead time. The many variations can be tested via network modeling, as we discuss later.

Segmenting customers leads to differentiated supply chains

There is a subtle but important difference between segmenting customers in the target market and segmenting supply chains.[6] As explained earlier, we segment or group customers using an understanding of the hierarchy of different attributes they value in a given service offer, for a given product or service category. These attributes are supplemented by their own values that are hard-wired over time and the situation in the market at the time of purchase. The combination of all three factors is manifested in the choice(s) they make, which, in effect, represents a type of in-built bias.

Then it is possible to develop an array of differentiated *value propositions* and corresponding supply chain operational strategies to precisely align with each of the behavioral segments identified.

Of course, the type of research and analysis that we propose as the basis of designing enterprise supply chains is exactly the same research relevant to other parts of the business as well. Why? Because we are looking at the same customer and treating them as a whole being. They don't split hairs when making choices. Therefore, we can use the results of the same research when making decisions about new product introductions, branding, pricing, service levels, etc. This insight represents a fabulous spin-off benefit of the customer-focused work in the supply chain and should be leveraged by the other functions in the business.

Sadly, in many companies we have worked in around the world, the commercial side of the business, which invariably drives segmentation, limits its use of it to easily collected, but much less informative, classifications such as: industry sector; institutional type; size; geography; and profitability, to name just a few. These are all valid ways of grouping customers, but they tell us very little about customers' preferences and how these developed.

It is all the more mystifying when you realize that some of the other methods of segmentation can, potentially, be downright misleading if used alone. For example, inside a single 'institutional' segment such as 'retailers', it is possible to identify up to five buying behaviors for the same categories of products, all leading to slightly differing service and engagement requirements.

Behavioral segmentation provides insight into what customers value most and, thus, it carries with it a predictive capability that other methods lack. This is a winning edge that is going to prove vital in the coming years of intense competition, where the difference between success and failure in a market is wafer thin.

Insight about customer behavior informs supply chain design

The five common supply chains, introduced in Chapter 2, resulted from the research described above conducted across a large number of diverse industries. They are shown again in Figure 3.7, in more detail, with the typical characteristics that come through in the research.

It is very apparent, once these different expectations and characteristics are defined, that a single supply chain solution would struggle to deliver high levels of satisfaction. It is also clear that the resource utilization, and thus

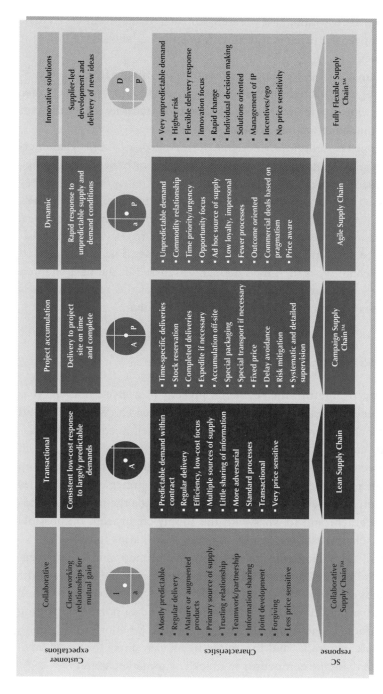

FIGURE 3.7 ◆ **The five most common behavioral segments and the appropriate supply chain response**

Source: Adapted from Gattorna (2015) p. 58

cost levels, that are warranted are different for each segment. And even that, to be competitive, the pricing and market positioning should be different for each segment.

Based on this finding, we concluded that the equivalent number of supply chain configurations naturally would be required to service a particular target market, albeit in different combinations and intensities, depending on the business-market situations present at the time.

This approach to consciously design a 'fit-for-purpose' supply chain network, *directly* linked to its target market, is consistent with the *design thinking* principles already referenced in Chapter 2.

Thus, based on the insights gained in the deep-dive into the customer, we are able to reverse engineer the appropriate combination of processes, planning techniques, technology and organization design back into the business in order to develop a fully aligned set of responses. The details of each of the supply chain types identified here are discussed in the next chapter. As you will see, however, the naming of each indicates the overall emphasis of the strategies needed to satisfy the particular segment.

2 Business strategy defines focus

It is one thing to identify the segments present in a given market. It is another to decide the level of focus that each deserves. We have found that, by being able to articulate the segments and their needs and expectations, and to combine this with the more pedestrian classifications such as industry-sector, the senior commercial and/or business unit leadership teams are able to consider the growth potential and strategic opportunities that each segment presents. They are thus able to guide the relative emphasis for each segment and to work with the supply chain team on possible service offers, channel strategies and on network scenarios to test.

It is difficult, and dangerous, for a supply chain function in an organization to shift the strategy dramatically without doing it in the context of the overall business direction. The issues revealed in the type of primary research described earlier, however, can lay bare the risks and opportunities sitting below the surface. Large segments with an appetite for shorter lead times, for example, are exposed – and this might be an easy entry for a new business or a more dynamic competitor to quickly win market share.

3 Network modeling to test options

The level of complexity in most national and multinational supply chains is a barrier to significant major change. Fortunately, the supply chain design 'problem' is a classic application for mathematical optimization and network optimization modeling is now mature with off-the-shelf models suitable for all but the most difficult situations.

The difference in the use of network modeling in the methodology outlined here is the more robust inputs available as a result of customer research and the ability to define and test service and cost scenarios anchored by segmentation. So, instead of testing the typical network options for more or fewer distribution centers, or manufacturing locally or overseas – with a focus only on cost minimization, the model can be used to test *scenarios* to achieve the four or five different service offers that might be needed to satisfy the particular target market. The model is still minimizing cost, but the higher level of refinement of the service side of the equation provides much greater strategic power to the results.

The combination of primary research, segmentation and network modeling has proven to be a real breakthrough because it allows a fresh look at what could be different, along with an objective, fact-based way to safely test and cost options. Modeling can take a lot of the politics and emotion out of major change – testing a large range of options, with minimal on-the-ground risk. Without clarity around the market, and without the business discussions about where to focus, however, modeling inevitably becomes only a cost reduction exercise and misses its full potential.

CASE STUDY: (Demand-side): DHL Express Taiwan[7]

Realigning the service offering with customers' expectations

Situation

In 2005, Deutsche Post World Net (DPWN), the parent company of DHL Express, laid out a strategic vision for the Asia Pacific Region that was seen as stretching. Market share was already at 33 per cent, and forecast to increase to 35 per cent, even though DHL Express products had begun to commoditize in the face of stiff competition from the major global third-party logistics (3PLs) providers that had entered the Asian market, i.e. FedEx TNT and UPS.

DHL Express (Taiwan) was the first integrator into the Taiwan market (1973) with a DOX service and, by the end of 2006, it had the strongest network in Taiwan, with 1,200 employees, 10 service centers and 250 vehicles for delivery and pick-up. With this strength, DHL Express (Taiwan) was expected to nearly double its revenue by 2015 and increase EBITA from 19 per cent to 22.5 per cent, according to the DPWN strategic vision.

The challenge

DHL Express (Taiwan) was one of the 41 countries in the DHL Express Asia Pacific Region. In 2005, the Taiwan economy was slowing, due to a downturn in electronic high tech (EHT) markets worldwide.

The task facing the newly appointed DHL Express (Taiwan) general manager, Stuart Whiting, was how to ensure the country played its role in meeting the strategic vision, in what was effectively a declining market for express courier and logistics services.

New insights

Whiting decided to re-examine his marketplace and make a conscious effort to find new ways to better understand the expectations of the customers still operating in Taiwan and better align with their expectations. He jettisoned the conventional 'one-size-fits-all' approach that had been applied by his predecessor and the more recent advice from consultants that customers should be grouped based on 'existing spend' or 'revenue potential'. Neither of these approaches provided the insight he was looking for. Instead, Whiting adopted the Dynamic Alignment™ methodology, which started with an 'outside-in' examination of the market. His team interviewed 260 major and minor customers, spread across five sales channels that were buying express products and services.

Results

Results were received and analyzed from 212 customers, and four clear behavioral segments were identified, i.e. IA; AP; ID; and DP, using the Dynamic Alignment™ coding system.[8] The IA segment is characterized by customers who value high levels of relationship support and, at that time, DHL was ill-equipped to meet this expectation. At the other end of the spectrum, the ID segment was expecting user-friendly, creative solutions and the DP segment was expecting creative solutions, delivered fast. At the time, DHL, through its Singapore-based Asia Pacific Quality

Control Center, was just moving to launch a capability that would cater for these two segments that Taiwan can draw on.

In regard to the AP segment that expected an urgent, time-based response, on an orderly basis, DHL already had it well in hand. As a result of these insights, Stuart Whiting was able to repackage DHL's express products and services and reorganize his sales and operations functions to better align with customers' expectations. The end result was a 20 per cent increase in profit within 12 months. In addition, customer and employee satisfaction increased significantly, as did share of wallet and retention of customers.

What can we learn?

This case is an example of the success that can be achieved, in a relatively short time, by segmenting customers according to their underlying expectations (buying behaviors). And, once you have this frame-of-reference firmly in mind, it is possible to precisely reconfigure your sales offerings and operations to ensure customers receive what they expect, no more, no less.

In the process, over-servicing and under-servicing are reduced and available resources are focused exactly where they should be, leading to lower cost-to-serve and higher revenues due to an improved satisfaction profile across the customer base. In turn, this opens up margin improvement, even in the face of stiff competition and price sensitivity.

Segue – to the supply-side

We will leave the discussion on the customer at this point and go to the other end of the supply chain to explore how we might give similar treatment to our suppliers. Our view is that, right now, there is nothing much going on in this space except for periodic cost-cutting initiatives such as strategic sourcing and supplier and product rationalizations. These initiatives are usually undertaken when margins are being squeezed because prices are under pressure and/or costs are escalating. But the underlying expectations and operating models of suppliers in all of this are rarely, if ever, factored into the equation. It's all done in a very mechanical way, which explains why the benefits, if any, are transitory at best.

The way that we have used segmentation as the cornerstone for design on the customer-facing side of a business is also relevant when we turn back to look at the supply-side.

Supplier segmentation can provide insight and clarity around the *capabilities* embedded in the supply base. This, in turn, will enable a more 'design-driven' approach to selecting suppliers and to managing the appropriate range of supplier relationships needed to support the market strategy of the business.

It is our very strong view that the *procurement function must act in unison with the strategies that address the customer buying behaviors identified at the front-end of the business.* The signals come from there in any comprehensive end-to-end supply chain design, especially if the firm has implemented digitization throughout. And the metrics that procurement managers are judged on should be tied to customer-driven metrics overall. Sadly, this is not the case in most enterprises, so there is a lot of upside in getting this right.

It is true that the effectiveness of an end-to-end supply chain can be either constrained or enhanced by upstream supplier and plant capabilities. Just as in the customer-base, however, the supplier-base usually contains great diversity and complexity, and special methods are required to focus on what really matters in the context of the organization's current business priorities.

Supply-side procurement with an 'alignment' mindset

A form of segmentation has been used for some time in procurement. An early version by Peter Kraljic,[9] in the 1980s, pushed procurement professionals to think more strategically – and the result was, perhaps, the first attempted classification of supply. The Kraljic method classifies sourced materials on their 'profit impact' and 'supply risk' and has four segments: *non-critical*; *leverage*; *strategic*; and *bottleneck*. Later work by Diane Bueler[10] suggested a segmentation regime based on a combination of product and supplier characteristics.

However, we would argue that, without an added behavioral dimension, all these methods of segmentation are inadequate because they are internally focused and lack a predictive capability. Behavioral segmentation enables supplier capability to be fully defined and, thus, the best methods for working with particular suppliers to be inferred. It also allows proactive alignment between the market-facing strategy of the enterprise and the corresponding sourcing strategy. And it helps us better understand where critical buffers (such as inventory) may be needed along the way to create closer alignment with customers.

We need to be able to identify those suppliers that are well-suited to *collaborative* supply arrangements; those that can provide *reliable supply at lowest cost* – but do not have the long-term mindset needed for collaboration; those that may be more expensive but have *spare capacity* to respond quickly to unplanned demand; and, particularly in this environment, those that have strong *innovation capabilities* to find solutions in times of unexpected disruptions.

Combining key segmentation criteria in an ordered hierarchy, starting with behavioral, enables focused sourcing strategies and clarifies risks and opportunities. The supply-side of the business can also be a rich source of opportunity and the starting point for new product offerings. For mature businesses, *collaborative innovation* with a supplier may be a more comfortable path than trying to initiate and drive change internally.

So, it's time to start listening to our suppliers and measuring them in meaningful ways. Segmenting them just on *what* they supply reveals little about the opportunities they present or indeed the risks they represent. Are you measuring the wrong things – 'lean' suppliers for innovation; and 'innovative' suppliers on driving cost down? Not surprisingly, these combinations simply don't work.

Similar to the customer-side, we have used the 16 archetypal selling behaviors to classify the supply base for a range of product and service categories. Once again, the supply base for any particular organization typically can be depicted well within four to five of the segments. The five segments indicated in Figure 3.8 have been seen often, but, as the case study that follows shows, other combinations can and do occur.

To demonstrate the new insights available when you view your suppliers through their own lens, we have documented a piece of work (Figure 3.9 and following case study) that we did in 2008 in Brazil in conjunction with our associates, Axia Consulting. The client was JBS S.A., the Brazilian-based global meat-processing business.

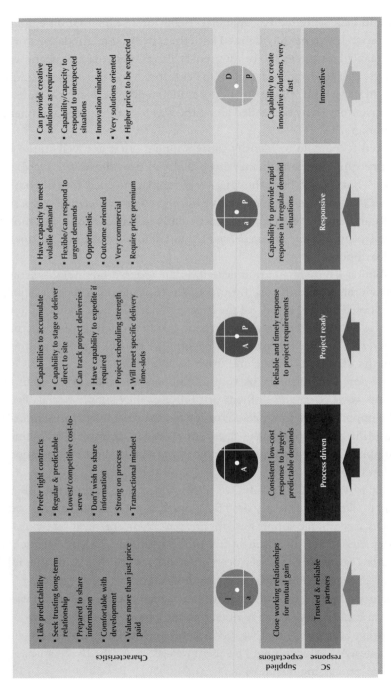

FIGURE 3.8 ◆ **Supply-side behavioral segmentation characteristics – common segments**

Source: Adapted from Gattorna (2015) p. 381

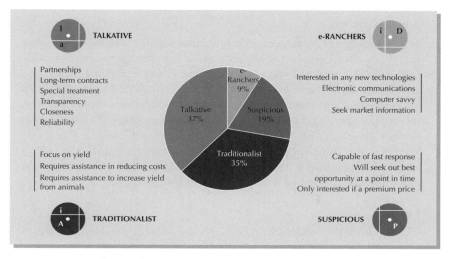

FIGURE 3.9 ◆ Cattle suppliers' (ranchers') segmentation at JBS S.A. in Brazil in 2008

Source: Adapted from Gattorna (2015) p. 381

CASE STUDY: Supply-side alignment – JBS S.A[11]

Looking from the supplier side of the fence

Situation

JBS is the Brazil-based largest meat processor in the world. Because it has continued to grow at a rapid rate for the last two decades, JBS requires an ever-increasing share of the available live cattle market, for processing and distribution to service its domestic and export markets.

Supply constraints

As its demands for live cattle increase, it places pressure on the available grazing land and brings it into conflict with sustainability requirements, i.e. the need to stop deforestation of the Amazon biome and achieve greater productivity from non-deforested land. It reached agreement with Greenpeace about sustainable sourcing practices some time around 2009. At the same time, it does not want to be dependent only on price levers and bidding at saleyards for its supply of live cattle, something their own procurement department were advising they should do at the time.

A new paradigm

In 2008, Gattorna Alignment, in conjunction with our Brazilian associates, Axia Consulting, conducted research in the supplier market for live cattle in Brazil. The objective was to ascertain the selling expectations among a sample of ranchers across a region of Brazil. Around the same time, JBS introduced several other initiatives designed to increase cooperation with its supplier base, e.g. to provide digital maps of properties of suppliers that did not have one already (Easy Map); together with Instituto Centro de Vida they also launched a program in 2013 to encourage ranchers to adopt sustainable practices with a view to increasing productivity and quality, and reforest degraded land (the New Field program).

Results

The results of this landmark research into the selling behaviors of Brazilian cattlemen were quite unexpected. We found that 81 per cent of the sample had some element of 'relationship' (I logic) in their expectations, and only 19 per cent were primarily driven to get top price. In detail, 37 per cent of the sample were motivated to enter long-term contracts for the sake of stability and to partner with processors, if possible. Another 35 per cent were interested in a better yield from their animals and, for that reason, were eager to cooperate with processors to find ways to increase yield. And 9 per cent of the sample were interested in modern techniques and prepared to experiment jointly to improve the productivity of their herd. Only the residual 19 per cent sought to opportunistically sell to the highest bidder for top dollar. This somewhat unexpected finding provided information to allow JBS to realign its buying propositions to the various rancher segments and include significant non-price relationship components, rather than just talk down the price.

Following its sustainability effort, McDonald's partnered with JBS to produce a verified sustainable hamburger from suppliers within the Amazon basin. Suppliers also benefited through reduced emissions, reduced slaughtering age and increased productivity.

What can we learn?

This case has several lessons. The first is that it is possible to grow a business and practice sustainable methods at the same time. This benefits all stakeholders in the red meat supply chain. The other lesson is that a simple focus on procurement price paid for inputs is flawed because it assumes that all suppliers have the same selling expectations. Wrong! Suppliers, like customers at the other end of the supply chain, have varying expectations, priced-based and non-priced-based, and we need to align our offers with this in mind.

The magic of linking customer and supplier segments

The best of all worlds occurs if an enterprise can consciously link the buying behaviors on the customer-side, with the selling behaviors on the supply-side, and to manage their operation in the middle in this context. To facilitate this, a powerful approach to developing end-to-end strategy is to link all three subsystems using a network optimization model, which allows various service and cost scenarios to be tested. We will talk in more detail about this idea when we discuss the CBH Grains case study in Chapter 5.

Points of view

1   Customer segmentation is the starting point for an *'outside-in'* approach that guides appropriate and market-aligned transformation.

2   Customer research and demand analytics are the key methods to inform behavioral segmentation and thus should be the first step for supply chain design or redesign.

3   The *'one-size-fits-all'* supply chain design philosophy is flawed because it assumes all customers have the same expectations. All of our research to date disproves this assumption.

4   Once we understand the expectations of our customers, it is possible to reverse-engineer these back into the enterprise. In other words, these insights about our customers directly inform the design of the supply chain.

5   Network optimization modeling cuts through the complexity and risk-aversion that can be the major barriers to change. It enables cool-headed testing of various service scenarios associated with the different customer behavior segments.

6   Segmentation and modeling are also key support tools to engage commercial and marketing functions in the supply chain of the future.

7   The supply-side is a mirror image of the demand-side, and offers much potential for value extraction if suppliers are managed in a more appropriate way, according to their selling expectations.

Kick-start your thinking

AN OUTSIDE-IN LENS

How well informed is your supply chain/organization about the market it serves? Do you . . .

Research customer expectations or only customer satisfaction?	Use segmentation to focus on the key differences in what customers need from the supply chain?
Treat demand patterns as an input to supply chain strategy?	Know the cost-to-serve of different types of customers?
Know how your lead times compare to your competitors?	Understand the Product Pareto for your range?

CHAPTER 4

Tailored supply chains give flexibility

Competing on differentiation

Introduction

F ollowing on from the core concepts of alignment introduced in Chapter 2 and the 'outside-in' premise explored in Chapter 3, we will now examine in more detail the implications of these ideas for the management of the supply chain. In particular, we will develop a profile of the five key supply chain configurations needed to support differentiated responses to the most common buying segments. Once hardwired into the enterprise, a portfolio drawn from these supply chain types can enable more effective alignment with customers in a range of target markets to be achieved without undermining efficiency. Taken together, they constitute what has become known by some of our clients as *Tailored Supply Chains*.[1]

The five supply chain types that we will focus on align with the most common customer segments:

- *Collaborative* Supply Chains™, that align with the *collaborative* segment;

- *Lean* Supply Chains, that align with the *transactional* segment;

- *Agile* Supply Chains, that align with the *dynamic* segment;

- *Campaign*[2] Supply Chains™, that align with the *project accumulation* segment; and

- *Fully Flexible* Supply Chains™, that align with the *innovative solutions* segment.

For each supply chain type, we will:

◆ propose a *value proposition* that summarizes how this supply chain delivers differentiated value to the target customer segment;

◆ suggest elements of an ideal, cross-functional, *operational strategy* to deliver each value proposition;

◆ consider the supply chain network and planning implications of each type.

Collaborative Supply Chains™

This is a unique supply chain type. It is, effectively, a subset of the more commonly known Lean Supply Chain. Through our work on behavioral segmentation, we were able to recognize the existence of this particular group of customers in many different markets. They look similar to *transactional* customers and share many of the same characteristics, but there are also some defining differences, e.g. willingness to share information and data; trusting a few selected suppliers as primary sources; and interest in participating in joint developments, to name a few.

We always suggest to our clients that the first thing they should do is identify which of their customers fit into this category because, if managed appropriately, they will be a continuing source of revenue and margin, unlike some of their other customers who come and go at will.

This type of customer craves acknowledgment and recognition, demonstrates brand loyalty and is not especially price-sensitive. If they like a company or brand, they will stay loyal until they lose faith, which is mostly due to being constantly ignored and under-valued.

Collaboration often is treated in 'motherhood' terms, an aspirational mode of operating with all customers. Our experience has been that this is rarely appropriate. First, for many customers, the commitment to one organization and the dedication and patience required to be loyal buyers or effective collaborators, does not synch with their own mindset or their organization's DNA.

And, second, this is often only a fraction of the market. Except for very high-end, premium branded product categories, *Collaborative* customers are rarely the largest segment in a market in terms of the numbers of customers.

The *Collaborative* segment, though, tends to represent a much larger proportion of sales or margin than their numbers suggest.

A typical value proposition for the *Collaborative* Supply Chain™ is shown in Figure 4.1. Notice how it is represented as cutting right across the entire enterprise. We contend that all functions contribute aspects of the customer's experience of value and that they all must buy-in if this supply chain is to be a success.

In industrial buying situations and where customers are few and relatively large, you may need to limit the number of customers singled out for the special treatment that the Collaborative Supply Chain™ implies. It is, by definition, a very labor-intensive supply chain type, because large customers in this category expect personal attention in a world that is rapidly going digital. They can't be switched over easily to an impersonal arms-length, system-driven relationship, for the sake of efficiency.

On the other hand, some of these customers may be happy to work on a joint systems/IT project connecting the two organizations, but only if the personal touch is kept intact as well.

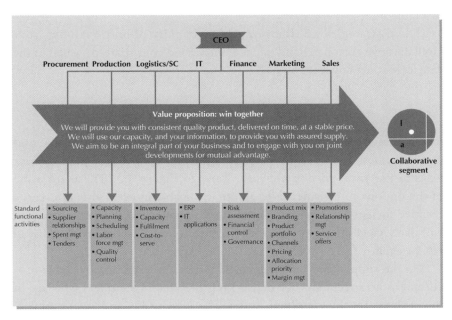

FIGURE 4.1 ◆ **Value proposition for Collaborative Supply Chains™**

Source: Adapted from Gattorna (2009) p. 140

In the consumer market, or industrial situations where there are a large number of smaller Collaborative customers, the relationship must be necessarily built and managed by the brand and systematic personalized engagement. The most important factors here are that the consistency and 'assurance' that the brand represents are backed up by supply chain performance.

Protective strategy

In the 'Strategy recipe' for each supply chain type, we have included 16 Strategic Dimensions, which are drawn from across all the functions depicted in Figure 4.1. For each Strategic Dimension we have suggested an 'Ideal Operations Strategy', and the combination of all 16 represents the way the business can shape its Collaborative Supply Chain™ for the purposes of servicing the Collaborative customer segment. There are, of course, other ways to achieve the same end but these give a guide to the types of strategies to consider.

The collection of Ideal Operations Strategies, which together represent the Protective Strategy for the Collaborative Supply Chain™, are detailed in Figure 4.2.

These strategies will improve the probability of both retaining your Collaborative customers and, indeed, increasing your share-of-wallet in the categories they buy from you.

Network implications

The potential stability and visibility of demand associated with Collaborative customers can open up new and more efficient supply paths and/or ways to use your existing network. Refer to Figure 4.3. These are some of the options to consider. Not all are applicable in every situation and a creative focus on the particulars of the customer and their own network will likely yield other options. But we have found this a good checklist to review against.

On the supply-side, stable demand can be underpinned by stable procurement arrangements for major inputs. Reliable suppliers who are in the business for the long-haul, and will be responsible and loyal suppliers to you, are the best fit to give the certainty and low risk needed for these customers.

	STRATEGIC DIMENSION	IDEAL STRATEGY
Marketing/sales	Product mix	Emphasis on mature, branded and augmented products
	Marketing emphasis	Build brand loyalty
	Channels of distribution	Either direct or via trusted outlets
	Pricing regime	Price according to strength of brand; moderate price sensitivity
	Promotional activity	Low promotional activity – not needed
Positioning	Innovation emphasis	Big emphasis on product quality and joint product development. Innovate to improve relationship
	Service emphasis	Empathy with loyal customers; consistency of service; trust
	Relationship intensity	Mutual dependence between customer and supplier
	Resource allocation priorities	Focus on supporting the relationship to retain customer
	Strategic risk profile	Low
Fulfilment	Procurement/sourcing approach	Select suppliers on basis of relationships
	Production	Low volume – high value add. Collaborate to reduce costs
	Capacity considerations	Maximum utilization achievable consistent with serving customers
	Logistics approach	Reliable/scheduled delivery; shared forecasts
	Systems/IT support	Emphasis on customer management, CRM essential
Finance & Administration	Financial considerations	Relax credit terms. Undertake customer account profitability analysis

FIGURE 4.2 ◆ Collaborative Supply Chain™ Strategy – Protective

Source: Adapted from Gattorna (2015) p. 202

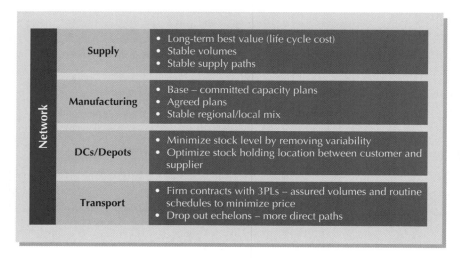

Network	Supply	• Long-term best value (life cycle cost) • Stable volumes • Stable supply paths
	Manufacturing	• Base – committed capacity plans • Agreed plans • Stable regional/local mix
	DCs/Depots	• Minimize stock level by removing variability • Optimize stock holding location between customer and supplier
	Transport	• Firm contracts with 3PLs – assured volumes and routine schedules to minimize price • Drop out echelons – more direct paths

FIGURE 4.3 ◆ **Practical implications of the Collaborative Supply Chain™ configuration**

In manufacturing terms, it is likely we will have forecasts from these customers that are highly accurate, so capacity commitments and production plans can be locked further in advance.

In the wider downstream distribution of finished goods, it is very likely that demand from these *Collaborative* customers will form a convenient 'baseload' in terms of stocking points and inventory levels. We might even be able to treat our customers' inbound networks and our outbound network as one, thereby reducing the overall level of inventory carried in the system and lowering overall holding costs.

Finally, considering transport across our network and that of our customers, we should be able to offer firm contracts to selected 3PLs, as well as find innovative ways to drop out nodes. For example, DKSH in Thailand was able to take soft drinks from the end of the supplier's production line in Thailand and deliver direct to retail outlets such as 7-Eleven, bypassing the need to take the product through its own distribution centers (DCs), with all the additional time and handling costs involved.

Planning implications

Planning in the case of *Collaborative* customers should be relatively easy and straightforward. Why? Because in most, if not all, cases, these customers will

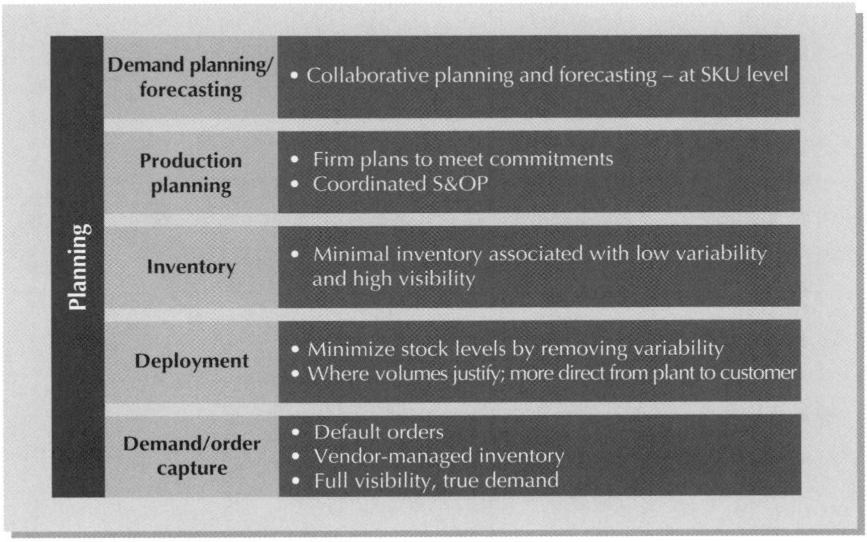

Planning	Demand planning/ forecasting	• Collaborative planning and forecasting – at SKU level
	Production planning	• Firm plans to meet commitments • Coordinated S&OP
	Inventory	• Minimal inventory associated with low variability and high visibility
	Deployment	• Minimize stock levels by removing variability • Where volumes justify; more direct from plant to customer
	Demand/order capture	• Default orders • Vendor-managed inventory • Full visibility, true demand

FIGURE 4.4 ◆ **Practical implications of the Collaborative Supply Chain™ configuration**

happily share their own forecasts of demand and make firm order commitments. The sales and operations planning (S&OP) process is greatly simplified. Customers can even be sitting in on our planning discussions or we can implant a planning executive in the customer's facility. Either way, it takes a lot of the unknowns out of forward planning.

In removing variability, we are able to carry less stock and produce product to an agreed schedule.

The planning implications are summarized in Figure 4.4.

Lean and Agile Supply Chains

In most industries that we are familiar with, Lean and Agile Supply Chains work in parallel, the *yin* and *yang* of the supply chain. For that reason, we will discuss them together and compare their respective properties, which are largely complementary.

While the Lean Supply Chain is designed to deliver product on a reliable basis at lowest cost, the Agile Supply Chain is designed with enough in-built capacity to be able to respond to unpredictable demand, cost-effectively, but not at the same low cost as Lean.

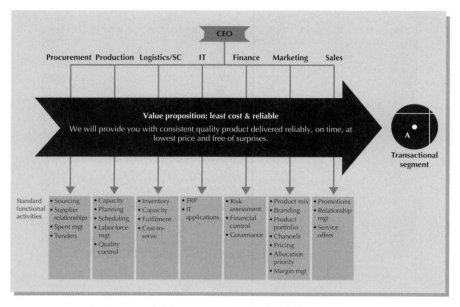

FIGURE 4.5A ◆ Value proposition for Lean Supply Chains

Source: Adapted from Gattorna (2009) p. 140

The respective *value propositions* for Lean and Agile say it all; see Figure 4.5A and 4.5B.

Whereas Lean focuses on meeting customer expectations for reliable, low-cost service, Agile is for customers who expect fast and flexible delivery under sometimes uncertain market conditions. The same customers could, conceivably, use both pathways on different occasions, under different circumstances.

Incremental strategy

The whole thrust of the Lean Supply Chain is to deliver a stable product line at lowest cost and on time. As such, all the functions must input to this supply chain in ways that are consistent with this objective.

In turn, this allows marketing and sales to offer these stable products on an 'everyday low prices' basis, making them very competitive. But, remember, this is usually for just part of the product range.

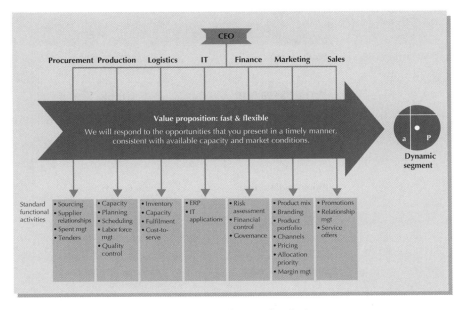

FIGURE 4.5B ◆ **Value proposition for Agile Supply Chains**

Source: Adapted from Gattorna (2009) p. 140

Innovation in this supply chain focuses mostly on engineering out cost through clever industrial engineering and removing waste wherever identified in the upstream and downstream subsystems.

Production can usually make long runs of standard product to reduce unit cost. And finance and accounting emphasize cost control throughout this supply chain.

The cross-functional dimensions that contribute to the incremental strategy needed for Lean Supply Chains are outlined in Figure 4.6.

In the case of the Agile Supply Chain, the product range usually would be larger in order to offer more choice, price is pitched at a competitive level (not always the lowest, as these customers factor in speed and availability) and, ideally, there are smaller batch sizes, which may require flexible manufacturing or even make-to-order (MTO). And because demand is difficult to predict, the shorter lead times involved require buffers at one or more points along the supply chain. These buffers can come in several

	STRATEGIC DIMENSION	IDEAL STRATEGY
Marketing/sales	**Product mix**	Stable product line; minimal variants
	Marketing emphasis	Lowest price; reliability
	Channels of distribution	Wide distribution through multiple channels
	Pricing regime	Lowest price. Every day low prices
	Promotional activity	Periodical, planned promotions
Positioning	**Innovation emphasis**	Focus on ways to reduce cost of inputs and processes
	Service emphasis	Efficiency and process engineering
	Relationship intensity	Low
	Resource allocation priorities	Focus on cost reduction
	Strategic risk profile	Low
Fulfilment	**Procurement/sourcing approach**	Outsource standard products to gain lowest cost production
	Production	High volume – low cost; commodity
	Capacity considerations	High utilization
	Logistics approach	High reliability; predictable service and availability
	Systems/IT support	Emphasis on transactional systems
Finance & Administration	**Financial considerations**	Focus on cost control/ management. Possibly use ABC costing

FIGURE 4.6 ◆ Lean Supply Chain™ Strategy – Incremental

Source: Adapted from Gattorna (2015) p. 242

forms, i.e. labor, inventory, production capacity and transport capacity. See Figure 4.7 for a list of ideal operational strategies that can be deployed.

For best results, it is recommended that decision support system, be deployed to help decide which orders of this type should be accepted and on what terms.

	STRATEGIC DIMENSION	IDEAL STRATEGY
Marketing/sales	Product mix	Larger range; choice important
	Marketing emphasis	Quick response to changing customer requirements
	Channels of distribution	Provide easy access to consumers; convenience
	Pricing regime	Competitive; moderate price sensitivity
	Promotional activity	High; fashion-style approaches
Positioning	Innovation emphasis	Seek product differentiation
	Service emphasis	Performance to specifications
	Relationship intensity	Low
	Resource allocation priorities	Build spare capacity to cater for volatile demand
	Strategic risk profile	Higher risk
Fulfilment	Procurement/sourcing approach	Market knowledge and distribution
	Production	Shorter runs; flexible scheduling; Make-to-Order
	Capacity considerations	Lower utilization because of 'buffers' in the system
	Logistics approach	Short lead times; use postponement
	Systems/IT support	Use modeling and analysis
Finance & Administration	Financial considerations	Focus on cost of additional (redundant) capacity. Monitor cash flow

FIGURE 4.7 ◆ Agile Supply Chain Strategy – Operational

Source: Adapted from Gattorna (2015) p. 282

Network implications

The pathways for Lean and Agile Supply Chains through the same enterprise network are very different.

In the case of Lean, everything is focused on low-cost repeatable processes, minimal stock-holding, and firm baseload contracts with 3PLs. However, for Agile, we have to build 'flex' somewhere in the network, on the supply-side (contracts), headroom capacity in manufacturing, using postponement protocols and/or variable labor and 3PL contracts.

This reality of opposing conditions available in the same network and a checklist for considering the network options for each supply chain configuration are shown in Figure 4.8A.

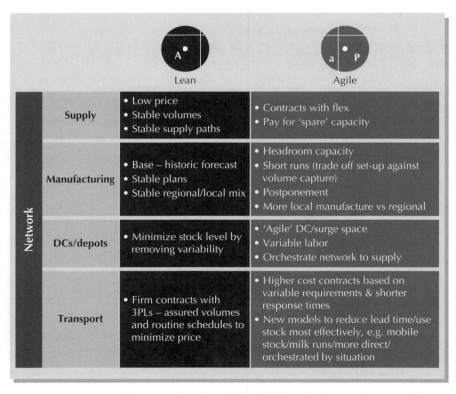

FIGURE 4.8A ◆ **Practical implications of Lean and Agile Supply Chain configurations**

Planning

And the same applies to planning regimes. Whereas in the Lean Supply Chain, we tend to forecast at the (stock keeping unit) SKU level and work on batch sizes through manufacturing, with high availability targets; in the Agile Supply Chain, things couldn't be more different.

Here we tend to forecast 'capacity' and book at that level with 3PLs and outsourced producers, while keeping everything as flexible as possible, to the very last moment. Another way of coping with this type of volatility is to ramp up the *clockspeed* of the entire organization to the point that net disruption levels are minimized.

The comparative situation for planning in each type of supply chain is depicted in Figure 4.8B.

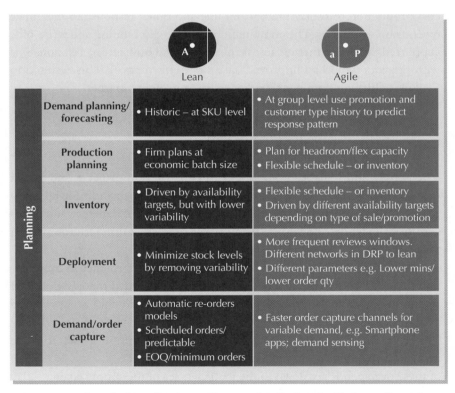

		Lean	Agile
Planning	**Demand planning/ forecasting**	• Historic – at SKU level	• At group level use promotion and customer type history to predict response pattern
	Production planning	• Firm plans at economic batch size	• Plan for headroom/flex capacity • Flexible schedule – or inventory
	Inventory	• Driven by availability targets, but with lower variability	• Flexible schedule – or inventory • Driven by different availability targets depending on type of sale/promotion
	Deployment	• Minimize stock levels by removing variability	• More frequent reviews windows. Different networks in DRP to lean • Different parameters e.g. Lower mins/ lower order qty
	Demand/order capture	• Automatic re-orders models • Scheduled orders/ predictable • EOQ/minimum orders	• Faster order capture channels for variable demand, e.g. Smartphone apps; demand sensing

FIGURE 4.8B ◆ **Practical implications of Lean and Agile Supply Chain configurations**

Seafolly, an Australian swimwear company, now dominates market share in its home country and has built a highly successful global brand. A key part of the strategy that enabled it to grow dramatically in a notoriously difficult fashion category was its savvy use of parallel Lean and Agile Supply Chains.

While its competitors were using the traditional 'push' strategy, loading up department stores at the start of the season with their best estimates of what would sell, and assuming either lost sales or deep discounting by the end of the season, Seafolly decided to take a different path.

Prior to the start of the season, it purchased fabric for the season's range and split its shipments of each fabric between its low-cost manufacturers in China and its local operation. At the start of the season, the initial shipment of finished goods arrived by sea from China and was distributed to department stores – a smaller 'push'; but, after that, the model turned to replenishment, based on monitoring sales and then fast, local production of the lines that were moving well. This *best of both worlds* strategy enabled low-cost production to satisfy the bottom line and quick response to maximize revenue opportunities. The combination reduced discounting and write-offs, supported the brand further across the season and built strong relationships with retailers (who had improved category performance). This resulted in Seafolly achieving dominant market share in its home market.

Campaign Supply Chains™

The supply and logistics component of construction projects and major engineering events, such as gas plant shutdowns, can account for up to 60 per cent of total cost. And, on many projects, liquidated damages and exposure from extended downtime bring risks sufficient to undermine project profitability.

The UK has been focusing on improving project performance in construction since 1994 when the first of a series of highly regarded reports identified significant losses to the economy of poor project performance and proposed new directions for the industry.[3] A follow-up review in 2009 found that: 'eleven years of KPIs have shown that projects are still only 50% likely to come in on budget and the average cost overrun of the remainder . . . was 26%. Half of these overspends are down to the inefficiencies of the supply chain . . . '.[4]

Despite the criticality of inbound supply, there has been very little adoption of the end-to-end 'supply chain' mindset or the tools of the supply chain profession, such as network optimization modeling, in the construction and heavy engineering industries. There has also been a tendency for manufacturers supplying these industries to treat project demand as just one more transactional order. Out-of-stocks, despite six months' notice and missed crane lifts, are the symptoms of mismatched processes and misaligned KPIs.

Major project-driven demand requires specialized supply chain capability. We have labeled the supply chain response needed as the Campaign Supply Chain™. The timing, positioning and configuration of materials are directly driven by the project schedule. The suppliers' operations need transparency of the various schedules and site locations in the planning processes.

Demand on suppliers is usually quite 'lumpy' and accumulation, quarantining of stock, staging and precision delivery are key processes needed to support major capital projects.

This pattern of demand, and the accumulation and staging expectation, is typical of the construction and engineering industries, but can also be seen in some large-scale promotions in the consumer goods industry.

The relationship between project duration and cost means that suppliers of projects are also increasingly competing on lead times.

Our field experience, on both sides of the project supply chain, suggests that few suppliers and subcontractors have the precise capabilities to reliably deliver the complex requirements of major project supply on an ongoing basis. Many suppliers have been accustomed to selling discrete products through various downstream channels to end users.

And, on the customer or project side, while there is a lot of experience managing projects at the site level, few of even the largest contractors are sophisticated in their end-to-end supply chain practices. They have been used to focusing on the procurement activity in terms of fit-for-purpose materials and price, but not so much on the flow of materials, cost-to-use and aspects such as supplier reliability and lead-time performance, which are, invariably, critical to meeting overall project timelines and cost projections.

So, overall, there is significant opportunity for misalignment between the two sides. By articulating the particular supply chain characteristics that are appropriate, in the form of the *Campaign* Supply Chain™, we hope to help project owners, suppliers and the third-party operators that often sit between them to understand each of their roles and to realize the enormous potential for improvement available.

A *value proposition* for the *Campaign* Supply Chain™ is depicted in Figure 4.9. Here, the clear emphasis is on complying to the terms and

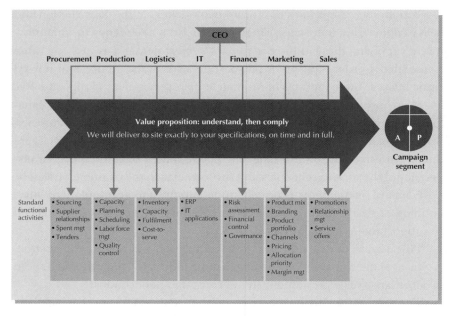

FIGURE 4.9 ◆ **Value proposition for Campaign Supply Chains™**

conditions of the contract, meeting specification at an agreed cost and delivering to a specific time schedule. These are the important criteria that all functions in the business must factor into the way the end-to-end process is managed.

Impact of collaboration on project outcomes

The P-A-D-I logics that we use for the Campaign Supply Chain™ – 'PA' – emphasize the time critical and the results focus aspects (P) as well as the reliability and control aspects (A). These are important in almost every major project and dictate the primary requirements for this type of situation. We recognize, however, that this is the most complex supply chain and that underneath the surface there are other requirements at different stages of the project life cycle. It could even be said that the Campaign Supply Chain™ is actually a hybrid. In the early design stages, especially, often there will need to be high levels of collaboration; when the project schedule is at risk, expediting and solutions at any cost may be required (what we will later describe as the Fully Flexible Supply Chain™).

It is also apparent that there are different styles of project: some with a much higher level of innovation required (where price should be secondary); others that follow a time-worn, predictable path where the experience curve should be leveraged to drive down cost and drive up project delivery reliability; and others that are difficult to specify and cost up front, and a flexible, stage-gated approach to execution is preferable (the ideal candidate for 'Agile' project delivery; and likely to require support from an 'Agile' or 'Fully Flexible' Supply Chain™).

Across those variations in emphasis, however, on very large capital projects, the strongest message coming through is that high levels of collaboration between project owners and major suppliers is associated with more successful outcomes.

The UK reports mentioned above, and much of the academic research on major construction projects, emphasize the improved probability of meeting time and cost targets with integration and collaboration along the chain. Although the UK Government has still not seen widespread adoption of the recommendations, two massive UK projects that have very publicly followed and benefited from the insights are the construction of the London Olympics facilities and the building of Heathrow's Terminal 5. Both have come in largely on time and on budget (the Olympics, even under budget). Initiatives such as pooled risk payments to encourage vendors to work together to solve problems and open-book costing were used at Heathrow to create a more open, cooperative contract environment.

The lack of a supply chain mindset lies on both sides, but it is the large engineering, procurement and construction contractors and project owners that have the most influence and should take the lead in upgrading their own operational practices and contracting approaches.

The big global industrial companies who are supplying these major projects might also re-examine their own practices in light of the shift away from mass manufacturing of products to project assemblies. One company we are aware of that is doing just that is Schneider Electric.[5] It has taken up this challenge and is examining how best to configure its network, on a region-by-region basis, to align with the particular mix of product/project business in these regions. It has also recognized that project business is different and needs specialized supply chain focus if it is to have a competitive advantage in this segment of customers.

Network options

Because of the 'one-off' nature of projects, the flow of materials onto the site is not given the same level of scrutiny as where the flow is continuous and long term. Considering the level of spend and the impact this flow can have, both on project performance and site efficiency, there is a strong incentive to consider how best to support projects and to use network modeling tools to 'design' the optimal arrangement on a project by project basis.

Examples of some of the network options that might emerge to service a major project are depicted in Figure 4.10.

These could include:

◆ A dedicated Project distribution center (DC) is built to handle all project-related business. This will receive products and subassemblies from all sources and build these into larger assemblies. At the appointed time, special packaging and special transport may be required to deliver aggregated inputs and assemblies to a site to meet the current project plan.

◆ On the other hand, a contractor may opt to outsource the specialist task of handling project-style work to a Campaign 3PL. Companies such as DHL, Kuehne + Nagel, and GEODIS have divisions specializing in this type of work.

◆ Finally, is the 'pop-up' warehouse model set up by a supplier at or near the project site to consolidate deliveries and conduct quality assurance (QA) close to where needed?

The particular choice of network facility is a function of the particular needs of the project; the key point being that this can, and should, be proactively designed and that analytical and mathematical tools can support that decision.

Building a knowledge exchange for projects

One of the glaring weaknesses inherent in the way large projects have been managed to date is the project by project method adopted. The learning and accumulated knowledge acquired in one project is not necessarily passed to the next. This knowledge largely resides in the heads of individual project managers, and they may or may not transfer it to the next project. What is needed are two improvements on this ad hoc process:

1. Adoption of an *end-to-end (E2E) supply chain philosophy* for projects that incorporates full visibility of supply-side and demand-side flows of

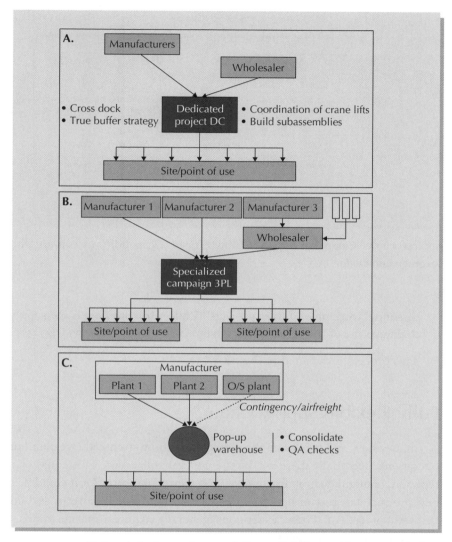

FIGURE 4.10 ◆ Network design options to deliver reliability and low-cost solutions to project schedules

materials, products and labor, as well as addressing disposal issues at the end of the life of the project.

2. Knowledge capture, using tools such as project dashboards, which capture and record the lessons learned on a project, which can then be aggregated in a *knowledge exchange*. This becomes a reference point for

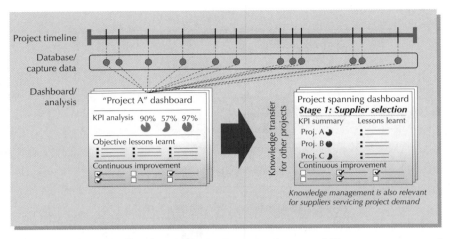

FIGURE 4.11 ◆ Campaign Supply Chains™ need a capability to capture and leverage knowledge

personnel working on future projects. While our focus here is the supply chain aspects of the project, this obviously has value more widely.

This process is depicted in Figure 4.11.

Fully Flexible Supply Chain™

No matter how well we design the network and how attentively we plan our operations, eventually there will be the unplannable event. This could be a typhoon, tsunami, factory fire or a key supplier bankruptcy. Or it could be a new product category or new channel, with no established patterns and little useful precedent. These 'exceptions' generally require a specific mindset and capability to optimize the situation at hand. Although a specific type of event may be infrequent, most large organizations are exposed to many such disruptive events each year. In recognition of this fact, and aware of the advantages of isolating such activity and developing a specialized capability around it, we have defined the *Fully Flexible* Supply Chain™ type.

The Fully Flexible Supply Chain™ does not replace contingency planning. There is a core requirement to plan and manage risk in each part of the operation. But when the risk goes beyond the contingency plan or we

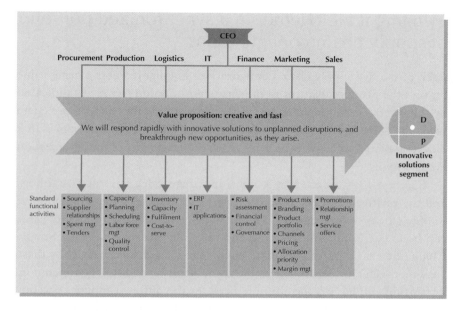

FIGURE 4.12 ◆ **Value proposition for Fully Flexible Supply Chains™**

are dealing with dramatic opportunities (the next iPhone), this is the capability needed to go 'off script' and quickly resolve a solution, no matter at what cost.

Unlike the other supply chains, there are no guidelines regarding the network or the planning approach that normally would be required; the high levels of variability preclude commitments to infrastructure and usually even processes and systems. The key resource requirement is experienced staff with a 'solutions' mindset, and the authority to make the quick decisions required when necessary. This could be a small team with a national (even global) responsibility, ready to spring into action when needed. The type of value proposition they would be working to is shown in Figure 4.12.

It has also become apparent to us and it clearly emerges from the value proposition that this is also the capability set that every organization now needs in its armory to drive innovation. The proactive and open-minded search for new solutions and the willingness and leeway to experiment are essential in fast-changing markets with fast-evolving digital tools. The Fully Flexible Supply Chain™ team could well drive innovation as their day job and emergency response as their night job!

Bringing it all together in a synchronized portfolio of supply chain configurations

Each of the five supply chain configurations highlighted above bring value beyond the product features to the customer in unique ways. As indicated by the way we have depicted the value propositions for each supply chain type, one of the most important implications of tailored supply chains is that differentiation may actually be achieved in different parts of the organization for each type.

Figure 4.13 is an attempt to consider where value is created and how, and the relative contribution of different functions. For the Collaborative Supply Chain™, for example, considerable 'relationship' and 'brand' value can be created only in marketing and sales. Whereas in the Agile Supply Chain, the lead time and responsiveness that are weighted heavily by these customers is highly dependent on the manufacturing and logistics operation. This again emphasizes the absolute need for the different functions to buy in to the horizontal supply chain flow philosophy. It's a matter of the chain is only as strong as its weakest link!

The degree of differentiation

In practical terms, even organizations that have identified the need for three, four or five different supply chain options to service their market fully often will find that the differentiation does not need to extend to all aspects of the organization. Mapping where value is generated for different types of customers, as depicted in Figure 4.13, can also identify the inverse – where it doesn't matter! The level of common versus differentiated network, processes and information technology is an important consideration in coming up with a practical result that can be implemented.

In some situations, the core requirement is for reliability and predictability so the Lean base is most suitable, and differentiation for Project, Agile and Collaborative can be confined to a few processes and systems. In another situation, however, fully independent end-to-end operations are required for the different segments and these may be fully outsourced or set up as physically discrete operations.

Different variations along this theme are depicted in Figure 4.14.

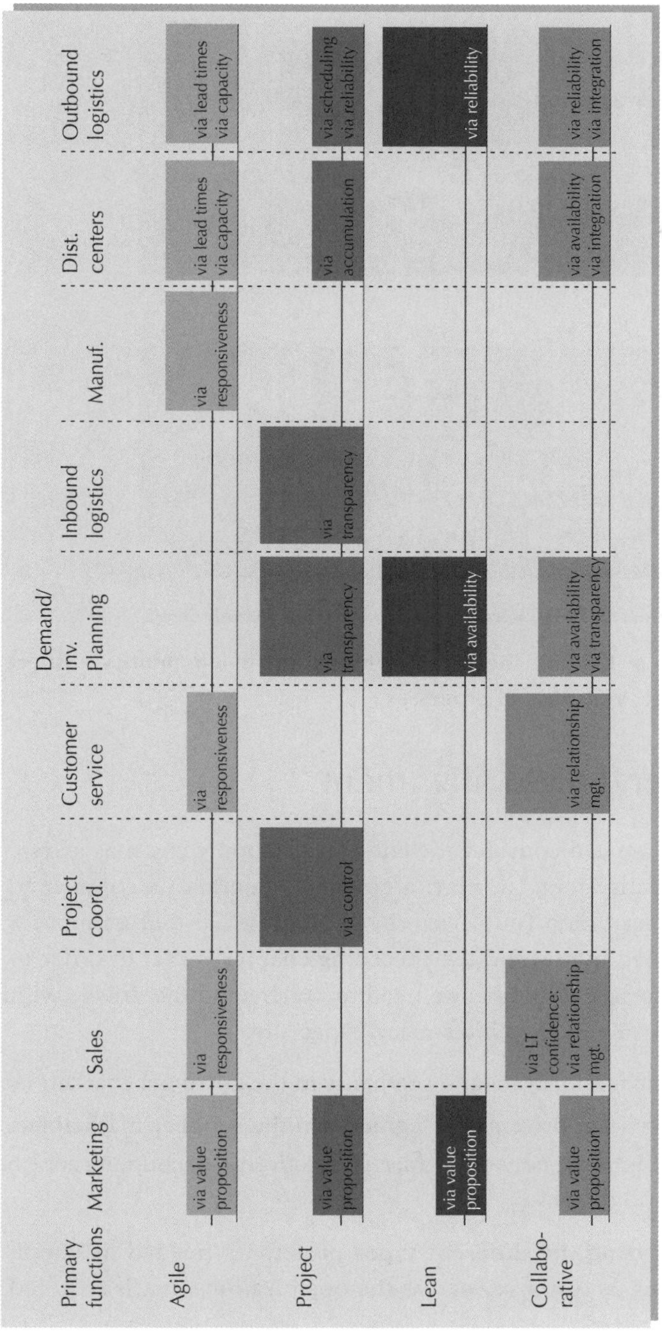

FIGURE 4.13 ◆ Value creation by function in the supply chain

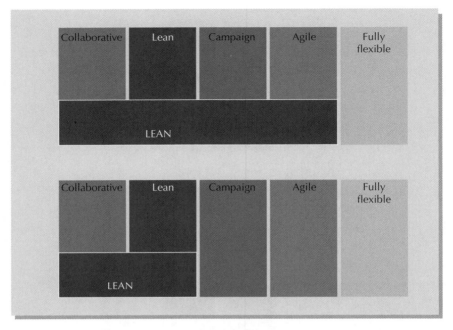

FIGURE 4.14 ◆ **Finding the right combination of common vs differentiated infrastructure, systems and processes**

End-to-end (E2E) alignment

Ultimately, we can consider the end-to-end supply chain as a system with three key 'subsystems' at play: a customer 'market'; a supplier 'market'; and the organization (ourselves) in the middle. In that context, what we have identified in this and the preceding chapter is that in order to design more appropriate responses we need to understand the drivers within each subsystem and how they inter-react, especially:

1. The behavioral drivers and segments in the customer marketplace.
2. The behavioral drivers and segments in the supplier marketplace.
3. Our own inhouse network, which is effectively a decoupling zone between supply and demand.

Summarizing the different types of activity needed as supply chain types enables us to convey across the organization what is required on the demand-side; and the capabilities we need to draw on from the supply-side. It also enables us to proactively design the network in a more considered way, including how and where to buffer or decouple along the chain/network.

These aspects of the overall E2E 'system' are depicted in Figure 4.15.

What this diagram suggests is that there are multiple potential pathways through an enterprise, from supply-side to customer-side. The key is setting up an internal organization structure that can intercept and interpret the demand signals from the marketplace and determine which supply-side and demand-side combinations to engage. Usually, there will be a small number that take most of the load.

Using this framework has allowed us to understand that customer activity in the marketplace is the starting point for all design and, once patterns become evident, it is possible to develop them further into repeatable processes that underpin product and service flows.

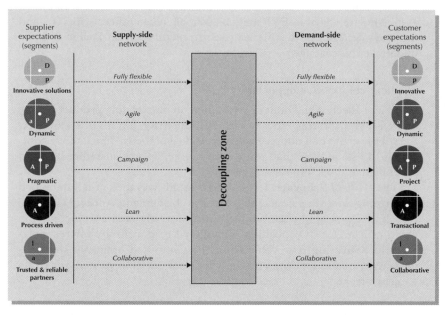

FIGURE 4.15 ◆ **End-to-end alignment implies a portfolio of supply chain paths**

Source: Figure 13.1 in Gattorna (2015), p. 404

CASE STUDY: Schneider Electric

Pioneering the roll-out of the Tailored Supply Chain solution for global customers

Situation

Schneider Electric is a French multinational supplier of energy management and automation solutions, serving a wide range of customers including utilities, data centers, industry and consumers. Its global revenue in 2017 was €25 billion, supported by 207 factories and 98 distribution centers worldwide. The business has been on a dramatic growth trajectory, nearly doubling in size in 12 years through mergers, acquisitions and organic growth. This growth was also accompanied by enormous complexity, exemplified by a legacy of 125 enterprise planning systems and numerous subcultures.

Schneider Electric has undertaken a massive supply chain transformation program over the last seven years. From a standing start in 2011, by 2018, Schneider Electric was ranked number 12 on the Gartner Top 25 Global Supply Chains and number 5 in Europe. Much of the credit must go to Annette Clayton, EVP and chief supply chain officer (CSCO) (and now president of North America region), recruited from Dell in 2011 to undertake this massive transformation.

The next competitive opportunity

Schneider Electric had built its reputation on outstanding product quality and on manufacturing efficiency and productivity. Until 2012, however, the supply chain had not received a great deal of focus. The rate of acquisitions (49 since 1988) had resulted in a large, diverse customer base but no unified approach to serving them.

The CEO of Schneider recognized that this was their great, untapped opportunity and set a course to address it, bringing in Annette Clayton, who had led supply chain at Dell, into a newly created chief supply chain officer (CSCO) position with global responsibility for recognizing and delivering new value from the combined operations of procurement, manufacturing and logistics. His decision turned out to be a masterstroke.

Connecting with the customer – the evolution of tailored supply chains

The key theme that Schneider Electric used to drive the first stage of its lift in focus was 'Connect-to-Customers', and the emphasis was on building an 'outside-in' supply chain culture and a set of global capabilities and tools to enable proactive design and execution of a customer-driven and simplified strategy. As the strategy evolved, the theme became more specific, focusing on 'differentiation' and 'the right to win'.

One of the critical first initiatives was to understand more about what customers really expected (and move beyond just knowing how satisfied/ dissatisfied they were at a point in time). After initial pilots, a methodology was developed, based on the Dynamic Alignment™ framework, to research customer buying behaviors across business units and geographies. This provided insight into the buying segments in the served markets and, thus, a way to reduce the complexity of such a diverse customer base into a more meaningful grouping.

After this research was conducted in several countries, it became apparent that five key segments could be used to describe the buying behavior differences in any country (albeit in different mixes). These were then converted into the five supply chain types that became the basis for the Schneider Tailored Supply Chains: Collaborative, Lean, Agile, Project and Fully Flexible.

Customer process capabilities have been developed to support differentiated supply chains; both at the Tailored Supply Chain and the industry level (e.g. OEMs versus panel builders) and 18 key capabilities enable the customer to experience an aligned service without the complexity that naturally accompanies customization.

Strategic decision support was a pivotal capability developed early to support the new direction and the Tailored Supply Chains strategy. Modeling is used to test service and cost scenarios; and country-level, regional and global flow models now cover much of the total Schneider network. From one person to a team of seven centrally, and nine regionally, network modeling, simulation, inventory optimization and analytics have become core competencies and support almost all major infrastructure and network decisions. These projects have identified very substantial savings, as well as defining the structure needed to gain a service advantage within a country.

Like most major multinationals, especially those that have grown by acquisition, data consistency and master data took a lot of work in early modeling projects and so this area has been, and continues to be, an area of focus, especially as Schneider's operations become more digitized. In parallel, and in pursuit of scale efficiencies, simplification and access to digital visibility, Schneider has also consolidated its third-party provider (3PL) network from 1,450 in 2013, to 300 today.

▶

Sustainability is also a key priority for Schneider Electric, heavily championed by the CEO and senior leadership team. During these years of transformation to an 'outside-in' philosophy, the supply chain team have also made substantial reductions in the CO_2 emissions across the network.

With so many initiatives in a short period, the building of project management disciplines and a project management office (PMO) to oversee change has also been fundamental to continued success.

Impact

The results of Schneider's intense focus on building a customer-centric logistics platform tailored to customers' buying behavior have been impressive. Using the easiest metrics to measure performance, in five years, the strategy has doubled the customer satisfaction score on the broad 'delivery' metric, improved on-time delivery by 3.2 points (to 95.8 per cent) and reduced logistics (DC and transport) savings at the rate of €150 million a year.

Transformation has also delivered wide industry recognition including high performance on the Gartner rating, bringing increased support for the brand. Supply chain is now a key plank in Schneider's competitive positioning.

What can we learn?

Although major transformation is not easy, a focused effort can make a dramatic shift in a relatively short time, as clearly evidenced by the substantial progress made by Schneider Electric since 2012.

As with all important change, strong, relentless leadership, conveying a coherent and compelling vision and continuing to reinforce *and* resource that vision has underpinned the success of this major initiative, undertaken and achieved not without a lot of internal resistance to change.

The Tailored Supply Chain strategy adopted by Schneider Electric provided a simple and robust framework to enable a genuine customer-centric focus and the results followed. Modeling and a menu of process capabilities then became the practical way to implement and cement in place the most appropriate version of the global strategy in each country.

Points of view

1 The most common behavioral segments point to five different supply chain configurations; three or four of these are applicable in a wide range of markets.

2 The importance of knowing and building capability to support loyal, stable customers cannot be underestimated. The Collaborative Supply Chain™ should be the first focus area of a tailored supply chain strategy.

3 Lean and Agile Supply Chains respond to different needs and usually would have different cost profiles. Distinguishing these activities will allow more rational decisions about appropriate service levels, cost-to-serve and pricing strategies.

4 Campaign (or project) supply chains have existed since the pyramids were built. But poor project performance demands a more considered and more specialized project supply chain capability, on both the supplier and contractor side.

5 The structure to support Tailored Supply Chains will vary, depending on the level of differentiation required in a particular target market.

6 Ultimately, the organization becomes an *orchestrator*, managing a portfolio of pathways through the enterprise to most effectively satisfy end customer demand.

Kick-start your thinking

DEFINING VALUE

Typical Dynamic Alignment™ VALUE PROPOSITION	Your Supply Chain VALUE PROPOSITION

Collaborative: win together

We will provide you with consistent quality product, delivered on time, at a stable price. We will use our capacity, and your information, to provide you with assured supply. We aim to be an integral part of your business and to engage with you on joint developments for mutual advantage.

Lean: least cost & reliable

We will provide you with consistent quality product delivered reliably, on time, at lowest price and free of surprises.

Agile: fast & flexible

We will respond to the opportunities that you present in a timely manner, consistent with available capacity and market conditions.

Campaign: understand, then comply

We will deliver to site exactly to your specifications, on time and in full.

Fully flexible: creative & fast

We will respond rapidly with innovative solutions to unplanned disruptions, and breakthrough new opportunities, as they arise.

♦ Can we articulate our supply chain value propositions?

♦ Which segments do they align well with?

♦ Are there segments where we are not delivering value?

CHAPTER 5

Decision making at a faster clockspeed

Decision support systems, analytics and tools for faster, better decisions

Introduction – the evolution of the decision

Decision making in operational environments is changing. The quantity and quality of data available to support decisions are growing exponentially; focus is on exceptions, with more routine tasks automated. But, in a more volatile environment, risk is higher and assumptions harder to make.

What hasn't changed, however, is that, despite all of the decision support available, the critical strategic decisions will still come down to individuals and leadership teams. And, despite the most educated cohort of business leaders in history, with the best tools and the most data, strategic decision making in many organizations is no faster or more assured than it was 30 years ago.

In this chapter, we explore various dimensions of strategic decision making in today's operating environment, particularly relating to data-supported decisions.

Analytics is core business

It would be fair to say that, if a company with $1 billion in sales revenue doesn't have an analytics group continually culling through its operational numbers, day-to-day, then it's going backwards.

Analytics is a bit like taking a blood test. Despite what you tell the doctor about your lifestyle, he is able to see the truth in the blood test results. The facts are inexorable and the patterns significant, which, once established, are ignored at your peril.

We need people looking at the numbers who are curious and who have the courage to act on what they see. We have to move beyond relying just on experience and intuition and get ahead of the game with predictive analytics and decision support systems that give experienced decision makers much more curated information to work with.

Fully leveraging the juxtaposition between experienced managers and the numbers is at the heart of the analytics opportunity that we see in front of us today; one without the other is inadequate in complex environments. And, yet, it appears that many senior executives do not fully appreciate what analytics and 'big data' can bring to the table and what their role is in relation to it.

The significance of the question

At the heart of analytics is *the question*. When it is the same question every month, one could argue the outcome is a dashboard or a report – but the very existence of information in these formats originated from a series of questions. When analytics is informing a new strategy, it's likely to be a new question. It could be as broad as – *which customers are we losing and why?* Or as specific as – *how much and what type of extra capacity would I need to turn orders around in two hours?*

If an analytics capability is to bring true value to the organization, the senior management team must understand the scope of the data and tools the analytics teams have at their disposal. If this knowledge is confined only to the department where they reside, their value will never be fully realized.

At a strategic level, the questioning sequence might look something like that depicted in Figure 5.1. Senior executives are asking the 'big' questions, which analytics teams then need to break down to a structured set of more specific questions that can be answered in the data; the next stage is extracting insight from the 'answers' – using visualizations and the operational experience that analytics cannot yet replace; and, finally, taking the answer to the original strategic question back to the originator in a simple logical structure that justifies the conclusion (Barbara Minto wrote the book – literally – on how to do this in *The Pyramid Principle*[1]).

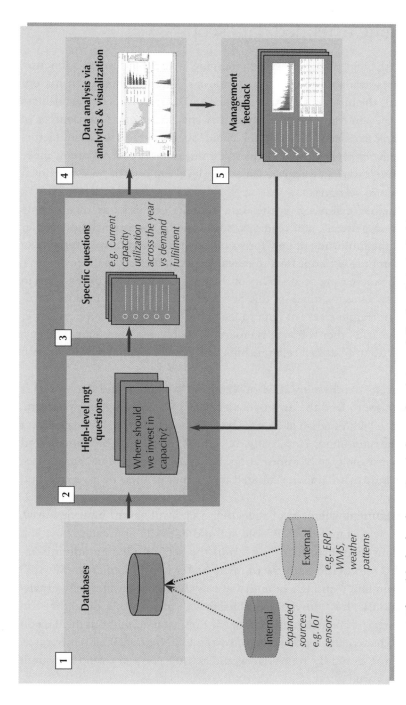

FIGURE 5.1 ◆ The critical role of questions in leveraging data analytics for strategic decisions

Leveraging extended data scope

Of course, the insights and answers emerging in such a quest are a function of the inputs available to inform the analysis. The core source in mature businesses is the historic sales transactions and the record of doing business over time seen in transport files, inventory snapshots, etc. New sources of data, coming from sensors along the chain, such as along the manufacturing and delivery processes, are expanding this dataset and making it more granular. What was once analyzed at a daily level can now be analyzed down to minutes and seconds.

The further extension is the data sources beyond our own supply chain. Traffic patterns, soil readings, social media sentiment and weather events . . . the multitude of new forms of structured and unstructured data that can combine with our own to reveal 'cause and effect' patterns.

With the increasing accessibility of software that can look for patterns in large diverse datasets, much of this data becomes of value. Machine learning looks at 'training' sets of data to learn the patterns that support better predictions. And other software is emerging that 'centrifuges' large, diverse datasets to identify causal relationships that previously may not have been evident.

The recent purchase by IBM of Weather Co's digital and data assets is seen as a move to feed the data needs of IBM's Watson cognitive platform. According to Jack Vaughan at SearchDataManagement,[2] '. . . we can expect more of the same now. And, truly, beyond Watson, data on climate and weather is just the type of information that companies in retail, agriculture and other industries are keen to feed into a mix of their own reports and projections.'

The chief data scientist of the USA, D.J. Patil, in an interview with Michael Lewis, stated that: 'People still didn't really appreciate how you can use data to transform.'[3] His job in the second Obama administration was '. . . to figure out how to make better use of data created by the US Government,'[4] and the quantity of raw data is of an incredible scale. The question is: how do you glean insights from such 'big data' that can become the basis of meaningful decisions? For instance, without the data on weather collected and made sense of by the US National Weather Service, '. . . no plane would fly, no bridge would be built, no war would be fought – at least not well'.[5]

Analyzing and seeing deeper into the data is vital because it holds many secrets. Most problems can be solved through collecting and analyzing the right data – and this is just as true in the case of complex supply chain operations spread across the globe.

Get the basics right – master data

Despite the increasing level of sophistication of the tools available and the analyses that can be conducted, in many, many organizations there is one enormous barrier standing in the way of using these tools well, for supply chain decisions – the quality of the master data.

There is a basic set of master data files in any product or material supply chain that define the fundamentals of the flow. Typically, these would include some form of 'product master' that uniquely identifies the product and should include logistics characteristics, especially the dimensions and weight; customer master files that define the commercial customer and related files that capture the delivery customer and corresponding location (ideally down to a geocode level).

The linkages between commercial and delivery customers are very relevant to the supply chain – they enable the cost-to-serve to be compared to net revenue to indicate the customer account profitability. Buying groups and multiple chains under the same stewardship are also relevant to collaborative opportunities. Our experience, however, is that very often the information to put the customer puzzle together is dispersed across functional silos. This lack of visibility precludes consideration of strategic supply chain options at the customer or group level.

Similarly, the absence of comprehensive comparable information about a product starves analytics and decision support systems of meaningful insights without a great deal of pre-work. The simple absence of accurate weight and cube information, for example, makes network modeling and strategic evaluation of different flow options near impossible.

Maintaining reliable master data, particularly across a large multinational operation, is hard work. It requires terms that could be considered old-fashioned, such as process discipline and rigor; and it needs to be owned by someone! But, without the certainty of a solid master database, it's unlikely that analytics teams will be able to produce convincing and useful guidance.

Harnessing the power of data to drive alignment

After considering data in some detail, we return to the consideration of *the question* – in particular, the question of focus. The use of analytics and big data are recognized as having a growing role in supply chain decision making. The potential scope is massive – but where should we focus and what are we looking for?

Our experience is that the primary effort should be on analyzing demand patterns and supply patterns.

Understanding how, when and, possibly, why current customers buy and creating meaningful demand groupings to capture these patterns is the key to being able to predict future demand with more accuracy. But, beyond this, it provides insight into the structure needed to serve them well, at an appropriate level of cost: it thus guides capacity planning and the design of the network. And, within these patterns, are clues to the reaction to new products, promotions and new channels and service offers.

One of the difficulties many firms have in seeing their demand patterns, however, is that they are collecting inadequate information from their commercial interaction with the customer – essentially from the initiation of an order. An order potentially can carry with it a richness of surrounding information: was this the original requirement or was the requested product not available; is it for stock replenishment or a one-off project; is it a promotional order or a promotional top-up; is the customer currently out-of-stock – and many variations beyond, particular to the industry. Especially in business-to-business purchasing, these insights are often lost.

Some of this information can be used to classify the type of demand, as shown in Figure 5.2.

In attaching, or 'tagging' relevant information at order receipt, analytics can be more revealing and demand planning can be conducted at a more granular level. Beyond this, there is also much more information available to vary the operational response.

Where there is not a way to identify the driver of the order, the different order types blur together at the product and customer levels. The underlying patterns are quite opaque and therefore difficult to manage proactively.

Without a mechanism to identify more about the order, valuable information about the customer is lost, for example, in Figure 5.3, where four different order types are coming from a single *Collaborative* customer on a

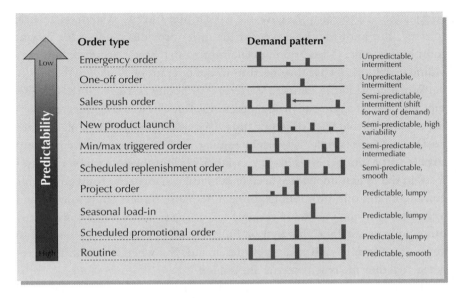

FIGURE 5.2 ◆ **Unpacking demand**

Source: Gattorna Alignment research. *Variations shown influenced by LLamasoft Whitepaper 'The Next Generation of Inventory Optimisation Has Arrived' (2013)

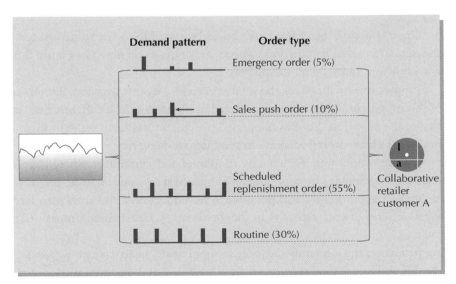

FIGURE 5.3 ◆ **Unpacking demand from a collaborative retailer**

regular basis. Typically, these would be captured in the system as generic 'orders'. But knowing the driver for the order provides much more insight into the customers' demand pattern, improving forecast accuracy and providing insight into what they need from the operation.

When considering demand patterns, variability is a key dimension. We typically look at aggregate product patterns. But within the aggregate sit layers of patterns that tell a different story. Demand coming from collaborative customers, for example, is typically regular, and the range more consistent than for other customers. This low variability brings the potential for a 'baseload' in the operation. More variable demand can emanate from customers coming in and out, promotions, project demand, traders (in resources and agriculture) or the inevitably variable tail of the product range – and many other sources. Agile, Campaign or Fully Flexible responses are needed to cover these various different types of demand. But when all of this is aggregated together the true patterns are hidden.

The coefficient of variation (CoV) is a key method to compare and discern these differences. In fact, this simple ratio may well be the single most useful statistic in the supply chain! Although it is a purely relative measure, it can highlight those customers and products that are more or less predictable. See Lean versus Agile buying patterns in the data depicted in Figure 5.4.

Once analyzed using the CoV, it will be possible to see some layers of the demand driven by customer action, generally as depicted in Figure 5.5, and shown in more detail in Chapter 2.

Promotions by suppliers and retailers can also distort demand. Examples of several potential patterns are depicted in Figure 5.6. You will note that, in two of the cases, all that has happened is demand has been pulled forward in time, with no overall increase in total demand levels.

On the supply-side, particularly in mining and agriculture where supply can be quite variable, the combination of historical data and statistics on probability can allow supply and demand to be understood and thus managed together, end-to-end, rather than independently which is much more often the case.

Just as on the demand-side, on the supply-side, analytics can be used to identify and understand the nature of the 'baseload' and the more and less consistent vendors. Particularly in supply-constrained industries, such as agriculture and resources, insight into the reliable, consistent suppliers or the more stable mines is valuable – particularly if they can be matched with stable demand.

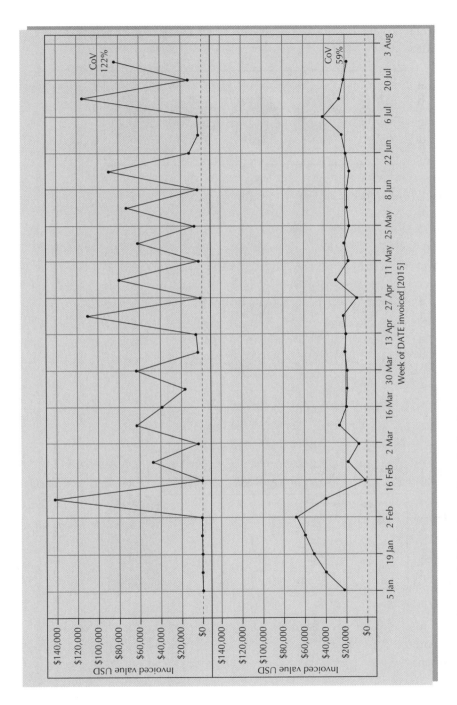

FIGURE 5.4 ◆ Lean vs Agile buying patterns in the data

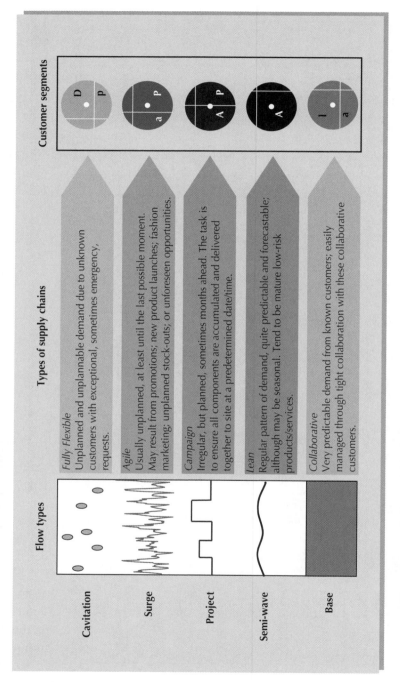

FIGURE 5.5 ◆ Flow characteristics typical of each customer segment–supply chain configuration

Source: Adapted from Gattorna (2015), p. 64

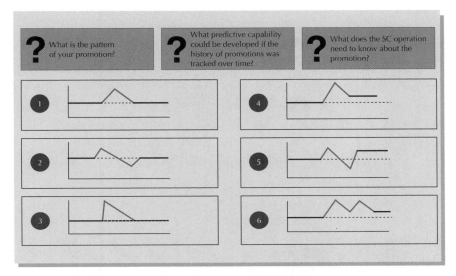

FIGURE 5.6 ◆ **Promotions – how do you handle them?**

A good example of this end-to-end approach is depicted in Figure 5.7, which is an analysis from the grain industry. Here you see depicted on the left, the variable supply coming through from three different seasons; and the partially stable patterns on the demand-side, all linked by the company's ideal supply chain network in the middle. The three subsystems ideally have to be managed in synch for best results.

Decision support systems and their critical role in designing and operating a complex supply chain

Structured decision support is the natural extension of analytics. There are three or four accepted levels of supply chain decision support corresponding to the different levels of decision making: strategic, tactical and operational/executional.

Network optimization modeling is a core strategic tool and is used for supply chain network design decisions. In most supply chains, the network configuration defines the most critical strategic choices including the service levels, sourcing paths, manufacturing and distribution locations. The 'design' should now also consider broader issues impacting the chain

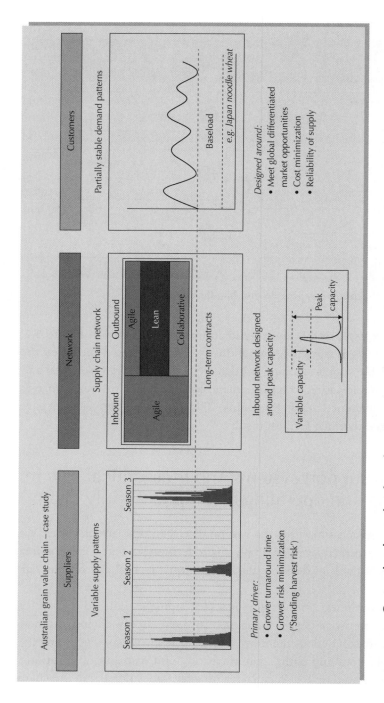

FIGURE 5.7 ◆ Connecting demand and supply patterns in an end-to-end supply chain

including distribution channels, risk profile and sustainability. Where the stocking profile is complex, network models should be supplemented with multi-level inventory optimization. Where asset utilization and timing and sequencing of activity are an issue, simulation may be the primary tool. But network modeling's superior ability to trade-off cost and select the optimal scenario is an important accompaniment to simulation.

The larger the scope included in a network model, the more optimal the result. Optimization is essentially about evaluating the supply chain trade-offs. Network models depict a supply chain network as shown in Figure 5.8, with multiple echelons starting at the supply end. Demand essentially 'pulls' volume through the network. Alternative scenarios of satisfying that demand can be tested or the optimizer can be given its head to find the best con-figuration for a specified set of service levels. Network models are some of the most well-established decision support tools used in the supply chain and companies such as LLamasoft, Solvoyo, AIMMS and River Logic have rigorous models built around the supply chain problem.

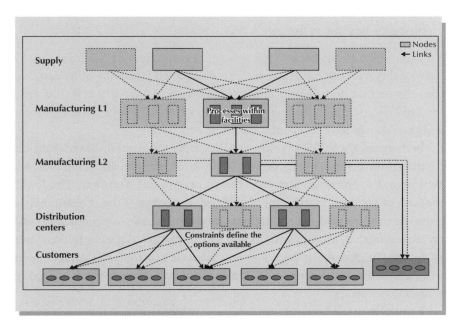

FIGURE 5.8 ◆ Network modeling – schematic diagram of a typical network and scenario options

Network modeling is one of the most important tools for both small- and large-scale supply chain transformation. And, while many organizations now use these tools, their full capability often is underutilized, in our opinion. Too many strategic network models are built with inadequate understanding of the core drivers in the customer and intermediary market and without fully considering the constraints and opportunities on the supply-side. This becomes a least cost solution to the current paradigm, rather than the true end-to-end re-design that such a major project opens up.

To get insightful and robust guidance from strategic modeling we consider there are five essentials:

1 Meaningful and logistically consistent aggregations of products, customers and suppliers.

2 Experienced operational managers heavily involved in designing and assessing scenarios.

3 Wider versus narrow scope.

4 Room for creative/off-the-wall scenarios.

5 Good communication with the final decision makers throughout the process – not just at the end.

This last point comes back to the issue of decision making. There are many high-quality network modeling projects conducted internally or by external consultants that never get to implementation; and, very often, it's because the final decision makers have not been involved intimately in the process and thus do not have full confidence in the results.

Increasingly, with faster solution times, the optimization-based decision support tools that were feasible only at the strategic level are being used for tactical and operational, and even day-of-operations, decisions. The lower the level of application, the more 'confined' the scope of the problem needs to be. At the strategic level, a national, or even global, supply chain is conceivably modeled, as aggregations and assumptions reduce complexity. But as the level of granularity increases and the time horizon reduces, the speed and rigor of the solution needs to improve and thus a smaller problem space is usually necessary.

Examples of the types of supply chain problems, within the various time horizons, where decision support tools can be of benefit, are indicated in Figure 5.9.

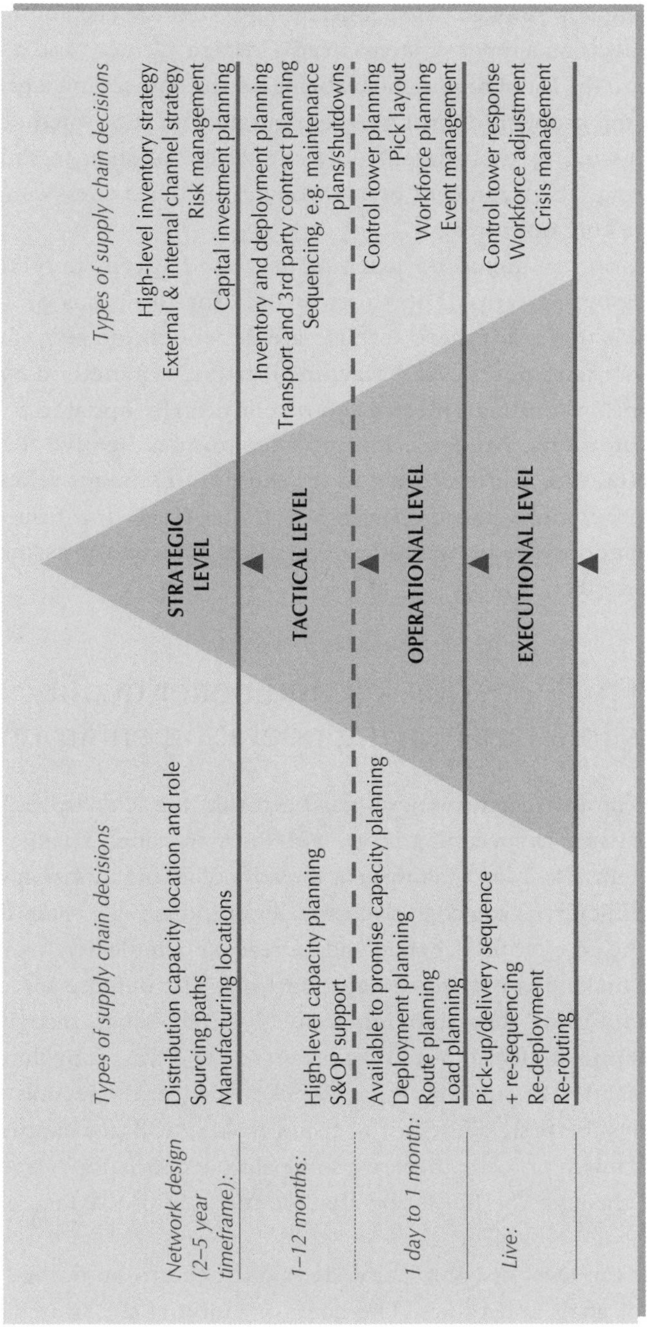

FIGURE 5.9 ◆ **The levels of decision support and examples of applications**

A point often overlooked when considering systems at each of these levels is that all decision support systems need a 'design' element and a 'design' phase – prior to the list of requirements being issued. Project managers often assume that the problem defines the configuration of the system; but this is similar to assuming that there is only one design of chair to satisfy the need for seating. The significant breakthroughs in effectiveness come from rethinking the core objectives.

The question of machine learning is raised often in relation to decision support systems. The short answer for the types of systems shown above is that all of these systems are dependent on sets of critical assumptions or parameters. And machine learning is a method by which these assumptions and parameters can be continually updated to reflect changing conditions. Machine learning techniques involve 'learning' from past data, thus route driving time assumptions might reflect road congestion predictions based on weather, time of year and time of day, but, as the relationships between these variables change, the assumptions must be updated.

Decision making: quicker and better quality decisions in a fast-moving operating environment

A key theme in our recent research has been that the 'clockspeed' of our organizations needs to speed up to cope with the increasingly volatile operating environment. Decision making is at the core of an organization's clockspeed. The difficulty is the cognitive capacity of individuals to understand and resolve the accelerating change and increasing complexity.

Decision making is part *science* and part *art*. The defense forces, who probably spend more time thinking about this than most, recognize the *science* by training on decision-making processes, and the *art* by developing leadership qualities. In our view, business acknowledges the second of these but underplays the first. While fast decision making will not happen if too weighed down with process, there are some simple heuristics or guidelines that can cut through the hesitation that we now see in the face of rising complexity.

Whatever the level of complexity, decisions need to be framed within the context of goals and values. The goal (or vision at the strategic level) structures the decision problem and thus the acceptable alternatives and guides the evaluation of options.

In supply chain strategic decision making, an important consideration is – what is the 'system' under consideration? Too narrow a perspective can hide the interdependencies and the 'cause and effect' relationships at play. A decision on a new transport mode, for example, needs to be viewed within the context of the 'network' or system that includes service levels, inventory levels, etc. The tools of systems dynamics, and simpler versions, such as the network diagram in Figure 5.8, are useful for capturing the essence of the situation and to implant 'systems thinking'.

As we have seen before, reducing complexity very often requires categorization. Understanding the type of issue allows more clarity around the path to resolution and the role of the leader. Snowden and Boone[6] identified four situations and the corresponding responses. Our slightly simplified version is shown in Figure 5.10.

Knowing where to focus and how to allocate resources is critical to effective strategy, i.e. which issues need our attention. The *Critical Issues Matrix* in Figure 5.11 is a highly effective tool for prioritizing – using only two dimensions: Impact and Urgency.

There are many tools for investigating, exploring and selecting: some quantitative, some qualitative. The trick is to know what to employ when.

Simple – 'known-knowns'	*Sense* (establish the facts), *categorize, respond.* Use best practice.
Complicated – 'known-unknowns'	*Sense, analyze, respond.* Logic-based. Expert knowledge. AI copes well here.
Complex – 'unknown-unknowns'	*Probe, sense, respond.* Experience, intuition, experiments, design thinking.
Chaotic – too confusing and too critical to wait	*Act, sense, respond.* Experience, intuition, judgment.

FIGURE 5.10 ◆ **Four possible grades of complexity**

Source: Adapted from Snowden and Boone

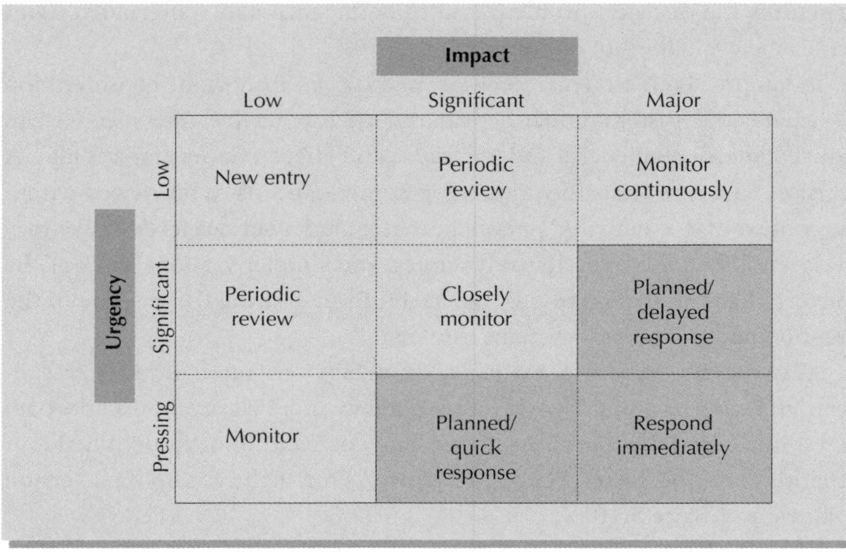

		Impact		
		Low	Significant	Major
Urgency	Low	New entry	Periodic review	Monitor continuously
	Significant	Periodic review	Closely monitor	Planned/ delayed response
	Pressing	Monitor	Planned/ quick response	Respond immediately

FIGURE 5.11 ◆ **Critical Issues Matrix**

Apart from the well-known financial comparison tools (such as discounted cash flows), some other tools that are helpful in specific situations are:

◆ decision trees;

◆ the decision matrix;

◆ risk analysis;

◆ root cause analysis;

◆ integrative thinking process (Roger Martin);

◆ checklists, e.g. ORAPAPA;

◆ Crawford Slips (now usually sticky notes);

◆ red team challenge.

Intuition and experience should not be underestimated, particularly in complex, chaotic and new situations. Daniel Kahneman[7] calls this System 1 thinking, and the pattern recognition and speed of response of experienced individuals are key attributes in these situations. This is the *art* aspect of decision making and *art* that can be honed and refined with time and practice.

The word of caution in this regard, though, comes from the same source. The greatest risk in both organizational and individual decision making comes from our own in-built biases. Kahneman and Tversky won a Nobel Prize for a

Framing	Anchoring	Overconfidence	Availability
Influenced by how a problem or fact is expressed.	Fixate on initial information and fail to adjust for subsequent information.	Misjudge probabilities; unfounded confidence.	Rely unduly on known/easy to access knowledge rather than examine alternatives.

DECISION-MAKING BIASES

Group think	Sunk costs & constraints	Confirmation	Selective perception
Desire for harmony and consensus overrides critical thinking.	'Honor' already committed expenditure or current resources without fully evaluating alternatives.	Search for and value information that supports pre-existing beliefs.	Interpret via own perceptions. Ignore perceptions beyond own.

FIGURE 5.12 ◆ Categorization of decision-making biases

Source: Kahneman and Tversky

series of studies[8] on how our decision making is impacted by common distortions that undermine objectivity. Some of the most common biases that can undo an objective evaluation of a situation are shown in Figure 5.12.

Even when we are using analytics, we need to be conscious of how the questions we use to frame the analysis, and our interpretation, can be prejudiced by some of these natural tendencies.

In the context of speeding up the organizational clockspeed, the operating conditions for faster decision making are also important. The levers for more responsive organizational culture and capabilities will be discussed in Chapter 7.

CASE STUDY: CBH GROUP, Western Australia

Strategic modeling of the end-to-end grain supply chain generates long-term grower value

Situation

CBH is an 85-year-old grain handling and trading cooperative owned by 4,200 grain growers in Western Australia (WA). The grain handling assets owned by CBH include approximately 200 storage sites, four grain ports and a fleet of trains. CBH is the largest cooperative in Australia.

On the supply-side, high climatic variability in Western Australia results in dramatically different annual harvests from year-to-year. In the three consecutive years studied in this project, for example, the harvest was 11, 7 and 15 million tonnes respectively.

By contrast, the demand-side of the equation is, at its core, a picture of stability. The main crops, wheat, barley and canola, are key inputs in everyday staples – bread, noodles, beer and cooking oil. WA noodle wheat is top quality and highly prized in Japan.

Managing complexity

CBH is constantly trying to manage the storage and handling network under its control to maximize grower value – either by maximizing revenue, minimizing cost or minimizing risk.

But this is an extremely complex supply chain. In addition to harvest variability, there are 9,000 farm locations and each storage site has to decide how many quality segregations to offer growers each year. And the harvest period is highly concentrated – around 21 days in any area!

Up-country storage is located near the grower to allow fast turnaround during harvest. But grain close to port gives the most opportunity to maximize revenue. Thus, many important and strategic trade-off decisions are embodied in the configuration of the network – how close, how fast, how many quality segregations, when to move grain and how much storage and handling capacity at sites, ports and in the fleet.

Modeling breakthrough

It was acknowledged by CBH that the level of complexity was too great to undertake major strategic redesign without decision support.

It was also apparent that a complete end-to-end optimization approach was needed to reflect the different ways that value could be impacted by the supply chain. A strategic network optimization model of the CBH network was built.[9] It incorporated every grower farm location and every final customer.

The model was one of the largest, most comprehensive strategic supply chain models ever built. It considered 220 million decision points. Prior to building the network model, in-depth research was conducted with growers, buyers and end user customers and the results of this were inputs to the design of the model and the scenarios tested.

Results

After an intense period of testing scenarios and close collaboration between the project team, operations and zone management and growers, a 10-year network strategy was confirmed.

It involved upgrading 100 sites for fast turnaround and gradual closure of another 102 sites. Growers will travel slightly further, but gain through much faster turnaround at the site. Substantial savings for growers in storage and handling costs and more targeted investment will be the ongoing direct benefit.

The indirect benefit was the analytical capability built within CBH for future decision making. A structured, end-to-end data repository down to the farm level was built that now supports ongoing analytics and is available for the next stage of tactical decision support that CBH is pursuing.

CBH is rich with agricultural and operational experience. Another indirect benefit was the expertise that these operational managers developed in using decision support – assessing its outputs, understanding sensitivities and testing their theories.

What can we learn?

There are too many trade-offs in complex supply chains to make major infrastructure and network decisions without decision support technology.

For strategic decisions, a comprehensive end-to-end view of the system or supply chain network provides a more optimal overall result and generates more value than breaking the problem up into its component parts.

The combination of a strategic modeling and involved, experienced, operations management to pose and assess scenarios ('what if' questions) is highly synergistic and opens up significant value extraction opportunities.

Points of view

1 The speed of decision making is an issue for many mature businesses competing in volatile markets.

2 Collecting and analyzing the right data is key to the future design and operation of enterprise supply chains; companies must hasten to build a strong internal analytics capability if they are to have a chance of staying abreast of today's fast-moving digital development.

3 A strong analytics capability is core business for the supply chain group.

4 Demand patterns provide an X-ray of the market – study them carefully.

5 An order is not an order – more information about its context improves prediction and helps design appropriate responses.

6 Some simple decision heuristics and tools can reduce complexity and improve decision quality and speed.

7 We need to be sensitized to the common types of bias to ensure our logic remains sound and our conclusions are valid.

Kick-start your thinking

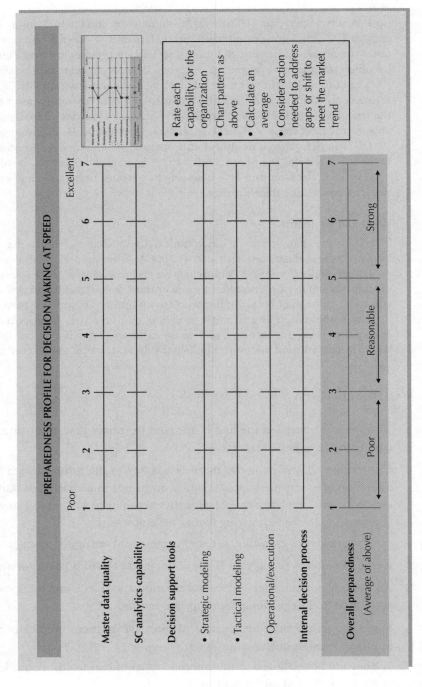

PREPAREDNESS PROFILE FOR DECISION MAKING AT SPEED

Poor   Excellent

1   2   3   4   5   6   7

Master data quality

SC analytics capability

Decision support tools

• Strategic modeling

• Tactical modeling

• Operational/execution

Internal decision process

Overall preparedness
(Average of above)

1   2   3   4   5   6   7

Poor   Reasonable   Strong

• Rate each capability for the organization
• Chart pattern as above
• Calculate an average
• Consider action needed to address gaps or shift to meet the market trend

CHAPTER 6

Working in an omni-channel world

Designing the optimal array of pathways to market

Introduction – reconsidering the routes to market

Brand manufacturers and retailers alike have, for different reasons, been forced to rethink how they wish to go to market. In both cases, pressure has come from users and consumers determined to find faster and more convenient ways to access products and services and from the new generation of businesses that have started with a clean sheet and trained consumers to expect those fast, easy solutions.

Thus, distribution channels have risen to be one of the most important strategic issues many businesses are facing in the rapidly changing operating environment. The key question to be answered is: what are the right commercial and physical arrangements to get our products or services into the hands of end users? Or for intermediaries such as distributors or retailers: what is our role and how do we protect it in the future? It is, in many respects, the elephant in the room for mature businesses, and disintermediation rather than direct competitors is the fear that keeps many CEOs awake at night.

Designing channel options – first principles

For any product or service category there are decisions to be made on the optimal routes to market. This revolves around which roles are needed to support the category; which should be conducted in-house, via which methods, and which can be conducted through external intermediaries.

Essentially, channels are 'value delivery systems'.[1] Each party in the channel is contributing to the value generated. And this value should exceed the additional cost (or margin loss) incurred as the product or service moves along its path, through to the ultimate user or consumer.

It is important to make a clear distinction when thinking about channels, between the customer and the end user. A customer is the next level downstream in the channel who takes title and pays for the products or services. This can be a national distributor, or Tier 1, 2 or even Tier 3 distributor. All are resellers and, to add value, must bring something new to the table, e.g. local proximity or an attractive and supportive assortment. The end user or consumer is the key decision maker, of course, because no matter how much you manipulate the location of inventory up and down a given channel, if it is not finally taken out and consumed, no one in the channel makes money.

The *golden rule* in channel design and operations is: he/she who 'owns' the customer (relationship) inherits the world![2]

The automotive industry historically has understood channel roles well, e.g. Ford is clearly the brand owner, manufacturer and connects with the buyer through advertising and promotions; its dealers provide local proximity, the relationship component, service and sometimes finance. Their roles are different, but generally complementary.

Channel fragmentation as choices increase

With the advent of e-commerce, channels have fragmented. In most product and service categories, there are more potential pathways to the consumer or end user than ever before and more variations in the way that value can be delivered. While a bricks and mortar retailer can enhance the product via the service experience, store ambience, immediate availability and comparative products, the e-commerce platforms enhance the product through delivery and ease of access.

Potential routes to market for a consumer durable product category are depicted in Figure 6.1.

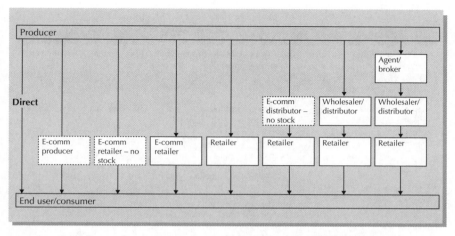

FIGURE 6.1 ◆ Channels to market – more complex, more fragmented

But adjusting to this new reality has not been easy for some and, indeed, many manufacturers are still tentative about their e-commerce arrangements, hedging bets wherever possible. Nonetheless, we cannot take our current routes to market for granted. We must get below the surface, understand customers' underlying needs and expectations and work out which combination of channels will best deliver value, while meeting our own commercial and strategic objectives.

It is also clear that, in some traditional industries, poor practices and ineffective splits in functions have crept in over time so that channel relationships are no longer effective. Distortions have often been created by inappropriate KPIs and objectives, such as unrealistic growth targets from brand manufacturers. Not only the channel, but the relationship between the parties needs scrutiny when channels are re-examined.

Getting 'below the surface' requires a methodical assessment from different viewpoints. A manufacturer needs to focus on what a particular channel brings to the consumer/end user; as well as what it brings to its own business. The position, as seen from the customer perspective, is depicted in Figure 6.2, and likewise from the supplier perspective in Figure 6.3.

END CUSTOMER PERSPECTIVE		
For any given product category a particular customer has an 'optimal' supply channel. It is that where the combination of supply characteristics aligns most closely with their needs.		
Channel choice factors – customer (example)		
Supply conditions	**Service proposition**	**Sourcing cost**
Availability of appropriate assortment	Lead time on Lean	Price after discounts
	Lead time on Agile	Credit terms
Ease of doing business	Minimum order quantity	
Relationship support: network ; peer engagement; advice	Availability of technical/product advice	
Supply assurance (e.g. brand)	Response time	
	Warranties	

FIGURE 6.2 ◆ **Channel optimization – from the customer perspective**

SUPPLIER PERSPECTIVE		
For any given product category a particular supplier has an 'optimal' fulfilment channel. It is also that where the combination of supply characteristics aligns most closely with their needs.		
Channel choice factors – supplier perspective vs direct (example)		
Supply conditions	**Service proposition**	**Net revenue**
Availability of complementary assortment	Lead time on Lean	Net price after discounts
	Lead time on Agile	Credit terms
Availability of relationship support: network; peer engagement; advice	Lower minimum order quantities	Order administration costs
		Selling costs
	Availability of technical advice	
Availability of supply assurance, e.g. brand	Response time	Advertising/promotion costs
Market enhancement, e.g. promotions; selling capability	Warranties	

FIGURE 6.3 ◆ **Channel optimization – from the supplier perspective**

Segmentation supports channel design

As noted above, if the customer does not perceive value from an interme-diary, the established paths are exposed. But how do we get close enough to a large customer base to interpret their perception of value?

As we have discussed in Chapter 2, we consider that behavioral seg-mentation of the customer base provides a way to reduce complexity and enable a more strategic focus on the market. It is thus also a very useful lens through which to assess the suitability of channel options. Supply chain modeling and cost-to-serve analyses can also be used to compare the cost (and service) of alternative channels.

Fundamentally, we need to review current channels and re-engineer them from the segment back into the enterprise. For example, the case depicted in Figure 6.4 reviews the direct versus intermediary options through the eyes of the Collaborative small original equipment manufacturer (OEM) customer segment.

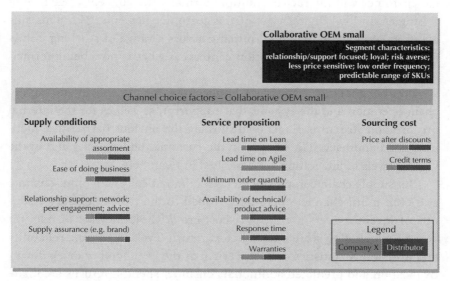

FIGURE 6.4 ◆ Channel value – comparison of direct and distributor channel from the customer perspective

On this basis, the distributor option appears to offer more value to this segment of customers. The other side of the equation can then be explored considering the advantages and disadvantages that the distributor channel brings to the supplier, using a similarly methodical approach. Combined with a cost-to-serve analysis, the various perspectives then enable a logical decision on the appropriateness of a specific channel to serve a particular segment of customers.

The use of multiple channels to respond to the needs of different segments of customers can be illustrated by considering the array of channels through which we can now buy a mobile phone and the particular needs that each channel is best suited to satisfy – see Figure 6.5.

From multi-channel to omni-channel design

In response to the multiple channels at their disposal, retailers and brand owners are now starting to recognize the strategic advantage of using them in concert rather than independently. By understanding that a single customer will interact in multiple formats, the concept of achieving a 'single window' digital view of the customer has emerged. This single view, along with dynamic sourcing across a range of stocking points (e.g. stores as well as distribution centers) is what is now being termed 'omni-channel'.

Omni-channel has significant implications for the end-to-end supply chain operation and the systems that support it, as well as for the internal organization structure. Functional silos are the obvious barrier to a more integrated approach. The impact on the customer and supplier end of the various levels of integration are described in Figure 6.6.

But supply chain complexity increases dramatically with omni-channel and even multi-channel operations. Added to the typical logistics trade-offs of inventory versus transport cost are a whole new set of relevant variables including store packing cost, return levels, lead time reliability and probability statistics on factors such as the likelihood of mark-downs by location and predicted additional consumer spend if returns are made to store.

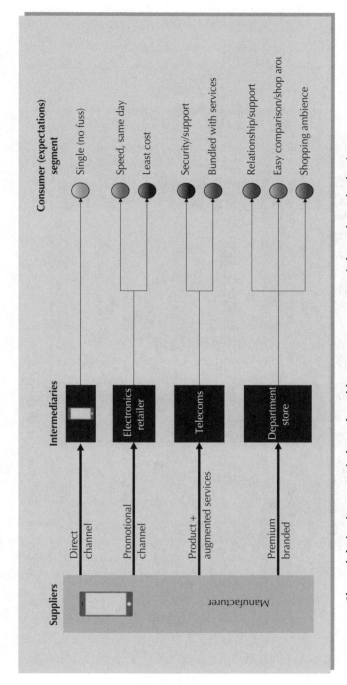

FIGURE 6.5 ◆ Channel design in an omni-channel world: consumer segments inform channel selection

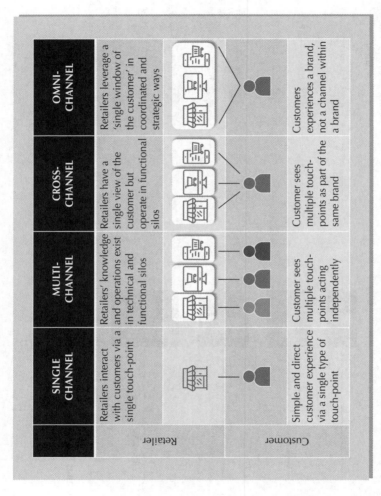

FIGURE 6.6 ◆ Evolution of retail channels

Source: "Omni Channel Retail: The future of retail", https://www.shopify.com.au/retail/119924675-10-slideshare-presentations-on-the-future-of-omni-channel-retail

This problem is too difficult for even the most talented planners and the software companies that have developed optimization-based decision support systems (such as Solvoyo and Quintiq) are now turning their attention to optimizing omni-channel fulfilment in real time. Patents are emerging for sophisticated new techniques to solve aspects of the problem. And this is an obvious application for machine learning to monitor and maintain the key statistical relationships.

Digitization is also providing important breakthroughs that will support omni-channel strategies. Macy's, for example, have found that the improved visibility from RFID tags on merchandise allows them to sell online that pesky 'last unit in store' that they, like many other retailers, excluded from e-commerce because of the high risk it would actually be out of stock. For Macy's and much of the fashion industry, 15–20 per cent of inventory is that last unit in store!

Channel cost visibility

Whether considering a complex multi-channel or omni-channel route to market or simply evaluating e-commerce options, the issue of cost-to-serve is critical. Any of the optimization systems mentioned above will require activity-based cost inputs (along with pricing and discounts) to produce meaningful outcomes. And strategic channel questions, such as 'should we also sell through Alibaba?', require a close look at the supply chain cost implications.

Few businesses are yet well placed to do either of these, i.e. evaluating the true cost of alternative channels at the strategic level or using detailed activity-based cost trade-offs at the point of omni-channel fulfilment. More typically, fixed costs, indirect costs and often even labor costs are allocated arbitrarily without an analysis of the cost drivers in the different channels. We need to be able to assess channel profitability and even customer account profitability (CAP) if the quality of decision making around channel design is to improve going forward.

Activity-based cost analysis, combined with price variances, can provide a picture of the true cost-to-serve of the different pathways, as indicated in Figure 6.7.

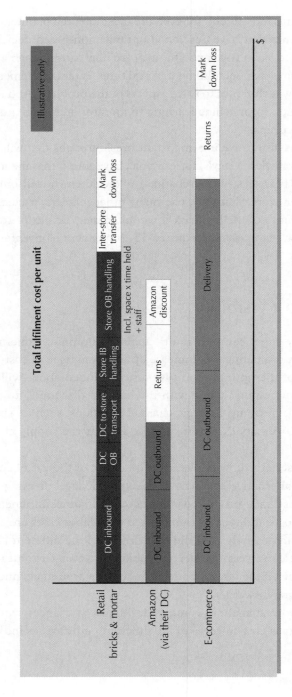

FIGURE 6.7 ◆ Channel cost comparison

The logistics costs of e-commerce fulfilment are generally said to be three to four times higher than the same item sold through a 'bricks and mortar' store. With increasing levels of small order automation and as throughput declines in some retail outlets (and thus fixed cost/unit increases), these rules of thumb are unlikely to be useful and should be abandoned. The actual cost-to-serve calculated to reflect the particular characteristics of the order and situation provides a much sounder base for channel decisions.

Returns are one of the most complex, and potentially crippling, aspects of e-commerce. In addition to the cost of freight and processing, a percentage end up as write-offs and rework. Part of the e-commerce equation has been supporting growth with lenient returns policies. These policies require close monitoring of both the cost for different types of merchandise and the customer sensitivity to policy changes.

There is considerable academic work being undertaken on e-commerce returns, some of which is summarized in Figure 6.8. It is apparent that this is another area where the pragmatic aspects of logistics hit up against the behavioral drivers of the customer – and that neither can be looked at, or managed, in isolation. More refined approaches to returns are obviously needed, such as differentiated policies by customer segment (related to loyalty, for example) and product category (more stringent where the value of the product deteriorates faster).

Level 2 maturity

It is very early days in the evolution of these new channels – as evidenced by the growth projections. Global e-commerce sales have doubled in the last five years and are forecast to double again in the next five![3] In this context, we can assume that there is a lot still to learn. But while we are doing that, our view is that the 'first principles' of channels – that they add value and that we know what they cost and that the cost makes sense in the context of a market strategy – are a good starting point.

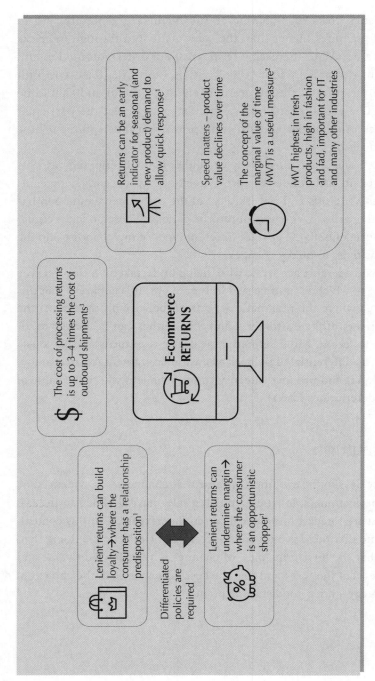

FIGURE 6.8 ◆ E-commerce returns – what the research says

Source 1: Hjort, K., Ericsson, D. and Gattorna J. (2013) 'Customer segmentation based on buying and returning behaviour', *International Journal of Physical Distribution & Logistics Management* (2013) Vol. 43, No. 10

Source 2: Blackburn, J.D. *et al.* (2006) 'Time value of commercial product returns', *Management Science*, Vol. 52, No. 8, August

Source 3: Andel, T. *et al.* (2002) 'Turning returns into cash', *Transportation Distribution*, 43(8)

CASE STUDY: ARGOS omni-channel

Transforming from a catalog-centric business to an omni-channel network

Situation

Argos is a general merchandise retailer with more than 840 stores in the UK. Its wide range includes homeware, consumer electrical, electronics and toys, with sales of approximately £4 billion.[4] Its history has been based largely on catalog selling and this proved a good base as it made its initial transition to internet sales. But with a difficult retail environment and Amazon's growing strength in the market, Argos management decided it needed to make a quantum shift in order to build a real competitive advantage as a leading digital retailer.[5]

Lagging, but with potential

Argos recognized that a key strength that it had to work with was its store network. Unlike Amazon, it already had a multi-channel capability in the UK. This had not been exploited, though, and the fulfilment system was still locked into the catalog approach with paper-based customer ordering and no visibility to stock across the network. The store network was also unevenly equipped, with many smaller stores with limited scope for range and larger stores with more range but inappropriate locations for wider distribution.

Designing optimized omni-channel paths

Argos started its transformation by researching customers' expectations. The feedback, while perhaps not a surprise, created a clear focus for all that followed. It found that the online shopper wanted 'fast, convenient and consistently reliable home delivery; the ability to choose between home and other points of pickup; a seamless link between e-commerce, mobile commerce and physical stores; and a simple means of returning any product.'[6]

It then moved on to working out how it could best leverage its store network. Argos wanted to know the optimal network to achieve same day pickup or delivery of essential items – up to 20,000 stock keeping units (SKUs). To do this, it used network modeling to test multiple scenarios. Inputs included each store's geographic coverage, delivery time and cost, backroom storage, space for loading and parking of vans, replenishment costs and distances between facilities.

What emerged was a new hub and spoke fulfilment model with 173 hubs acting as 'mini-warehouses'. A set of 'dark hubs' – non-retail fulfilment centers – were also designed to fill gaps in the geographic coverage. A fleet of approximately 500 vans with 2,500 drivers was recruited to support the hubs. Each shipping point was no more than an hour from its target customers, and operated 24/7 and together they enabled 95 per cent of UK households to receive same day service, seven days a week.

Argos has also focused heavily on technology and the in-store experience. Most notably, it has replaced the laminated catalogs and mini pens for which it was famous, with tablet devices at digital kiosks. Employees use portable devices and headsets to find stock quickly and prioritize tasks. Stores include a Fast Track 'click and collect' area to support online purchases. And, critically, Argos has achieved a single view of stock across its whole network. Its website uses this information to guide customers regarding pickup choices, in addition to its role in replenishment.

The new operating model is now well-established and, by 2018, its mix of sales was 41 per cent walk-in and 59 per cent digital (with digital sales across four channels, 'check and reserve', 'internet home delivery', 'fast track collection' and 'fast track delivery').

Impact

Part way through the five-year transformation project, Argos was bought by Sainsbury's and commentators focused on the strength that Argos had built in omni-channel as one of the key attractions for the grocery retailer. And Argos has received wide industry recognition for its transition and the results achieved. *Retail Week* in the UK named it as the best UK multi-channel retailer in 2017. And the modeling project that Argos and LLamasoft conducted to design the omni-channel fulfilment network has received innovation awards in Europe and the USA.[7]

But the most important result of the transformation has been holding ground in the volatile retail environment. As Phil Hull, distribution director of Sainsbury's Argos told SupplyChainBrain, 'If we hadn't done this . . . I'm not sure we would have been here today.'

What can we learn?

Argos started its transformation by researching customer expectations. We often think we know what customers want, but we are also often, if not mostly, wrong! For major shifts, as this project involved, it is essential to have a frame-of-reference based on the customer.

There were too many options, trade-offs and decision variables for the Argos fulfilment network to be redesigned without sophisticated network modeling support. Omni-channel multiplies the choices and requires a deep dive into low-level data on demographics and consumer behavior. Any reasonably large omni-channel strategy requires strategic decision support tools.

Bricks and mortar stores can be a real advantage in the age of e-commerce, but only if treated as a part of a comprehensive and integrated strategy.

And, finally, Argos has demonstrated that even a very traditional retailer 'renowned for their slightly dated stores and peculiar shopping experience' can leapfrog to the leading edge of the multi-channel supply chain in a relatively short time with a strong and well-articulated vision.

Points of view

1   Two of the most disruptive forces encroaching on mature businesses are disintermediation, or the reduction in the use of intermediaries between producers and consumers, and fragmentation of the market across multiple channels, e.g. e-commerce, bricks and mortar, Amazon.

2   Channels, both old and new, need a grass-roots review, regularly – starting with the end customer's perception of value.

3   Multi-channel and omni-channels are a critical driver of growth for consumer goods and retail, but the level of supply chain complexity is a step-change higher.

4   Sophisticated decision support systems are essential for omni-channel profitability. And inventory visibility is a critical input to manage margin.

5   Knowing the true cost-to-serve, by channel and customer segment, is needed to ensure the appropriate channels are selected and appropriate policies are set (e.g. on delivery, sourcing, returns).

Kick-start your thinking

CHANNELS AT RISK?

Supplier (Us)

Intermediaries

End customers

New?
Alternative?

Refer to Figure 6.1

Draw current routes to end customers and estimate the percentage of business flowing down each channel.

Are any of these channels at risk of disintermediation from low value add?

Could alternative business models offer lower cost/more value?

Are any new channels indicated?

CHAPTER 7

Critical internal capabilities

Shaping the appropriate subcultures to propel operational strategies forward

Introduction

Designing and implementing new supply chain configurations is not necessarily a purely rational exercise, because it is subject to the vagaries of external customers and the behaviors of internal personnel. Indeed, our field work indicates that up to 60 per cent of *intended strategies* are never delivered on the ground in established businesses. And, perhaps surprisingly, this slippage is usually not due to competitive action. Rather, it is due to internal constraints, particularly the resistance to change embedded in the organization, which has the effect of impeding progress.

The proposition that the Dynamic Alignment™ framework embodies is that to consistently perform well in particular parts of a market requires strategies that are specifically aligned; *plus* internal capabilities that can deliver those strategies.

The idea is to interpret the subcultures (or buying behaviors) present among the target customer population, and then attempt to mirror these inside the business using different combinations of *capabilities* to develop precisely aligned subcultures. The objective is to develop an internal operating environment in synch with particular strategies and the customers to which they are ultimately directed. And thus, to provide more fertile ground for the strategic seeds we are sowing.

Where customers and markets are known, and the products or services are well-established, the different capabilities needed can be clearly defined. We will discuss the major types of subculture that are best suited to different market segments later in this chapter.

But we will also discuss the 'innovation subculture'. To be on the front foot in the world of fast and continuous change that we now face, we need to have a part of the organization exploring 'what's next' – new products, markets, technologies and business models. In a departure from the 'mirroring' of the market proposed above; this mindset and capability must be independent, open and unconstrained by the current paradigm. But it is not suitable for more stable business – and there's the rub!

But first, the foundations . . .

What is organizational culture?

Organizational culture is the combination of unwritten values, beliefs and deeply held underlying assumptions that have developed inside the organization over time. In effect, it is a statement of 'how we do things around here'. Organizational culture, as with all categorizations around behavior, is relative rather than absolute. Culture should not be confused with 'climate' – the current mood of the organization. Culture drives strategic capability; climate does not.

Culture is best depicted as an iceberg, with the *visible conscious* behavior above the waterline for all to see and the other 10/11 hidden from view below the waterline; this is the *invisible unconscious* component that is difficult to change. This situation is depicted in Figure 7.1.

As already inferred above, culture can either provide sustenance to a new strategy, if it sits comfortably within current norms, or derail it if it doesn't. Differentiated market strategies require subcultures to be created, which are aligned with the appropriate value proposition. Thus, strategy needs to be developed with a view to how it will be implemented within the organization, as well as externally. The P-A-D-I coding system introduced in Chapter 2, can also be used to describe and map organizational culture and corresponding subcultures.

This allows us to define and specify the appropriate subculture(s) required to drive success in different situations. The four generic enterprise types of subcultures are depicted below in Figure 7.2.

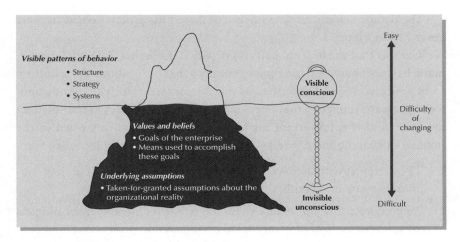

FIGURE 7.1 ◆ What is organizational culture?

Sources: Schein, E.H. (1988), p. 9[1]; and adapted from Gattorna (2015), p. 107

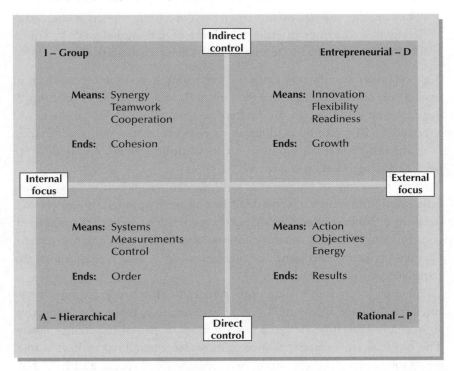

FIGURE 7.2 ◆ The four generic types of subcultures showing the moiety effect of opposing subcultures

Source: Adapted from Gattorna (2015) p. 111

The detailed characteristics of each of these four generic subcultures are described in Figure 7.3.

The way that the four subcultures depicted in Figures 7.2 and 7.3 interact is best explained by the moiety concept that '. . . allows for a culture to be conceived of and described as two distinct subcultures'.[2] 'Anthropological research suggests that opposing subcultures interact in four distinct modes',[3] and it is important for leaders to understand this when in the process of shaping the desired subcultures. The four distinct modes are:

1 'They interact with *antithesis* when values and behaviours of moiety subcultures come into conflict.

2 They interact through *rivalry* when the two sides engage in sociological struggles for control of institutional processes and products.

3 They interact with *reciprocity*, indicated by "give-and-take" social exchanges, which might be transactional and/or transformational.

4 They interact *complementarily* when each half of the moiety assumes differentiated functions in order to achieve organisational goals.'[4] This is obviously a preferred state that supports external alignment.

This explanation of moiety helps us better understand the mechanisms at work inside an enterprise, where the Group (I) and Rational (P) subcultures oppose each other; as do the Entrepreneurial (D) and Hierarchical (A) subcultures. But, given that all these subcultures exist in our target market as evidenced by the behavioral segments identified, all are required, so we need to manage their co-existence.

The *dimensions* of culture that typically are recognized to be the most influential, and which are included in culture mapping, are: autonomy/decision making; change tolerance; communication; conflict management; control; external coping; identity; internal organizing; performance-reward. Change programs can either be 'evolutionary' – slowly adapting to the requirement – or 'revolutionary'.

Change levers for shifting organizational culture or building subcultures are depicted in Figure 7.4. Our experience suggests that leadership style and organization design are the most powerful of the change levers. The physical environment is increasingly also considered to have a role, e.g. 'Googleplex', the corporate headquarters for Google and its parent Alphabet has redefined the physical work environment. Its playful environment is clearly reinforcing the unconstrained, innovation-focused culture that Google has driven.

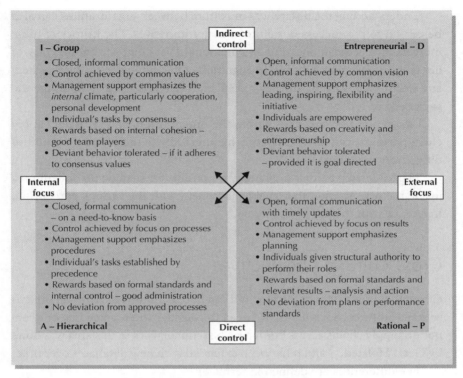

FIGURE 7.3 ◆ **Characteristics of the four generic subcultures**

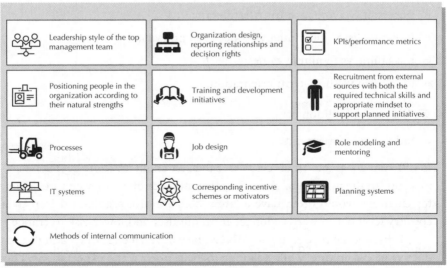

FIGURE 7.4 ◆ **Levers for changing culture**

Understanding the differences in culture between organizations can also be critical to the success or failure of major initiatives. The history of futile mergers and acquisitions, and dysfunctional JVs, point to the difficulty of integrating dissimilar cultures. Recognition of the differences is the first step; and decisions regarding the new 'ideal' culture and strategies to bridge the gaps need to follow.

Integration between silos within the organization, and between supply chain partners, can also be severely hampered by failing to take account of differences in culture.

The leadership team is ultimately responsible for shaping the subcultures inside the organization that enable alignment with the various parts of the market or with the key stakeholders.

Cross-cultural perspectives

Country cultures sit over the top, and can have a modifying effect on organizational cultures. So, what do we need to consider when managing our corporate supply chains across borders? The seminal work in this area was done by Geert Hofstede,[5] and it has been extended with new databases over time.

The differences are defined in terms of:

- power distance (egalitarian vs hierarchical);
- uncertainty avoidance (or risk tolerance);
- individualism (individual vs collective mindset);
- masculine vs feminine values;
- long-term vs short-term orientation.

With a recent addition of:

- indulgence vs restraint.

In different geographic markets, we see that, although the same buying behaviors appear, the mix can be skewed by the influence of country culture. Japan, for example, would often have a larger collaborative segment, driven by a country level bias towards a longer-term mindset and lower-risk tolerance.

Multinational corporations (MNCs) face the challenge of creating a productive global culture, while adapting to local 'norms' and expectations. This has proved to be an ongoing challenge for many, often resulting in internal resistance to global strategies and inappropriate strategies hitting the local scene in the first place.

The concept of 'global hubs', which act as a two-way conduit in MNCs, has emerged. Their role is to shape and articulate the company's core cultural values and assist in the process of localizing them.

At the individual level, we are often doing business across boundaries arising from different cultural perspectives. In summary, country cultures influence the mix of segments seen in a market; but the most common segments still appear to feature.

They also impact the organizational culture and the deployment of culture change levers. Sensitivity to the underlying differentiators, such as those identified by Hofstede, enable more finely tuned responses both to the market and to managing across borders. We also need to be conscious that our own cultural paradigm will influence how we view the rest of the world.

Cultural change – current state

Prior to making changes to internal culture, it is important to have a shared view on the starting point – the current culture and constituent subcultures. This process is usually described as 'mapping' the culture, and there are formal and detailed ways of conducting culture assessments. Fortunately, the tools for this are often from the same theoretical base that we have used here. In smaller organizations and business units, the descriptors given earlier are often enough for a leadership team to make a good assessment and to categorize the 'way we do things around here'; and to identify the groups (or subcultures) who appear to collectively hear a somewhat different drum.

Cultural change – shaping the underpinning subcultures

Once you have assessed the particular customer segmentation (or external subcultures) in your target market and mapped the internal subcultures, you are in an ideal position to compare differences and begin making changes as needed, using the identified customer segments as a *frame-of-reference*. This will involve mixing the appropriate recipe of capabilities to derive the required subcultures. There follows discussion on how this can be done, for each supply chain archetype that we identified in Chapter 4.

Group subculture for the Collaborative Supply Chain™ configuration

Characteristics of the Group subculture are synergy, teamwork, cooperation and structure. Its *integrative* capability is supported by tight alignment with customer systems and processes, relationship-focused resourcing and information sharing.

The specific internal capabilities that make up this subculture are described in Figure 7.5.

Hierarchical subculture for the Lean Supply Chain configuration

Characteristics of the hierarchical subculture are adherence to procedures, measurement, control and order. Its *efficiency* capability is characterized by mature processes, stable systems, low-risk predictable performance and embedded Lean principles.

The specific internal capabilities that constitute this subculture are described in Figure 7.6.

Rational subculture for the Agile Supply Chain configuration

Characteristics of the rational subculture are action orientation, directness, energy and results-focus. Its *responsive* capability is characterized by processes and systems to support flexibility, fast decision making, risk tolerance and a focus on individual responsibility.

The specific internal capabilities that constitute this subculture are described in Figure 7.7.

Rational/hierarchical subculture for the Campaign Supply Chain™ configuration

The Campaign Supply Chain™ is a hybrid and thus the capability needed to support it is somewhat of a mix of the previous subcultures. Taking features of each, the result needs to be able to comply with tight schedules but adjusted when necessary. This is, perhaps, the most difficult configuration to achieve.

CAPABILITY AREA	CAPABILITY
Customer interaction	◆ Account management focus ◆ Multi-level engagement strategies across organizations
Processes	◆ Customer account management ◆ Key account management ◆ Collaborative planning & forecasting ◆ Joint innovation
IT systems	◆ CRM ◆ Cloud-based collaboration platform ◆ Control towers with joint visibility ◆ Early adoption for blockchain
KPIs	◆ Retention ◆ Share of wallet/share of spend ◆ Reliablity and availability ◆ Shared KPIs around common goals
Organization	◆ Risk management/mitigation ◆ Organization design: multi-disciplinary relationship cluster ◆ People selection and positioning: ensure bias of relationships (Ia) in cluster ◆ Strategic partnering capability
Culture	◆ Minimize change ◆ Internal collaboration-teaming ◆ Consensus decision making ◆ Incentives: encourage participative schemes ◆ Job design: degree of autonomy negotiated by consensus ◆ Internal communications: consultative/face-to-face ◆ Training & development: team building ◆ Role modeling: managers with ESFP MBTI profile ideal ◆ Recruiting: team players ◆ Leadership style = Coach: conscientious; leads by teaching; concerned for others; loyal; committed; politically astute; seeks agreement by consensus

FIGURE 7.5 ◆ **Internal capabilities required to propel Collaborative Supply Chains**™

Source: Adapted from Gattorna (2015) p. 206

CAPABILITY AREA	CAPABILITY
Customer interaction	◆ Routine & predictable ◆ Personal interaction is lower priority
Processes	◆ Forecasting critical ◆ Reliable information to support automation/decision support ◆ Relentless focus on cost ◆ Built on core 'lean' principles
IT systems	◆ Replace legacy systems with stable, common ERP system ◆ Automation ◆ Data warehousing & decision support ◆ Refined inventory management ◆ Strong track & trace
KPIs	◆ Reliability & accuracy focus: DIFOTEF ◆ Forecast accuracy ◆ Productivity ratios ◆ Cost/unit
Organization	◆ Minimize structural risk ◆ Organization design: Multi-disciplinary cluster built around core processes ◆ People selection and positioning: ensure bias of (A/Ap) consistency/repetition/efficiency in the cluster
Culture	◆ Minimize change ◆ Adhere to central policies ◆ Central decision making ◆ Incentives: conformance to policies ◆ Job design: centralized control ◆ Internal communications: regular; structured; 'need-to-know' basis ◆ Training and development: emphasis on analysis and measurement ◆ Role modeling: managers with ISTJ (A) MBTI profile ideal ◆ Recruiting: players with deep analytical skills ◆ Leadership style = Traditional: leads by procedure and precedent; implements only proven practices; cost controller; efficiency focus; uses information to control; seeks stability; is risk averse

FIGURE 7.6 ◆ **Internal capabilities required to propel Lean Supply Chains**

Source: Adapted from Gattorna (2015) p. 245

CAPABILITY AREA	CAPABILITY
Customer interaction	◆ Accessible
	◆ Proactive
	◆ Personal interaction at decision maker level may be necessary to capture opportunities
Processes	◆ Forecasting at capacity level
	◆ Simplified/process shortcuts
	◆ Flexible scheduling
	◆ Modularization
IT systems	◆ Customized/situational
	◆ Configurable applications
	◆ Scenario capability
	◆ Real time decision support
	◆ Demand sensing
KPIs	◆ Response time
	◆ Lead time focus
	◆ Opportunities captured
	◆ Revenue growth
Organization	◆ Risk tolerance with guidelines
	◆ Organization design: multi-disciplinary clusters focused on Pa segment [speed]
	◆ People selection and positioning: ensure bias of agility (Pa) in cluster
	◆ Limit organizational constraints
Culture	◆ Individual decision making
	◆ Incentives: cash and in-kind bonuses
	◆ Job design: authority levels established by clear and published limits
	◆ Internal communications: formal; regular; action oriented
	◆ Training and development: problem-solving; resource allocation
	◆ Role modeling: managers with ESTJ (Pa) MBTI profile are ideal
	◆ Recruitment: result-oriented personnel
	◆ Leadership style = Company Baron: leads by objectives; embraces change; goes for growth; focuses on what's important; analytical; fact-based negotiations

FIGURE 7.7 ◆ Internal capabilities required to propel Agile Supply Chains

Source: Adapted from Gattorna (2015) p. 245

Characteristics of the rational/hierarchical subculture are systems, control, order and result orientation (budget and timing). Its *delivery* capability is characterized by: a collaborative front-end; scheduling and project alignment; progress monitoring and expediting, if necessary; knowledge management; and risk management.

The specific internal capabilities that constitute this subculture are described in Figure 7.8.

Entrepreneurial subculture for the Fully Flexible Supply Chain™ configuration

Characteristics of the entrepreneurial subculture are flexibility, risk tolerance, low structure and individualism. Its solution capability is characterized by minimal processes, flexible systems, networks of alliances and empowerment of individuals.

The specific internal capabilities that constitute this subculture are described in Figure 7.9.

The increasing importance of an innovation subculture (D)

The entrepreneurial or innovation culture described above would once have been considered the domain of the start-up; and we would once have said that the Fully Flexible Supply Chain™ capability would have been used only intermittently. It is now apparent, however, that most established businesses need to build and maintain an innovation subculture that operates in parallel to current business.

The reason for this comes back to the constraints of business-as-usual. Significant product, market or business model initiatives and experimental technologies need an element of creativity, freedom to explore and risk tolerance that the more structured subcultures, driven by specific and directional KPIs, cannot usually accommodate. This subculture is also highly dependent on individuals (rather than systems and process) and the mindset of the people that do well in innovation is quite different from those that drive the other common types of subculture.

CAPABILITY AREA	CAPABILITY
Customer interaction	◆ Focused project customer service representatives ◆ Specialized sales and technical sales teams
Processes	◆ Project control tools – synchronized to customer's project plan ◆ Early warning processes & control towers to monitor progress vs plan dates ◆ Project BOMs ◆ Modularization/subassembly 'products'
IT systems	◆ Project planning linked to customer's plan ◆ Inventory visibility ◆ Stock reservation system ◆ Decision support for sequencing ◆ Network optimization modeling to position inputs
KPIs	◆ Project/bid wins ◆ Plan compliance: on time and in full delivery (DIFOT) ◆ Lead time (length & reliability to promise)
Organization	◆ Risk mitigation/contingency capability ◆ Organization design: Multi-disciplinary cluster with PA bias for compliance & response to variations ◆ People selection and positioning ensure bias towards timing, cost, reliability ◆ Analytics to build project knowledge base ◆ Project management/critical path planning capability
Culture	◆ Individual decision making ◆ Incentives: cash and in-kind bonuses ◆ Job design: authority established within clear guidelines ◆ Internal communications: formal, regular, scheduled ◆ Training and development: teaming; cost/time management ◆ Role modeling: combination of ISTJ (A) and ENTJ (P) MBTI profile is ideal ◆ Recruitment: detail-conscious and results-driven personnel ◆ Leadership style = Project Baron; focuses on meeting delivery schedules; meeting cost budgets; does not accept sloppy practices; manages a tight ship; uses PM tools; analytical; fact-based engineer

FIGURE 7.8 ◆ **Internal capabilities required to propel Campaign Supply Chains**[TM]

Source: Adapted from Gattorna (2015) p. 327

CAPABILITY AREA	CAPABILITY
Customer interaction	◆ Proactive with innovation or solution focus
Processes	◆ There are no processes – just local initiative, real-time
IT systems	◆ Low systems requirement; mainly event management ◆ Network optimization modeling ◆ Inventory management ◆ Track & trace
KPIs	◆ Individual KPIs aimed at encouraging creativity ◆ Solutions/initiatives ◆ Tolerance for failure (hit rates)
Organization	◆ Extreme risk taking ◆ Organization design: part-time emergency cluster ◆ People selection and positioning: ensure bias of creativity at speed (Dp) in cluster ◆ Analytics
Culture	◆ Individual decision making ◆ Incentives: reward individualism and risk-taking behavior ◆ Job design: autonomy through empowerment ◆ Internal communications: spontaneous and informed ◆ Training and development: lateral thinking; brainstorming ◆ Role modeling: managers with ENFP (D) MBTI profile are ideal ◆ Recruitment: enterprising; resourceful personnel; self-starting ◆ Leadership style = Visionary; leads by inspiration; is authentic; informal; decisive; cares about ideas; values innovation

FIGURE 7.9 ◆ Internal capabilities required to propel the Fully Flexible Supply Chain™

Source: Adapted from Gattorna (2015) p. 360

Although innovation requires a subculture unconstrained by the historic culture, it needs leaders that are aware of the strengths of the base. We reinforce again that cultural capability is a key responsibility of the leadership team; and building this future-facing capability could well be the key to survival!

A word about leadership

Referring back to our proprietary Dynamic Alignment™ model in Figure 2.1, Chapter 2, it is not an overstatement to say that the success of any enterprise is directly linked to the quality of the leadership team and the CEO who heads that team. Those leaders who are directly connected into the target market, and have real understanding and empathy with that market, set the stage for high performance of their respective enterprises. This connection is fundamental to success. With this established, there is a good chance that the leadership team will develop and launch operational strategies that are better aligned to the target market and, similarly, that they will shape the internal organizational capabilities (and corresponding subcultures) in such a way as to successfully deliver a large proportion of their *intended strategies* into the target marketplace.

So, it all starts and finishes with the leadership team. They need to be able to span the different parts of the market, and/or to have a range of embedded styles that help them to cater for and align with the range of customer segments visible in the target marketplace. As with the other three levels of our Dynamic Alignment™ model, there are four dominant leadership styles.

No doubt, the moiety concept referred to in the foregoing section on 'culture', also comes into play here, where the competing leadership styles are evident according to Figure 7.10. By definition, we need a healthy tension to exist in the leadership team to ensure vital decisions are well debated before being finalized. In these situations, the CEO has to be the final arbiter and sometimes this involves making tough calls. Ram Charan is adamant that making the tough calls is the role of a good leader.[6] He says that '. . . they cut through the complexity to get to the heart of the matter, without getting superficial. And they do it without losing sight of the customer'.[7]

From these four primary leadership styles, it is possible to derive up to 16 variants of leadership style, which is very consistent with the Myers–Briggs Type Indicator,[8] but those depicted below are the most recognized and widely understood types.

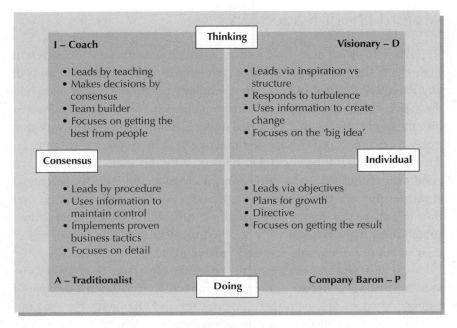

FIGURE 7.10 ◆ Leadership styles – the four generic types

Source: Adapted from Gattorna (2015) p. 149

A common thread?

If you study the successful enterprises worldwide, be they business or sporting, it becomes obvious that a key central theme is about *authenticity* of leadership. 'Authentic leaders listen to inner conscience to guide them in decision making and taking a stand on controversial issues.'[9] According to Gilbert Enoka, a member of the New Zealand All Blacks[10] coaching staff, 'development of the authentic self . . . is hugely powerful to performance'.[11]

These are the principles that have made the New Zealand rugby team, the All Blacks, not only the most successful rugby team in history, but the most successful sporting team, of any code, in the modern era. Perhaps they have something to teach business and politicians about leadership.

Bill George has a similar message, that the essence of a great leader is about '. . . being genuine, real and true to who you are . . . Authenticity – the mark of a true leader – begins with honesty and integrity'.[12]

Some of the other key ingredients of leadership are well articulated by Richard de Crespigny in his book *FLY!*[13] He was the Captain of QF32, the Qantas A380 that suffered a catastrophic explosion in one of its engines after take-off from Singapore on 4 November 2010. The aircraft was carrying 469 passengers and crew. In his book, he focuses on '. . . the underlying capabilities and techniques that ensured we survived the unthinkable that day: the teamwork, leadership, problem-solving, risk-assessment and deep understanding of how the human brain works that enabled everyone involved to perform at their best.'[14]

Richard states that leaders, to perform at their best, have to be *resilient* and master their mind. Of course, with the intense training undertaken by pilots, they are better positioned to dispel fear and remain calm in crisis situations. Unlike most of us, they have trained for potential unforeseeable situations.

For management in general, and supply chain executives in particular, since they don't usually undergo such intense training, we have to substitute by proactively building our own deep knowledge of that within our span of control. And now this can (and should be) supplemented with modeling and testing of possible future scenarios. Pilots have their simulators, we have modeling.

De Crespigny also makes a point that is particularly pertinent in the current business environment '. . . failing well is the hallmark of *resilience*. Failing well means understanding what happened and learning from the experience, figuring out how to improve, making the necessary changes, and being unafraid to try again'.[15] We agree with this notion (but we are hoping that Richard confines his failures to the simulator)!

More executives in the supply chain will be called upon to take calculated risks with the decisions they make in these unpredictable times, and they won't always get it right the first time. The secret is to 'fail well' and try again if the initial attempt did not work out. It is not an option any more simply to sit on your hands and 'do nothing'.

In our Dynamic Alignment™ model, introduced in Chapter 2, we stressed that everything starts and finishes with 'leadership'. By that, we mean that genuine leaders project themselves into their operating environment, and absorb it to the point that they fully understand and empathize with the situation there. It is only then, with this in-depth understanding of the market, and the expectations of customers, that they are able to precisely formulate strategy and the underlying subcultures that must, by definition, be present for success.

Richard de Crespigny goes even further. In his view, '. . . leadership is personal . . . be authentic and start acting and thinking like the leader you want to be'.[16] In his view, 'the leader doesn't set the culture; the leader IS the culture'.[17] And how true that statement is. Look at the performance of any successful enterprise in the Fortune 500 and elsewhere, and this statement rings true. It's the leadership every time, stupid!

Lessons specifically for the supply chain

Executives in senior supply chain leadership roles, such as the chief supply chain officer (CSCO) or SVP Supply Chain, have to be particularly courageous in the current volatile operating environment. They need to formulate a vision of how they see the 'supply chain of the future', clearly articulate what it looks like, communicate it to the rest of the enterprise, and sell the dream.

People want to be led, and this strong, uncompromising approach will be appreciated, even if some disagree with its content. What we don't want is the flip-flopping that we often see in response to share market shifts and in the political arena these days, because it leads to uncertainty, loss of confidence and inaction.

Leaders in the supply chain have to take a position, be counted and stand for something. At times, this will be difficult in the face of opposition, but leaders with the required tenacity and belief will win through in the end and put the enterprise in a better place.

'The urgency around being a (great) leader has skyrocketed. During the next 10 years we will experience an unprecedented storm of technological and demographic shifts. This storm will sweep in remarkable changes in the way we interact with each other, our devices, and the world around us, while also presenting new, unmatched opportunities.'[18] Nowhere is this more evident than in the supply chains that cut horizontally across all functions in the enterprise, like a giant central nervous system.

Finally, returning to the issue of *integrity*, mentioned earlier as a critical component of genuine leadership. Supply chain leaders are in pole position to ensure that ethical and accepted standards are met in the course of doing business. The environment has to be respected and suppliers must be held accountable for the treatment of their labor. A zero tolerance of slavery has to be applied. Such is the burden of responsibility on the new breed of CSCO.

CASE STUDY: The New Zealand All Blacks

Lessons business can learn from sport

Situation

'The [New Zealand] All Blacks are the most successful rugby team in history. They have been called the most successful sports team, in any code, ever. In the professional era, they have an extraordinary win rate of over 86 percent, and are current World Champions.'[19] The All Blacks know, as did the famous American football coach, Bill Walsh, '. . . that if you established a culture higher than your opposition, you would win'.[20] 'A values-based, purpose-driven culture is the foundation of the All Blacks approach and sustained success.'[21] The difference is they know how to deliver – these are not simply aspirations. The identity of the team matters most, and all the current players in the team buy into this principle, above all else.

The challenge

But it wasn't always like this. At the beginning of head coach Graham Henry's reign in the early 2000s, the All Blacks had been badly beaten by the South African Springboks, and come last in the annual Tri-Nations tournament. Worse still, it was the appalling behavior of many of the players after the match that led the assistant coach, Wayne Smith, to describe the team as 'dysfunctional'. It was time for change, big change. The mighty All Blacks were at a precipice.

Devising new operating principles

A plan was devised by Graham Henry and the coaching group that 'traversed years, seasons, series, weeks, days and even the seconds the match clock traveled as it counted down to the final whistle'.[22] Graham Henry, as teacher/coach, set out to remotivate his players, to stimulate them in order to make them want to be part of the team's future. He wanted to see leadership and responsibility come from within the team. In 2004, he laid out his blueprint for change in a report to the New Zealand Rugby Union. Henry identified his key areas of focus as follows:

> *Sufficient leadership, knowledge and confidence to implement the game plan; the transference of leadership and therefore responsibility from the coaches to the players; the development of leadership ability and composure; the necessity for the group to understand their identity – who they are, what they stand for, and their collective and individual responsibilities as All Blacks.*[23]

▶

The change program, which continues today, incorporated principles such as: play with purpose; accept responsibility; pass the ball – leaders create leaders; create a learning environment; embrace expectations; and practice under pressure. All ideas that are quite transferable to the world of business.

Results

Since that fateful meeting at the New Zealand Rugby Union in 2004, all concerned have been focused on turning the vision into action and, in this, they have succeeded, right up to the present day.

The All Blacks won the Rugby World Cup in 2011 and again in 2015, and are hot favorites to win in Japan in 2019. Graham Henry has retired, but the same style of leadership has continued through the appointment of his assistant, Steve Hansen. They have become practically unstoppable, but pride and humility remain in a fine balance.

What can we learn?

This case is as much about leadership as culture change. It takes inspired leadership to chart a path for a team (or commercial enterprise) and set the required disciplines in place to follow. In the case of the All Blacks, the cultural change program started in 2004, and culminated in success in 2011, winning the Rugby World Cup. It took seven years! So you can see how long it takes to change culture! And it requires significant tenacity to stay the course. In an enterprise, you can change your intended strategies relatively quickly, but realigning the culture (and constituent subcultures) to properly underpin these strategies can sometimes take years, especially if the organization is large. But persistence pays off, and the results will follow if you stick to your guns.

Points of view

On culture

1 The internal culture in the enterprise can either sustain or impede the implementation of strategy.

2 Differentiated market strategies require the equivalent differentiated subcultures to underpin them.

3 Subcultures are subject to the 'moeity' effect, where opposing subcultures are in tension with each other. This can be positive if recognized and managed.

4 It is possible to map the culture and subcultures present in an enterprise – and to compare this with current customer segments in the market to determine the degree of alignment/misalignment.

5 There are 13 change levers that can be applied to the task of shifting or creating subcultures.

6 Country cultures sit over the top of company subcultures and modify the way they work.

7 Recipes of internal capabilities also help shape the subcultures required to align the enterprise with its target market.

On leadership

1 Nothing good happens in the enterprise without inspired leadership.

2 Appropriate leadership styles are situational, depending on the 'season' the enterprise is in and external circumstances.

3 All the best leaders are authentic and operate with integrity towards the natural environment and the people that support their supply chain.

4 Operating in volatile market conditions requires courage, persistence and preparation to deal with disruptions.

5 Supply chain senior leaders are in the vanguard as the enterprise attempts to position itself to win in a changing marketplace. But they are faced with balancing the need to win against acting with integrity at all times.

Kick-start your thinking

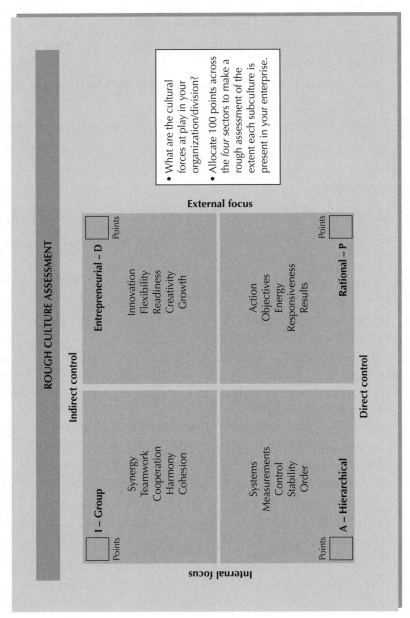

ROUGH CULTURE ASSESSMENT

- What are the cultural forces at play in your organization/division?
- Allocate 100 points across the *four* sectors to make a rough assessment of the extent each subculture is present in your enterprise.

External focus

Indirect control

Entrepreneurial – D   Points

Innovation
Flexibility
Readiness
Creativity
Growth

Rational – P   Points

Action
Objectives
Energy
Responsiveness
Results

I – Group   Points

Synergy
Teamwork
Cooperation
Harmony
Cohesion

A – Hierarchical   Points

Systems
Measurements
Control
Stability
Order

Direct control

Internal focus

CHAPTER 8

Digital strategies

Developing a digital supply chain via automation, digitization, IoT and blockchain

Introduction

Perhaps the best summary of the future logistics/supply chain landscape is depicted in Figure 8.1, prepared by DHL. This maps social and business trends against technology trends, and uses a high–low scale to assess the potential level of disruption caused by each phenomenon.

It is clear that contemporary supply chains will all have to be fully digitized end-to-end (E2E) to remain competitive in the future. This is going to require a lot of work internally and with trading partners in corresponding distribution channels.

Through the widescale adoption of digitization ' . . . computers can diagnose situations and identify challenges that humans don't see. Real-time information makes it possible to run experiments rather than guessing what might work'.[1] This use of technology combined with human judgment is the ideal outcome of digitization.

The four digital technologies that will likely have most impact on supply chain performance over the next 5–10 years are:

1 *Automation/robotics:* will become commonplace in logistics operations and take over many tasks that are currently manual.

2 *Artificial intelligence (AI):* will underpin a new level of predictive capability in the supply chain. By being able to mine and utilize the *patterns* in a wide range of datasets, AI can improve the quality and speed of decision making in the enterprise.

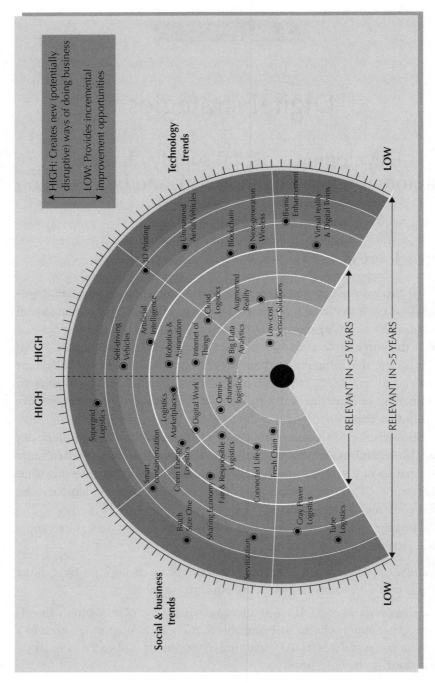

FIGURE 8.1 ◆ The DHL Logistics Trend Radar

Source: DHL Trend Research (2018), Logistics Trend Radar, p. 15. Available at: http://www.dhl.com/en/about_us/logistics_insights/dhl_trend_research/trendradar.html#.W5d3l-gzY2w

3 *Internet of Things (IoT):* a network of sensors will feed data across manufacturing and logistics. The opportunity is to increase visibility and trigger proactive response at key points along the supply chain.

4 *Blockchain:* distributed ledger technology that will speed up processes, reduce complexity, improve transparency and ensure reliable provenance. And to leverage all of the above, heavy-duty analytics, as discussed in Chapter 5.

These applications will form the backbone for digitized businesses and extended supply chains. We will examine each of these new technologies in turn, acknowledging that we also need a powerful analytics capability in place to drive the necessary decision support regimes.

Automation/robotics

Automation historically has been considered the domain of manufacturing rather than logistics. At the production stage, activities, components and processes tend to be standardized and thus easier to mechanize and manage with process control systems. Logistics has lagged because of variety. So, although there are big advances in manufacturing from automation, robotics and linking manufacturing processes to a network, perhaps the most significant step change could come from how products are distributed, post-manufacture.

A retail warehouse, for example, could easily handle 30,000 SKUs of different dimensions; and no store order would be the same configuration on a given day. But the second decade of the 21st century has seen warehouse and logistics automation move into the mainstream. Key enablers have been the developments in AI and optimization systems and smart, alternative ways of managing variety.

At the vanguard are a few operations that are taking automation and robotics to the extreme. A UK online grocery retailer, Ocado, has designed for itself what has been called a 'hive' warehouse – a huge chessboard-like grid, populated by 1,000 robots the size and shape of a washing machine. 'Each of the bots has a central cavity and a set of claws it uses to grab crates and pull them up into its interior, like an alien abduction in a supermarket aisle . . . imagine a huge machine, with groceries going in one end and shopping orders coming out the other. Humans do the unpacking and packing, while in the middle, robots sort and rearrange this vast inventory 24 hours a day.'[2] Ocado's development has caused so much interest they are now selling their system to other retailers.

While companies such as Ocado and Amazon have been early adopters (and creators) of the next wave of automation; we are now seeing major investments by the 'early majority'. Woolworths in Australia, for example, has invested US$160 million in a new facility in Melbourne, which includes 14 kilometers of conveyors and robots that pack 650 cases/hour – four times existing manual rates. This facility alone, serving only one State, is thought by some analysts to create sufficient savings to change the dynamics in the retail market in Woolworths' favor.[3]

The convergence of robotics and automation with AI and predictive analytics can reduce cost, reduce time to market and improve safety. However, the decision regarding the level and type of investment in automation is particularly difficult in a shifting business environment.

In many industries, the route to market, and with it the order size, is changing. Thus, the typical timeframes for investment evaluations hit up against a need for assumptions around order patterns and business models.

As depicted in Figure 8.2, warehouse investments can be particularly vulnerable to more direct consumer and business purchasing and the smaller order sizes that result. Because materials handling systems are increasingly capital intense, and can lack flexibility, scenarios regarding a range of future states should be closely reviewed as part of the capital evaluation process.

Artificial intelligence (AI)

Artificial Intelligence systems will be able to give managers real-time insights about their business operations – as well as detect early warnings of problems before they occur.[4]

After several decades of promise, AI is now delivering results and it has become part of daily life. We search for information, navigate across cities and buy online with guidance from machine-learning algorithms. For the 'digital native' mega-businesses, Google, Amazon and Alibaba, artificial intelligence is at the heart of their business model, and for many tech and automotive businesses it is fast becoming a core plank of the model.

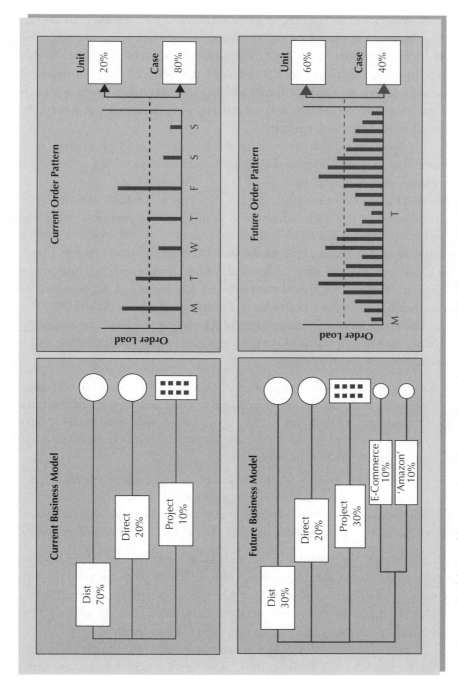

FIGURE 8.2 ◆ Decision making on automation needs to take account of business model shifts

Beyond these industries, in more traditional businesses, even though these everyday applications are taken for granted, the barrier to reliance on AI for key decisions is still high. A large survey of 3,000 AI-aware, C-level executives by McKinsey in 2017 showed that only 20 per cent used any form of AI in a core part of their business, and that many business leaders were uncertain of what it could do for them, what the applications were, the benefits or how to assess returns.[5]

It's likely that if you are reading this book you could be working for a more mature organization and asking yourself these questions, so let's see if we can answer some of them.

What can AI do for the supply chain? In the same McKinsey research, case studies of the early adopters in retail, utilities, manufacturing and healthcare highlighted AI's potential to 'improve forecasting and sourcing, optimize and automate operations, develop targeted marketing and pricing, and enhance the user experience'.[6] And, if we return to Amazon and Alibaba, it's apparent that these back-end and front-end applications are exactly where they have been able to flourish on the basis of AI.

The most heavily invested form of AI currently is machine learning.[7] The most common forms of machine learning are well-suited to the multi-faceted supply chain problem:

- *Supervised learning* is where labeled data is used to train the system to learn the relationship between specific identified inputs and outputs. For example, all customer details, order lines and delivery details for five years of orders could be the starting dataset to examine the response to price and off-invoice promotions.

- *Unsupervised learning* is where the system is looking for patterns or clusters in data without labels (or essentially an 'x' axis only). These could be images of e-commerce returns to explore handling and disposal issues, or social media feeds about the company to disclose emerging concerns.

In both cases, the barriers in the past have been the size of the dataset required and the computing power needed. Cloud computing and the data centers that support it have helped overcome both of these impediments and most organizations are now accustomed to accumulating large datasets (although, perhaps, not yet the type needed for unstructured data).

Many of the areas where AI can provide support are already well measured. We usually track KPIs on forecast accuracy, operating cost, customer satisfaction and spend per customer. The benefits of AI in this setting are usually associated with better, faster prediction and alerts to enable earlier, proactive responses, and return on investment is measured by the usual parameters of sales, share and margin changes over time. This pragmatic positioning is important to demystify AI and help it make sense in more traditional organizations.

The 'supply chain of one'?

The global ERP software company SAP is proposing its vision for a digitally enabled 'supply chain of one', i.e. a specific and customized path for every individual product going to every unique delivery point on a given day.

For SAP, this is a huge turnaround in philosophy, from a company not too many years ago intent on cementing into place a 'One supply chain for all' philosophy. The 'supply chain of one', as proposed by SAP, is, for many people, the natural extension of developments in AI. The questions we might ask ourselves are as follows:

1   Is this realistic and achievable?

2   Does this obviate the need for the predictive capability of customer segmentation and the limited number of differentiated supply chains as proposed in Chapter 4?

The answer to the first question is 'yes', at least in part. Sensing of demand signals, leveraging of IoT and preventive maintenance alerts and predictive analytics will give us better information for more reliable planning and order preparation. Smart manufacturing is heading towards more flexible, faster and more customized output.

But how to respond to a customer's request will always need to be driven by a set of 'rules'; and these rules will form the basis of the automated fulfilment logic.

The answer to the second question is a definite 'no'. What Dynamic Alignment™ brings to the table is a primary filter or heuristic, which proposes that the first level of 'rules' should be about the customer's buying *preferences,* i.e. what is important to them as buyers. In practical terms, we also invariably use another one or two filters such as industry, geographic location or type of business.

What tools, such as AI and optimization, allow is more filters and more rules; and these guide us towards the eventual path a product will take through the supply chain on its way to the customer. These are, effectively, 'If/Then' statements that will guide the automated response(s).

So, for example, *rules* for an industrial supplier might include:

Segment rules	If a collaborative customer, then . . . If a transactional customer, then . . .
Industry rules	If construction, then . . . If an OEM, then . . .
Application rules	If continuous manufacture, then . . . If subassembly, then . . .
Geographic rules	If metro, then . . . If remote, then . . .
Product rules	If category aa1, then . . . If category aa2, then . . .

Essentially, AI and digitization will employ the type of grouping and logic that is used to aggregate products, customers and delivery points in network modeling (and which enable the model to focus on what is strategically most important). In models, the grouping enables for testing strategic scenarios and to surface meaningful patterns; here the heuristics are used to determine the best way to serve the customer with this product, in this situation.

The key will be to work out in advance what those *most important* factors are. Some grouping, based on customer expectations, as used in Dynamic Alignment™, will be a very important starting point.

The Internet of Things (IoT)

The Internet of Things (IoT) are the everyday objects and physical devices that can be equipped with identifying, sensing, networking and processing capabilities that allow them to communicate with one another and with other devices and services over a network to achieve some useful purpose.

IoT is the enabler for many of the other advances discussed in this chapter. To achieve full value from automation, robotics and the blockchain will require the availability of networked data and feeds from the physical assets and products within the chain. The concept of Industry 4.0, and the fully networked manufacturing environment, is predicated on IoT and cyber-physical systems (CPS). CPS refers to the interaction between algorithms and connected devices: 'Embedded computers and networks monitor and control the physical processes, with feedback loops where physical processes affect computations and vice versa.'[8]

Beyond the factory walls, IoT also holds promise for faster, more stable end-to-end supply chains. Automated reordering; improved visibility along the chain; improved logistics asset performance (with proactive alerts to avoid breakdowns); and early warnings signaling any deviations from plan are some of the opportunities it opens up.

Interoperability and systems connectivity stand out as the potential constraints in taking advantage of IoT across the supply chain (rather than in closed systems). And this has implications for the nature of the relationships along the chain itself.

Beyond these barriers, however, many of the cost and communication constraints that stood in the way of widespread adoption of RFID have been left behind. Trackster™,[9] for example, an IoT start-up, is showing that containers, pallets and even packages can be cost-effectively tracked in real time within and between countries (except in the middle of the ocean where satellite communication becomes prohibitively expensive), without the need for expensive infrastructure to read sensors as they pass! In addition, the Trackster™ organization has adopted a unique leasing model rather than selling the devices outright. This changes the cost model from capital investment, to a variable operating cost and reduces the barriers to adoption.

The supply chain often is depicted as a physical flow of product, with a corresponding, but separate, information flow. IoT suggests a new version of the supply chain, with the physical and information flow inextricably linked and interdependent.

But, on the path to these visions of the future, we have some important decisions to make regarding IoT. The advances in technology and the reduction in the cost of sensing and communicating has opened up vastly new opportunities to collect data. The question now becomes one of where to focus and which data can bring value – especially in the first wave of investment.

One of the key opportunities, and thus focus areas, is to use IoT together with predictive analytics to reduce levels of volatility along supply chains. With this greater stability comes reduced cost and improved reliability, both much sought-after by customers. Applications that monitor the health of an installed base of equipment and those that monitor physical (as opposed to system) stock levels can reduce the incidence of unexpected 'shocks', thus stabilizing the load on the supply chain.

Another key opportunity is enhanced tracking, providing the certainty and confidence that customers are becoming accustomed to at a more sophisticated level. The combination of IoT and blockchain, as discussed below, is an important advance in this direction.

Simply collecting data across all potential tracking points through the supply chain at this stage, however, is unlikely to be either cost-effective or of value. We argue that it is necessary to have a very definite strategy linked to how the customer will eventually realize benefit from this investment in technology and resources. This strategy can then be used to more closely define the information required and thus the specific data that should be collected along the chain.

The thought process goes something like that depicted in Figure 8.3.

Competing on data

One of the most 'intensive' users of IoT is Formula 1. The facts are impressive; see Figure 8.4 for a summary of the Red Bull capability. This astounding level of focus involves analytics teams on the racetrack, as well as back at head office, continually monitoring the data and adjusting the strategy.

All the F1 teams have similar data capabilities, but the difference (sometimes only a fraction of a second in a race) lies in what each team does with it. And this too is the key message for those of us in more mundane industries!

Another example is the rapid development of data mining in yachting, in particular the America's Cup. On the Oracle Team USA boat, 1,000 real-time sensors collect data and generate hundreds of gigabytes of information.

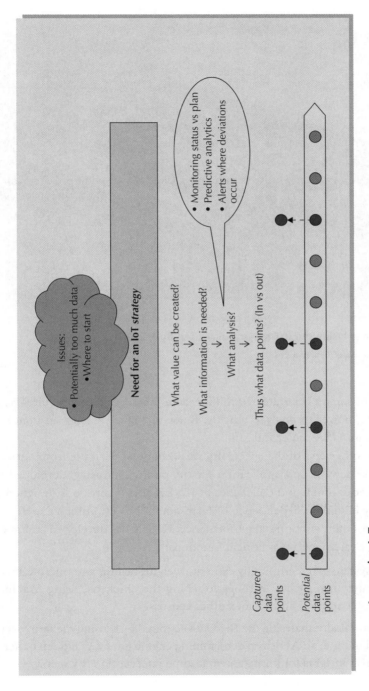

FIGURE 8.3 ◆ Leveraging IoT

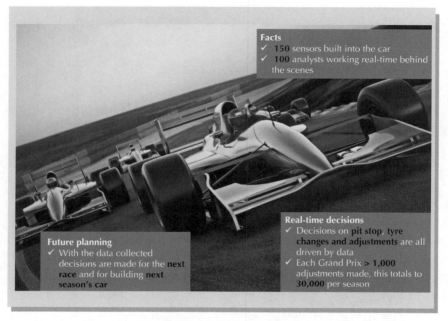

Facts
- ✓ **150** sensors built into the car
- ✓ **100** analysts working real-time behind the scenes

Real-time decisions
- ✓ Decisions on **pit stop, tyre changes and adjustments** are all driven by data
- ✓ Each Grand Prix **> 1,000** adjustments made, this totals to **30,000** per season

Future planning
- ✓ With the data collected decisions are made for the **next race** and for building **next season's car**

FIGURE 8.4 ◆ **Using the IoT in Formula1 (Red Bull, 2017)**

Source: Blackbox data in F1. Scott Betts/123RF

An hour of sailing generates 90 million data points, and this requires huge computing power to analyze quickly. Refer to Figure 8.5 for an image of Oracle Team USA under full sail.

At the other end of the spectrum, we see a great example from agriculture in the new Birdoo application for the poultry industry, developed by Dr Mahender Singh and colleagues at KNEX Inc.[10] Birdoo is designed to effectively eliminate dependence of farm operations on human expertise – the cause of most suboptimal performance. KNEX has developed an Expert Learning System with two critical functions:

1 'The system can 'continually estimate weight, health, and micro-climate attributes in real-time without touching the chickens, using Machine Vision techniques and various other sensors.'

2 'By continually analysing the Big Data acquired by sensing the farm over a period of time, an AI driven deep mining engine uncovers hidden patterns to deliver insights for immediate real-time intervention (by managers).'[11]

FIGURE 8.5 ◆ Oracle Team USA America's Cup Yacht under full sail

Source: Leightonoc/Shutterstock

See Figure 8.6 for a schematic of the Birdoo application. The current focus is on the Broiler Farm, but future developments will target other key locations along the overall Poultry Value Chain.

Blockchain

Blockchain is the other major development that we believe will dramatically change the operating landscape and will amplify the value of the other digitization initiatives discussed here.

Blockchain refers to a distributed or shared ledger that can store the history of transactions conducted between organizations and that can be viewed by parties involved in the transaction within an agreed set of controls and protocols.

As each transaction occurs, it becomes a 'block'. Each 'block' is connected to the one before in an irreversible chain or sequence over time – hence 'blockchain'. A key strength of the database that blockchain builds

Poultry value chain

The overall poultry value chain starts with grain procurement and ends with the consumer. Key activities range from planning and sourcing of feed ingredients such as soybean and corn to convert these into chicken feed. Next steps include processes such as breeder farming, egg hatching, broiler farming that result in production of eggs and meat. These products are sent further downstream to plants for processing, packaging and distribution. Each step in the value chain has its own unique challenges that limits the overall profitability.

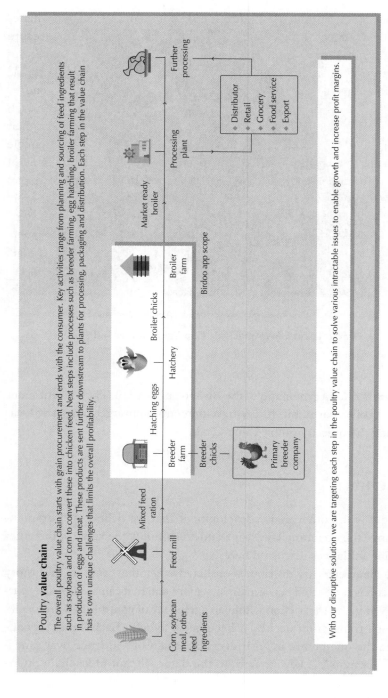

With our disruptive solution we are targeting each step in the poultry value chain to solve various intractable issues to enable growth and increase profit margins.

FIGURE 8.6 ◆ Digitizing the Poultry Value Chain

Source: Reproduced with permission, KNEX, Inc., 2018

is its trustworthiness. The blocks are recorded on many servers, simultaneously, and the wide distribution of information makes it much more secure than single instances of data. Blockchain is based on the same concept of security and validity, achieved via distributed computers capturing identical information, that is the underpinning of bitcoin, the cryptocurrency.

In supply chain terms, relationships traditionally occur between each adjacent party in the chain and banks have arrangements with each other. Although the relationships would stay the same, blockchain would enable many parties in a chain to have access to, and interact with, some or all of the same information embodied in the transactions. In Figure 8.7 we depict what today's supply chains look like, compared with tomorrow's supply chains operating with blockchain protocols.

An important aspect of blockchain development has been the emergence of 'smart contracts'. These are commonly agreed terms between parties which will execute automatically once specific conditions (e.g. delivery on time, within temperature bounds) are met.

One of the key benefits from blockchain is expected to be the increased efficiency, and thus reduced cost, of conducting transactions, particularly those associated with the transfer of ownership of goods or assets. The other key benefit is traceability – the ability to capture real-time (and to thus build historic) information about the origin of a product or material, and its physical condition and location at any time along the supply chain. This history and record-keeping aspect is known as the 'immutable record' feature.

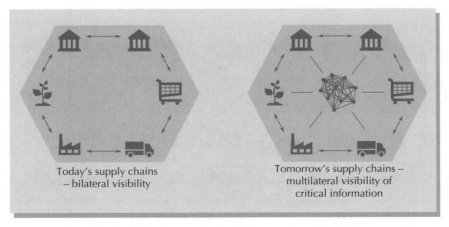

Today's supply chains
– bilateral visibility

Tomorrow's supply chains –
multilateral visibility of
critical information

FIGURE 8.7 ◆ **How blockchain protocols will increase end-to-end transparency**

Blockchain, when combined with IoT tracking and smart contracts, has the potential to bring major supply chain benefits via:

◆ reducing cost, reducing risk and increasing the speed of transactions;

◆ allowing the exchange of value within a network without relying on intermediaries;

◆ enabling verification of provenance and authenticity.

A potential blockchain and IoT application for a beef supply chain in Western Australia is depicted in Figure 8.8. Data capture points are IoT-enabled, and this data is automatically passed through to the blockchain. Australia has well-established RFID monitoring of cattle location and technology businesses that have been built to utilize and further extend the value of this information for the cattle owner. This provides the base data feeds enhanced by the addition of data on the growing characteristics (grass fed/days on grain), carcass characteristics and could, potentially, include information on hormones, antibiotics, genetics, etc. In transit, additional quality and tracking information can be captured, such as temperature readings and daily GPS locations. And for the retail customer and end consumer, the origin of the beef and the details of its journey can be verified.

At the extreme end of the disruption continuum, blockchain has also been proposed as a mechanism to underpin a radically new model for grocery. Under this proposal, consumers would be able to buy products directly from brand manufacturers, with transparent prices on a wide range of branded products. The platform would take a small transaction fee paid

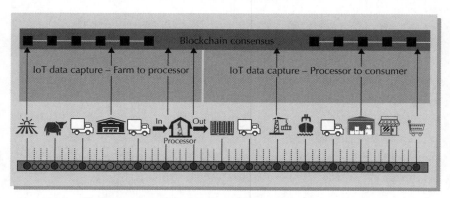

FIGURE 8.8 ◆ **Blockchain application for a beef supply chain**

Source: Gattorna Alignment[12]

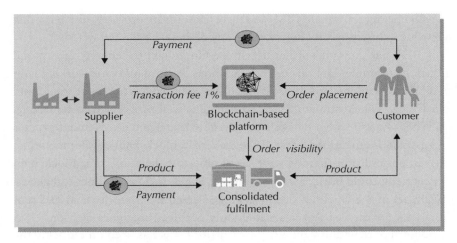

FIGURE 8.9 ◆ A decentralized marketplace disintermediating grocery retail

by the manufacturers, but the brands control all that the customer sees and the pricing. Logistics service providers are also represented on the platform. The usual middle party (the retailer) is not required, as the platform creates the aggregation and blockchain facilitates secure transfer of funds between each of the parties involved. This arrangement is depicted in Figure 8.9.

Current status of blockchain

Globally, there is significant investment occurring in developments and trials around the world and a large number of start-up companies working on specific aspects of distributed technology (the generalized version of blockchain). IBM has been a key driver and, in terms of supply chain, the most prominent, with joint trials conducted in 2016–7 with Maersk, the world's largest shipping company. Following encouraging results from the trials, they recently announced a joint venture business (TradeLens) to apply blockchain in global shipping supply chains.

An IBM and Economist Business Unit study of 200 banks in 16 countries indicates that 66 per cent of banks are likely to have commercial, scaled blockchain solutions in place by 2020.

IBM alone currently has 1,500 staff dedicated to blockchain development. Microsoft is partnering with JPMorgan Chase and several other large corporates on competing software to IBM, and there are software providers emerging that provide industry-specific solutions off any of these 'backbone' systems.

BHP has announced that it will use blockchain to securely record and track key sample data taken from its mines. Australia Post is working with Alibaba to explore ways to use it and other technologies to reduce food fraud in China. The Australian Stock Exchange is well progressed to replace its CHESS system with a blockchain system to manage the settlement process (Australia is emerging as one of the leaders in blockchain developments).

In agriculture, there is wide recognition of the value that blockchain potentially could bring, and trials are starting in various product categories. Walmart in the USA has been tracking selected fresh products in different markets for the last few years including Mexican mangoes into the USA and local pork within China.[13] Their major focus has been on reducing the impact of recalls, by being able to quickly trace the source of any problem. After strong results from the mango/pork trials, they have announced a coalition of nine major food companies, including Unilever, Nestlé, and Dole to further explore ways to leverage blockchain.

Bringing it all together

Essentially, each of the above described technologies are *enablers*. They can and will change the way we do business. But there is one simple question that needs to be asked in evaluating their applicability – where and how do they add value for the customer? The answer to this question will guide smart deployment of these smart tools.

The outline design for a shift towards a full digital supply chain strategy would look something like that depicted below in Figure 8.10. Ultimately, any digital strategy must support the broader business and supply chain strategy and enhance the alignment with the target customer segments.

Digitization: operating in the new, connected landscape

Digitization of the physical activity in the chain will be a major disruptor. The pace of change appears to be faster than we have seen for other major industrial technology adoptions.

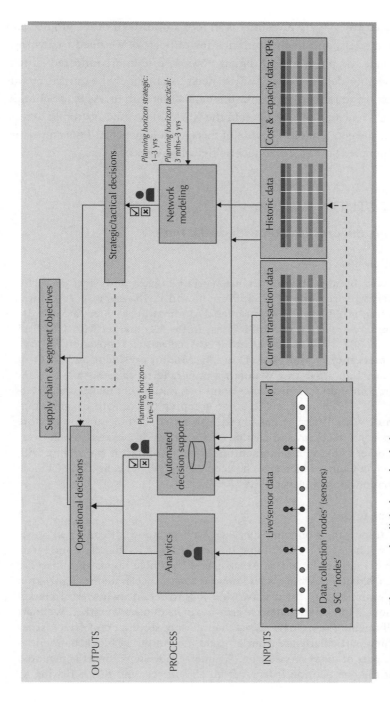

FIGURE 8.10 ◆ Elements of a digital supply chain strategy

We need to evaluate investments in terms of today's order profiles and business models, and likely scenarios for tomorrow. We need to envisage and manage the physical and digital flows as one interconnected system which together deliver value. And we need to ultimately be guided by our customers – and remember to take our staff along with us. As Eric Schmidt, Executive Chairman of Google, told the World Economic Forum at Davos:

'Everyone gets smarter because of this technology . . . and the empowerment of people is the secret to technological progress.'[14]

CASE STUDY: Walmart

Priming the organization with digital tools

Situation

Walmart, by any measure, is the world's biggest and most powerful retailer, with revenue of US$500 billion in 2018, from 11,700 stores operating in 28 countries. It serves 270 million customers a week. Its e-commerce revenue is climbing fast in the US market with US$11.5 billion in 2018.[15] Walmart's mantra is 'Accelerating Innovation', to save customers money and time. Doug McMillon, president and CEO of Walmart Inc. attributes Walmart's unparalleled success to '. . . our people, our culture, our purpose and our values that makes the difference . . . '.[16] There seems to be no stopping this growth-oriented juggernaut. What Walmart has found is that customers who shop in store and become e-commerce customers spend nearly twice as much overall. To keep the online momentum going, Walmart is partnering with JD.com in China, which gives it access to over 90 per cent of the Chinese population. A very clever move.

No time for hubris

But, despite their ongoing success, Walmart knows it can't rest on its laurels. There is a lot of competition out there in its domestic and international markets, including Amazon and its Whole Foods subsidiary, as well as Alibaba in China, so it knows it has to accelerate the digitization of its entire supply chain network if it is to retain its powerful market position. While online sales are growing in its domestic market, Walmart is still opening more new stores than closing stores. Food safety issues in China particularly are front of mind too, and their blockchain initiative is part of the response from Walmart. Indeed, Walmart is paranoid about the competition it faces, from all sources, and this is driving its transformation to a fully digitized enterprise, and top management makes no secret about this.

Full speed ahead with digitization

Walmart clearly sees E2E digitization of its supply chains as the core of the solution going forward, and they see this initiative as a way to both reduce cost and better serve customers. Walmart, together with some of the world's biggest suppliers (including Unilever and Dole Food Co), is combining to build a blockchain powered by IBM to '. . . remake how the industry tracks food worldwide . . . '.[17] For perhaps the first time, big competitors are collaborating, specifically, on this Food Trust initiative to bring food safety to consumers. And with this level of support it is bound to succeed. Apart from this project, one of the biggest problems that Walmart faces as it goes down the omni-channel route is the difficulty of managing inventory that is being accessed by consumers in different ways, as the same consumer potentially chooses to buy across several different channels.

Results

Walmart has risen to the challenge posed in its target markets. In 2018, Walmart delivered the highest comparable sales growth in its US domestic business for nine years, while e-commerce sales grew by 44 per cent.

In China, through its new arrangement with JD.com, Chinese shoppers 'can order items on the JD.com platform, have them picked from shelves in Walmart stores and delivered within 1 hour'.[18] That's service!

It is easy to see how Walmart has continued to drive its growth trajectory, from a theme of 'save money' in 2014, through 'moving with speed' in 2017 and 'accelerating Innovation' in 2018. Its leadership has the formula for ongoing success and the resources to back it up.

What can we learn?

Looking at what Walmart and Amazon are doing, working the market from both ends, the future of retailing is likely to be a blended bricks-and-mortar/e-commerce model. It just depends how each of these behemoths mix their particular blend.

In retailing particularly, but true also of other industries, digitization via the IoT offers opportunities in three critical areas: 'customer experience, the supply chain, and new channels and revenue streams'.[19]

But above all, Walmart is the standard bearer for others to follow. It has all the ingredients for success – an inspired and visionary leadership, who see the challenges and opportunities in the world of the future, form their plans and execute. They are the firm to follow as the world goes digital, in every respect.

Points of view

1 Contemporary supply chains have to be fully digitized end-to-end (E2E) in order to remain competitive in the future operating environment.

2 The four digital technologies likely to have most impact on supply chain performance over the next five years are: automation/robotics; artificial intelligence (AI); the Internet of Things (IoT); and blockchain.

3 All of these technologies are, effectively, enablers, which means they must justify their application through the value they deliver to business.

4 They all require an underlying analytics capability to be fully effective; and building this capability is a good starting point for 'thinking digital'.

Kick-start your thinking

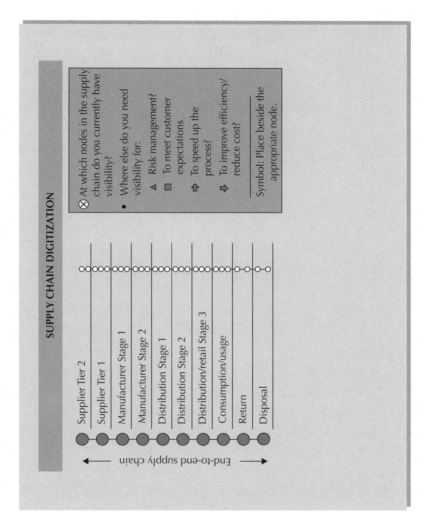

CHAPTER 9

From a 'static' to 'dynamic' supply chain philosophy

Disrupting the organization and increasing clockspeed

Where to from here

As we move deeper into the 21st century, it has become glaringly obvious that the legacy organization structures and processes that we have relied on for decades are now past their 'use-by' date.

And the reason is that they are just too slow! The new businesses and business models emerging to become the most dangerous competitor in the industry – across a great many industries – deliver their results faster than ever before. Whether those results are an e-commerce delivery to the consumer, new product innovations, the next wave of fashion or construction of a new rail line or bridge, speed is an essential factor.

Customers have become accustomed to the higher level of responsiveness available in some parts of their experience and have transferred that expectation to their other areas of commercial activity. If, as a consumer, they can achieve next day delivery when they order from home, they start to wonder why they are waiting a month for an industrial delivery to their workplace.

Technology has been an enabler, but it is the way an organization utilizes its internal and external resources to take advantage of technology that becomes the real differentiator. And, for many, this is quite a challenge.

You only have to look at Friedman and Teller's Adaption Gap in Figure 9.1 to understand the issue. The rate of change of technology may well have outstripped the rate at which humans can absorb change.

When interviewed by Thomas Friedman, Eric Teller, the CEO of Google's X research and development laboratory, arguably one of the drivers of much of the recent technological change, argues that we need a new

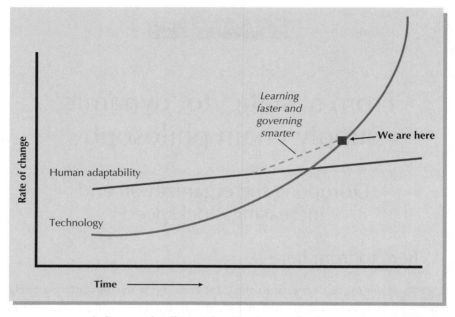

FIGURE 9.1 ◆ Friedman and Teller's Adaption Gap . . . in the age of accelerations

Source: Friedman, T.L. (2016) in conversation with Teller, E. *Thank You for Being Late: An Optimist's Guide to Thriving in the Age of Accelerations.* UK: Allen Lane, Penguin Random House, p. 35

mindset to cope with, and take advantage of, the multiple changes in technology and innovation upon us:

> . . . *the new kind of stability has to be dynamic stability. There are some ways of being, like riding a bicycle, where you cannot stand still, but once you are moving it is actually easier. It is not our natural state. But humanity has to learn to exist in this state.*[1]

This chapter reviews some of the elements we need to think about if our supply chains are going to be able to support dynamic stability and to work at the much faster clockspeed required to keep up in a constantly changing world.

Faster cadence = faster organizational clockspeed >>> increased competitiveness

One of the first to try to articulate this new story was Charles Fine. In his ground-breaking book *Clockspeed,*[2] Fine used the analogy of fruit flies, which he called a 'fast clockspeed species', evolving from eggs, through adulthood to death, all in under two weeks! Much of his research was concentrated on the industrial equivalents of these fast-evolving fruit flies.

One of the companies that he featured was Intel, which in turn had fast-evolving customers such as Compaq and Dell, whose products inevitably had short life cycles in the user marketplace. Clearly, then, as now, the real pressure was coming from the customer end of the chain, and that pressure has increased significantly in the two decades since Fine wrote his seminal book.

Fine studied whole industries, noting the different *rates* at which they evolved; he called these rates 'industry clockspeeds', which he defined as resulting from a combination of product, process and organization clockspeeds, respectively.

He drew the conclusion that any differences in clockspeed between businesses is manifested in the size/length of the decision-making window, and we fully agree with that. When it comes down to fundamentals, enterprises under pressure from their customer base and/or competitors must, by definition, find ways to make faster decisions if they are to survive. Indeed, given that competitive advantage is now regarded as only 'temporary', the enterprise must continually re-invent itself to stay ahead. The old concept of locking in a 'sustainable advantage' is no longer possible in fast-moving industries and markets.

We find it useful to think about this idea of 'clockspeed' or cadence in relative terms. There is a natural rhythm that a market or broader industry operates at; and then there is the clockspeed that our own organization is capable of achieving, on a regular basis. When the enterprise is moving slower than the market, there is a potentially dangerous misalignment; faster may be a competitive advantage, if customers value it, or a waste of resources if not. It is a useful starting point to describe this pattern, if only at the conceptual level, as illustrated in Figure 9.2.

With the coming of the e-commerce era and the direct access that this affords suppliers to their consumers or end users, coupled with digitization and the disintermediation effect of blockchain, we are likely to see many more disruptions across industries that are dragging their feet on clockspeed.

Faster rhythm (or clockspeed) is essential for maintaining competitiveness in the face of rising consumer expectations. But, not only that, as the Zara case study at the end of this chapter illustrates, it can also give the organization a way of combating increased volatility in the market.

An organization that is operating at a faster rhythm is usually less exposed when customers shift their preferences, because they are holding less inventory and are able to redirect their resources to better match the market. And,

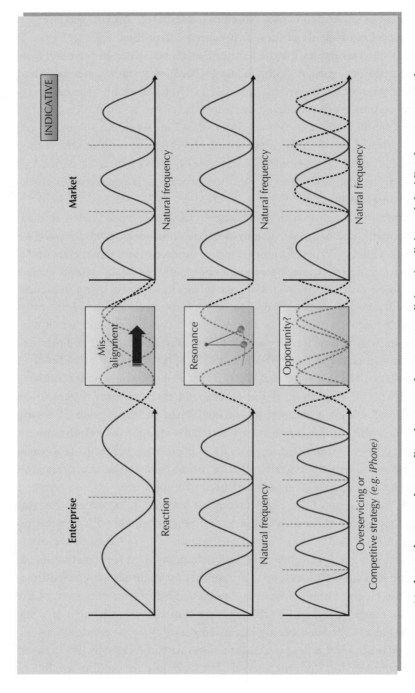

FIGURE 9.2 ◆ **Market cadence: understanding the natural pattern (explicit or implicit) and deciding how to respond**

because we are now talking about achieving faster split times in each element of the overall lead time, the time buckets are shorter and this has the effect of reducing the risk of forecasting error. As in the case of Zara, they are never more than three weeks away from the next cycle of product launches to their stores, so markdowns become much less of a problem. And stock-outs can even be something of a virtue!

Design and concurrency

Many of the operational decisions that result in faster cadence of enterprise supply chains are design-related. Charles Fine emphasized the need for concurrency,[3] the design of product, process and supply chains in parallel. His concept is depicted in Figure 9.3. In her recent book, Omera Khan also supports the importance of the design stage as a key enabler of supply chain agility. Her going-in proposition is that '. . . the supply chain begins on the drawing board'.[4]

This concept of concurrent and multi-faceted design is not only relevant for innovation and new product development, but is an important part of the efforts needed to retrofit a faster cadence across the organization.

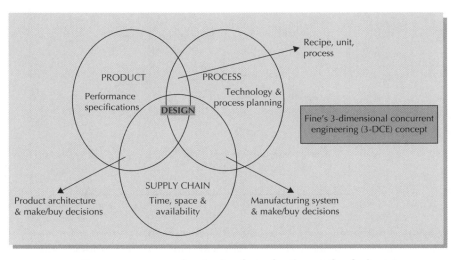

FIGURE 9.3 ◆ Concurrency – underpinning fast adaption at the design stage

Source: Adapted from Fine, C.H. (1998) *Clockspeed: Winning Industry Control in the Age of Temporary Advantage*. Basic Books, p. 146

By focusing on one step or process alone, we are rarely able to make fundamental and sustainable change. As we see in the new business models that disintermediate industries, it is usually more than one aspect of the traditional way of doing business that is reinvented.

Capturing the value of time

One of the reasons why time matters so much in today's operating environment is because of the faster decay rates of modern products, especially high-tech products. Fast technological development is causing rapid obsolescence in many contemporary products that are part of our modern lifestyle, so we need to find ways to adapt to this new reality.

Blackburn[5] and his colleagues have introduced a useful concept in this regard – the marginal value of time (MVT). They have used the notion of measuring the value of the time decay for commercial returns and for fresh produce; but we think that this method of factoring a financial impact into decisions has much wider applicability. Figure 9.4 compares two products with different decay rates.

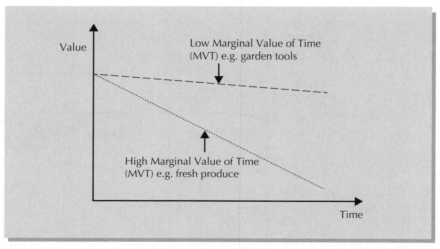

FIGURE 9.4 ◆ **Value inevitably reduces with time for most products; different products have different value decay rates**

Source: Based on Blackburn, J. D., Guide, D. R. Jr., Souza, G. C. and Van Wassenhove, L. N. (2004). Reverse Supply Chains for Commercial Returns. California Management Review, Berkeley 46.2, p 6–22

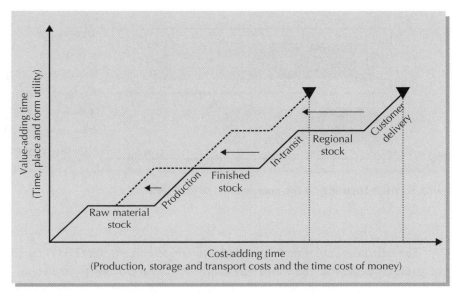

FIGURE 9.5 ◆ Mapping value and cost in relation to time

Source: Adapted from Christopher, M. (2011) *Logistics & Supply Chain Management.* 4th edn. Prentice Hall, pp. 132–33

Apart from looking at the market aspects of value decay, we can also potentially map the points at which value is and isn't added over time in the supply chain and when cost is incurred. Value Stream Mapping can be used to map value at a detailed level; but adding cost provides an additional level of insight. Some of the elements that contribute to the overall cost on a temporal basis are: inventory holding; space; additional processes and lost opportunity. Value decay can also be represented as risk and obsolescence or deterioration. At the strategic level, the generalized depiction alone can be powerful. When we map value against cost in this way, we get a profile like that depicted in Figure 9.5.

Customer lead times

The lead time that customers experience in all of this is, of course, the ultimate test. And, in many cases, by focusing on deconstructing this lead time, the non-value adding areas and activities that need new processes or systems become apparent.

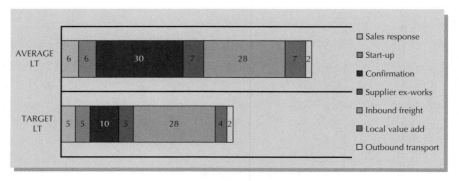

FIGURE 9.6 ◆ Focusing on the components of lead time

The customer lead time for a complex, engineered-to-order (ETO) range of products going into the construction industry, with globally sourced components, for example, is depicted in Figure 9.6. Customers were requesting shorter lead times. When the components of lead time were unpacked to understand what would be needed to achieve their ideal fulfilment ('target' in the figure) lead time, two things were apparent. The first was the amount of time used in the early 'admin' stages of the order (sales response, start-up and confirmation from the overseas plants and suppliers). We have seen this pattern across many industrial businesses – that the process of actually agreeing to, pricing and initiating the order can be unnecessarily cumbersome and slow.

The second aspect was the unreliability of their stated lead time. We have seen in our discussion of the *Campaign* Supply Chain™ configuration how important this is in the project setting, which is the relevant context for this example. But, it is, of course, critical across all industries where a customer is awaiting fulfilment. In our experience, all customers value reliability; it is just that for some it is the most important attribute and for others it is ranked a little further down the list.

And, as with the 'length' of the lead time, it is by focusing on the components that we are able to identify how to reengineer improvement. Martin Christopher illustrates how variability at the component level contributes to the overall variability experienced by the customer. See Figure 9.7.

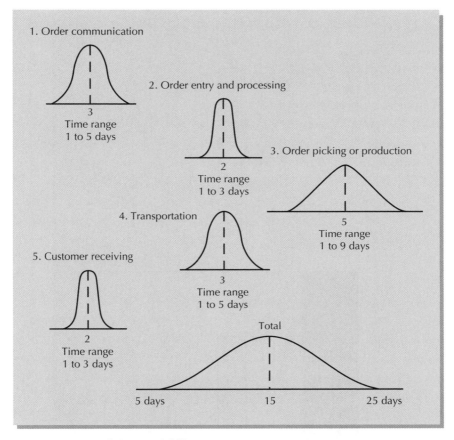

FIGURE 9.7 ◆ Lead-time variability

Source: Christopher, M. (2011) *Logistics & Supply Chain Management*, 4th edn. Prentice Hall, p. 126

In the ETO example provided, the combined focus on reducing the lead time and variability of components is depicted in Figure 9.8. A chart like this formed the basis of a successful project to drive a competitive advantage on project bids via building a reputation for faster and more predictable order fulfilment.

Once we would have thought about this in terms of six-sigma-type incremental improvement; but now we are very often looking at ways to drop out processes entirely or to use systems or technology to cut through more radically. AI or optimization-driven pricing decisions, modularization and/ or postponement of final assembly or moving the decoupling point closer

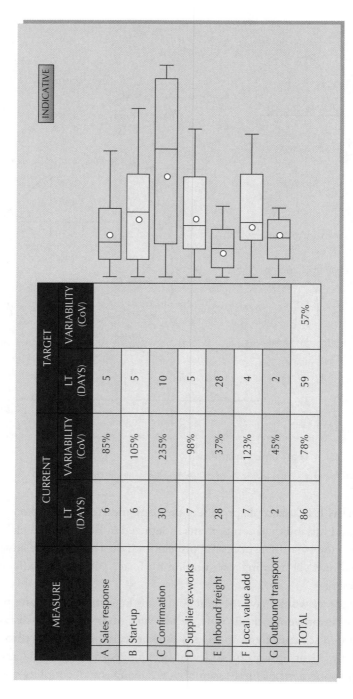

MEASURE	CURRENT		TARGET		
	LT (DAYS)	VARIABILITY (CoV)	LT (DAYS)	VARIABILITY (CoV)	
A Sales response	6	85%	5		
B Start-up	6	105%	5		
C Confirmation	30	235%	10		
D Supplier ex-works	7	98%	5		
E Inbound freight	28	37%	28		
F Local value add	7	123%	4		
G Outbound transport	2	45%	2		
TOTAL	86	78%	59	57%	

INDICATIVE

FIGURE 9.8 ◆ **Sample lead-time analysis**

to the customer are just some of the many ways that both lead time and reliability can be attacked.

In complex networks, it is also possible to use network optimization modeling techniques to identify and test lead-time scenarios. A project in China for another major industrial company,[6] identified that, by reconfiguring the network, the number of customers receiving next day delivery could be more than doubled (from 31 per cent to 68 per cent) and the reliability improved, with little impact on cost.

Capabilities to underpin faster rhythms

While reducing the lead time for customers is one aspect and, for some organizations, a key deliverable from faster clockspeed, it is not the only outcome.

We return now to the broader theme, and in particular how we need to organize ourselves if the goal is a faster rhythm right across the operation.

Once again, we turn to Fine and his definition of the company as a 'chain of continually evolving *capabilities*',[7] and, by this, he includes its own capabilities and those along the entire supply chain. In our terminology, he is referring to the *extended supply chain*.

From our experience, some of the key enterprise-wide *capabilities* required for success in the new faster clockspeed world are those briefly listed below. These sit underneath the specific capabilities already discussed in Chapter 7, which are needed for different types of supply chains to align with the corresponding segments of customers.

1 Organization designs that promote speed of decision making.

2 A design that supports both 'business as usual' and the continuous search for new innovations.

3 Appropriate KPIs to measure performance, free of conflicting demands.

4 A suite of different 'subcultures' inside the business that intuitively can underpin the different supply chain types.

5 Decision support systems (DSS) to aid fast decision making.

6 Appropriate and efficient sales & operations planning (S&OP) regimes to focus the entire organization on agreed priorities to meet customer demand.

7 Conscious development of digitization and analytics capability, including customer/supplier sensing.

8 Focus on managing *capacity* to levels appropriate to the volatility experienced.

9 Flexible and structured resilience to recover from major network disruptions.

10 Channel selection aligned with market cadence.

11 *Requisite* collaboration with appropriate network members.

These internal capabilities should be supplemented by targeted, supply chain–specific capabilities, also designed around the notion of fast rhythm, some of which have been mentioned earlier, such as:

- product design that is modular; concurrently engineered; supply chain friendly;

- manufacturing that can respond quickly, e.g. small batch; appropriate automation/robotics; AI informed; using flexible technology such as 3D-printing; group technology; flexible manufacturing systems;

- logistics that minimize pipeline time and can adjust; postponement; insourcing/outsourcing flexibility; control towers; 3PL portfolios; network optimization modeling supported.

Organization design – enabler or inhibitor of faster clockspeed?

But how we arrange our capabilities and resources becomes the next big question. The reality is that customers buy our many different capabilities horizontally across the enterprise, from procurement through to logistics fulfilment. Yet, we insist on managing our enterprises vertically, arrayed in functions, because it is easier to manage and supposedly more convenient. This means we are naturally 90 degrees out of phase with our customers, all the time! Now you know why you have so many crises and exceptions.

Since the introduction of this siloed structure around the time of the Industrial Revolution, we have loaded up our enterprise functions with the dual task of managing their respective specialisms, while at the same time contributing to the horizontal flow of the cross-functional supply chains, explicit and implicit. The 'as is' situation is depicted in Figure 9.9.

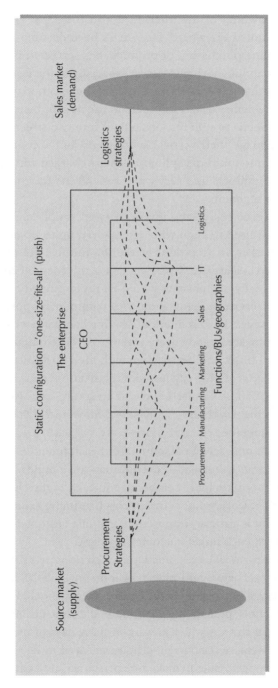

FIGURE 9.9 ◆ The conventional 'Static' organization design

Source: Adapted from Figure 1.1, Gattorna (2015) p. xxix

But, with the dawning of the internet era in the early 1990s, everything changed. As noted elsewhere, customers have become increasingly demanding and online purchasing of products has served to increase customer expectations about short lead times, especially in the last few years.

The net result is that this conventional style of organization design struggles to cope with the demands of customers in the new Industrial Age.

We think a solution is to split responsibilities into two streams, i.e. leave the functions to manage their vertical specialisms; but second personnel from each function into multi-disciplinary clusters charged with driving the horizontal flows of products and services across all the functions towards identified customer segments.

In Chapter 4, we discussed the five archetypal supply chains that we find are typically required to align with, and satisfy, up to 80 per cent of a particular target market. In situations where the full five are present, this would imply we need at least five clusters to create this focused and concentrated attention. Usually, the clusters would be underpinned and serviced by a central shared services organization with common support functions such as human resources, IT and finance. Leading companies such as Zara, Adidas and Li & Fung are already using variants of this configuration in an effort to reduce lead times and better align with their customers.

The customer-side of the suggested organization cluster design is depicted in Figure 9.10. A similarly focused structure can also provide a more aligned engagement with the supply-side. This would look like a mirror image of the customer-side.

The idea is to not only select personnel from each function on the basis of their technical expertise, but also to overlay this with a mindset dimension that ensures the appropriate bias is embedded in each of the clusters, e.g. a relationship bias in the *Collaborative* cluster; cost bias in the *Lean* cluster, etc. This micro-alignment is critically important if genuine customer eccentricity is to be achieved with each target customer segment.

We suggest that personnel be seconded from their respective functions for a period of up to two years before returning to their original roles all the better for the experience. In larger organizations, the clusters ideally should be populated with dedicated personnel, preferably co-located in the same facility, but, if this is not possible, virtual clusters will also work in these days of messaging and collaboration tools. Remote relationships, however, need to be supported by regular face-to-face opportunities to make sure personnel know each other well.

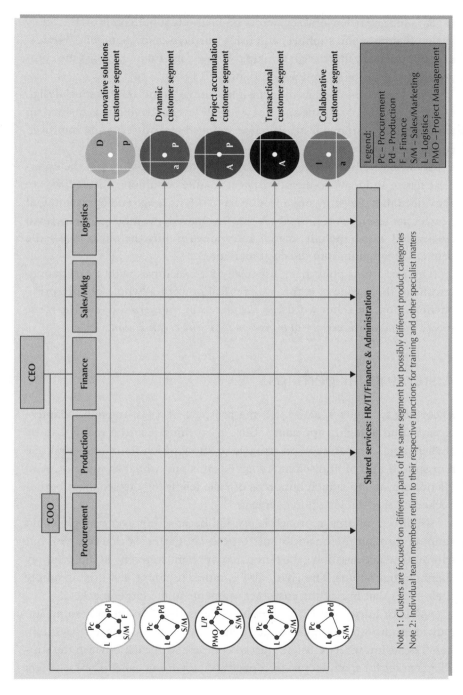

Note 1: Clusters are focused on different parts of the same segment but possibly different product categories
Note 2: Individual team members return to their respective functions for training and other specialist matters

FIGURE 9.10 ◆ Supply chain organization clusters

By adopting behavioral segmentation methods at both ends of the supply chain (customer and supplier) and using our Dynamic Alignment™ model as the heuristic in the 'design thinking' Knowledge Funnel, we get the comprehensive solution as outlined in Figure 9.11.

This future state signals the transition from a 'static' to 'dynamic' design of enterprise supply chains and a new higher level of flexibility is opened up with advantages from a faster cadence, reduced cost-to-serve and improved customer satisfaction.

So, when we talk about *clockspeed* we are not suggesting that the enterprise has to suddenly accelerate to meet volatile conditions. Instead, we are convinced that the entire organization has to lift its *tempo* and operate at that new higher level, *all the time*. Once this is achieved, the internally generated clockspeed will, hopefully, match and indeed nullify the effect of volatile demand emanating from the customer end.

The important point here, especially for executives with a mandate to transform the business, is that we are dealing with a 'whole-of-enterprise' phenomenon. In other words, *in the process of transforming your enterprise supply chains, it is necessary to transform the entire organization.*

A step too far perhaps

According to Rigby *et al.*,[8] '. . . the prospect of a fast-moving, adaptive organisation is highly appealing. But . . . turning it into a reality can be challenging. Companies often struggle to know which functions should be reorganised into multidisciplinary agile teams and which should not. And it's not unusual to launch hundreds of agile teams only to see them bottlenecked by slow-moving bureaucracies.'[9]

We also think this approach is overkill because not every supply chain running through the business has to be *agile*. Faster clockspeed, yes, but without the acceleration (start-stop) component inherent in agile supply chain configurations. The right configuration to adopt is a mix of supply chain types that mirror the customer segments in the target market.

As Victor Fung found at Li & Fung in the mid-2000s, creating some 300 individual customer-oriented multidisciplinary clusters can lead to dysfunctional behavior, where clusters start to compete with each other in the supplier market for manufacturing capacity. Victor Fung called these clusters

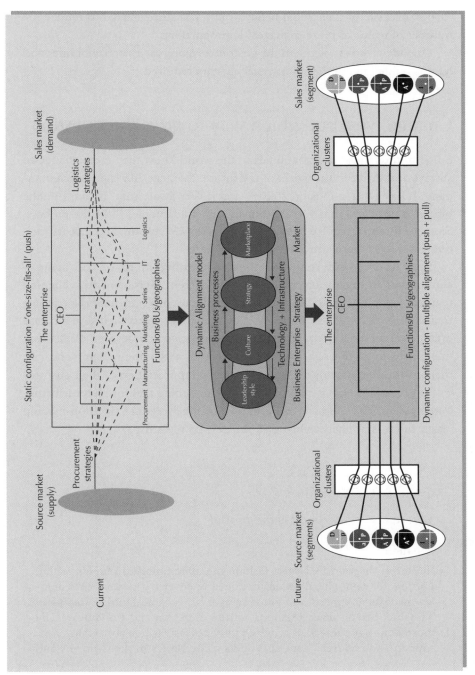

FIGURE 9.11 ◆ From 'Static' to 'Dynamic' design of enterprise supply chains

Source: Adapted from Figure 1.1, Gattorna (2015) p. xxix

'tribes' because of their tribal behavior and has since started to reduce the number of teams to more manageable proportions.

Our advice was to segment the customers along buyer behavior lines and let this guide the number of internal clusters required.

Change, yes, but which way to go is the question

Some of the largest multinationals in the world know they must change to survive and thrive in the world of the future. Siemens AG is one such company. It has a vision (Vision 2020+) and is very aware that 'It won't be the biggest companies that survive, but the most adaptable.'[10] In the process, Siemens intends to delve deeper into its *ownership* culture, and give its various businesses more entrepreneurial freedom.

But, having said that, are they just doing more of the same – eliminating an organizational level in the current divisions and realigning regional organizations to be more customer focused? This sounds like decentralization to us, which stops far short of a full makeover designed to increase organizational clockspeed. It seems that major companies still can't bring themselves to go through the very real pain of a genuine realignment with their customers, starting with a much deeper appreciation of their customers' expectations; that is the fundamental launching pad for all transformational action. The Siemens AG initiative may help reduce decision-making times, but it is unlikely to bring all the desired rewards.

CASE STUDY: Inditex/Zara[11]

Where fast clockspeed is the model

Situation

Inditex is the world's largest fashion manufacturer and retailer, with a portfolio of eight global brands designed to cover a wide consumer market for fashion apparel and homewares, i.e. Massimo Dutti; Zara; TRF/Trafaluc; Stradivarius; Oysho; Uterqüe; Bershka; and Pull&Bear. The most famous of these is Zara, which provides fast fashion apparel for men, women and children. Zara also offers some Basics in the women's and home décor segments. Each brand has a centralized DC in La Coruña, Spain, and all finished products are despatched from there by road or air to its chain of stores, worldwide. The Zara brand has two fashion categories: Basic and Trendy, and its supply chains are configured to respond to each, on the supply-side and demand-side, the classic *hybrid*.

The clockspeed challenge

Fabrics purchased from raw material suppliers around the world are brought into Spain via a *Lean* supply chain for Basic apparel and via an *Agile* supply chain for Trendy fashion lines. Basic fashion items have a longer life cycle and are mostly made in Asia. Trendy items, with a very short life cycle, are manufactured locally in Spain and nearby countries. Both Basic and Trendy lines are shipped out in Agile outbound supply chains at a fast rhythm. Zara stores are replenished with new product twice a week. The challenge is to keep up this fast clockspeed, relentlessly, week in week out.

Rewriting the rules

Zara is able to design, manufacture and distribute its product lines in around 15 days compared to double that for most of its competitors. There is no single factor that drives the fast clockspeed. It is a combination of many factors, all contributing to the short, predictable lead time. Perhaps the overall winning formula is provided by the *continuou change* culture that pervades all levels of the organization; it is in the DNA of all employees, instilled top-down by the owner and the leadership team around him. The focus is on fast adoption of new ideas. And the unique way Zara organizes itself into self-managed multidisciplinary teams plays a major role in achieving this *speed culture*, e.g. in La Coruña, three teams, Commercial, Design and Stores, all work as one to minimize lead times. Process is used sparingly, postponement techniques embraced and quick decisions are encouraged, together with use of the latest technology in design and manufacture.

Results

The results are there for all to see. From 2000 to 2017, Inditex sales and EBIT have both averaged 10 per cent growth per year. In terms of store numbers, Zara is well ahead of rivals such as Topshop, H&M and Mango, with 1,500 stores in 81 countries. Zara's winning strategy of absolute speed with its 'fast fashion' is the mountain-climbing equivalent of Reinhold Messner's direct alpine climbing technique[12] in which he climbed the

▶

highest mountains in the world by making a dash on the final assault, by himself, without oxygen, unhindered by all the other logistics that might otherwise create additional complexity and slow him down. So, too, Zara has found ways to scale back the complexity in its organization and thereby speed up its entire E2E supply chain cycle. It is akin to an entirely new business model that other companies across many industries are trying to emulate.

What can we learn?

If you are capable of fast clockspeeds inside the business, you can chase trends, be first with new products into the market and also reduce the risks and costs associated with getting it wrong on a large scale.

The clever separation of the supply chains for Basic and Trendy products allows Zara to refine its different speed and cost strategies.

And the short, fast cycles and flexible organization structure enables the adoption of new and innovative techniques as and when they are thought of.

Zara has an unrelenting focus on the customer to the point that it co-creates its products by leveraging customers' inputs. You can't get any more customer-centric than that!

Finally, there is no fear of failure at Zara. And that is the way it has to be going forward if you want to be successful in this volatile world.

Points of view

1 We need to achieve a cadence that enables us to match or lead the natural cadence of the market, which often now means we must be able to compete on speed.

2 Human adaption, in general, is lagging the technology curve. We must find ways to catch up, fast, because those that can adapt have a distinct advantage.

3 Charles Fine's concept of *clockspeed* gives us insight into the design of high-performance supply chains which compete on speed.

4 If the enterprise succeeds in lifting its tempo (clockspeed), it will be infinitely better placed to absorb the unpredictable shocks emanating out of the increasingly volatile marketplace.

5   To achieve the sought-after higher clockspeeds, all the enterprise's *internal capabilities* must be reviewed and re-engineered for speed.

6   This is central to the new supply chain philosophy being adopted by the *best-of-the-best* enterprises.

7   Measuring and accounting for lead times and capturing the value of time are important concepts in today's operating environment.

8   Our customers buy horizontally across the enterprise, while we stick to managing our functional silos vertically. Herein lies a fundamental problem in today's world, which features an ever-quickening pace of doing business.

9   Sorting out this organizational conundrum will release the enterprise to achieve new and higher levels of performance.

Kick-start your thinking

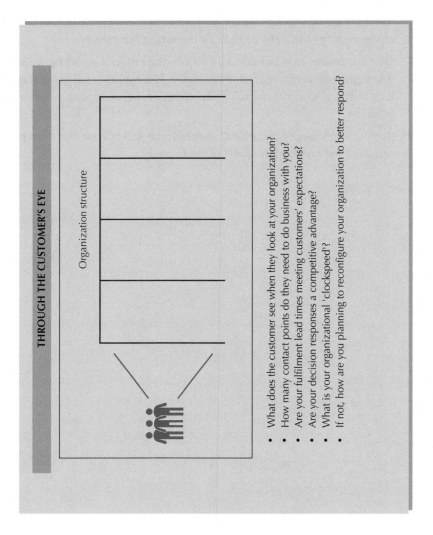

THROUGH THE CUSTOMER'S EYE

Organization structure

- What does the customer see when they look at your organization?
- How many contact points do they need to do business with you?
- Are your fulfilment lead times meeting customers' expectations?
- Are your decision responses a competitive advantage?
- What is your organizational 'clockspeed'?
- If not, how are you planning to reconfigure your organization to better respond?

CHAPTER 10

Future business models

Focusing on true value, scale and efficient
use of resources

Introduction

T he business model is how a business creates, delivers and captures value. And, for most industries, we thought we knew the basic formula pretty well – until about 2001, when a wave of new ways to create and deliver value started to impact our daily lives. Apple's iPod (2001) and iTunes (2003) delivered fast, easy music to our pocket; Amazon's Kindle (2007) gave us weightless (and wait-less) books; Skype (2004) gave us free international calls; Facebook (2005) gave us friends; and Airbnb (2008) gave us places to visit.

Some of the emerging models were fundamentally new ways to connect buyers and sellers. Amazon took aggregation to a whole new level and, in doing so, made a virtue of the long tail that has tormented many other businesses. Its e-commerce model has redefined retail. In China, Alibaba was creating value by connecting manufacturers and commercial buyers in a novel form of wholesale that focused on aggregation of interfaces rather than aggregation of inventory.

As with most true innovation, these business models were not responding to needs that customers expressed – they were supplier-led initiatives, developed in anticipation. They used technology to provide solutions to problems we didn't know we had . . . until they had been solved. And then we didn't know how to live without the solution!

In this chapter, we consider the internal business model, the drivers for change and some simplifying ways of thinking about new models. We also return to the theme of leadership and capabilities in this context. In both the developed and developing world, there are many highly educated, highly motivated (mainly) young entrepreneurs, with relatively easy access to capital. They are studying the underlying needs of customers and looking for new models to serve them (and serve the environment), more effectively than the mature businesses in the respective sectors. So, if we are those mature businesses, we need to bring a little of that same mindset inside the tent!

From a supply chain perspective, some of the potentially biggest opportunities to create and deliver value come from taking a much wider view – looking beyond our own operation. This is the physical world of 'networks of networks' and shared supply chains, and the technology-enabled world of the data 'lead-box' and the 'platform'. There are many industries and geographies where, we believe, these macro-level supply chain solutions offer a more efficient, and more sustainable, value-delivery model. So, we will also look at these later in this chapter.

Technology trend meets market need

The cornerstone of any business model is the customer value proposition. Simply put, '. . . your customer value proposition must solve a problem more effectively, simply, accessibly, or affordably than the alternatives'.[1] The way that resources, processes and pricing are arranged to deliver that value proposition is, essentially, a system.

In the past, a dominant business model or system would tend to emerge over time in any given industry and, 'in the absence of market distortions, the model will reflect the most efficient way to allocate and organize resources'[2] in that industry.

As the examples in the introduction suggest, however, this steady evolutionary process is not where many industries are sitting right now. Technology's potential significance in the resource set has increased and the customer and their operating environment have shifted. And both of these factors are driving development of new business models at a rapid rate; and even new ways to define whole industries.

Kavadias and his colleagues[3] at the University of Cambridge Business School, in trying to interpret the new status quo, studied 40 high-impact new business models. They concluded that many new models are emerging from the 'sweet spots' where emerging technologies meet new market needs. Figure 10.1 captures some of the trends and the convergence points resulting in new business models.

Our own experience with large businesses suggests that most of them are actually operating more than one business model already; competing in different parts of the market with a different combination of resources and value propositions. And the thrust of our earlier chapters is that we believe that many of these models need to be refined further and be more closely tuned to their markets, with a clear focus on the value proposition they are delivering, in order to stay viable. But it is also clear that, to counter the risk posed by new models and/or to support growth, every reasonably sized organization also needs a parallel stream of activity focused on the current juxtaposition of market and technology trends.

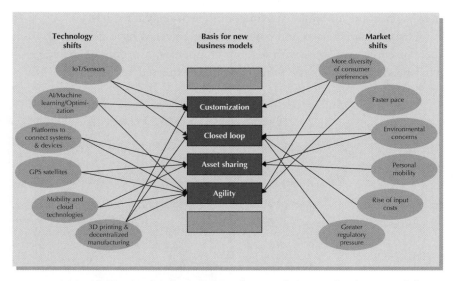

FIGURE 10.1 ◆ **Linking technology and market needs in new business models**

Reshaping, reinventing and venturing out

In many of the discussions about transformation and new business models that we encounter, we find that there is a lack of clarity about the extent and direction of the change in scope; and executives in the same room can be working on very different starting assumptions. Given this, and the points made above, it is probably prudent to go back to basics and better understand the range of options.

Typically, for established enterprises, the types of shifts in a business model that are relevant are those shown in Figure 10.2. Clarifying the level under consideration, or the scope in play for those teams working on 'transformation' or 'innovation', can avoid misaligned expectations.

Stages of business model innovation

There has been considerable focus recently on trying to codify the stages of business model innovation. Alexander Osterwalder and Yves Pigneur[4] have created a simple guiding framework known as the Business Model Canvas that has become a popular starting point, especially for start-ups.

Clayton Christensen and colleagues[5] at Harvard have developed, from their research and work with leading companies, a profile of the stages – what needs to happen and what should be expected, at each stage – for a

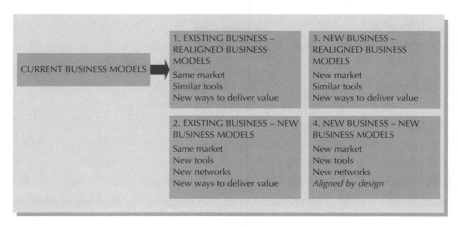

FIGURE 10.2 ◆ **Reshaping, reinventing and venturing out**

Priorities/output	Capabilities/input
1. Value proposition	**2. Resources**
A solution that meets the needs and expectations of a customer	Products, staff, external relationships, technology, facilities, equipment, brands and cash required to deliver this value proposition to the targeted customers
3. Profit formula	**4. Processes**
Assets and fixed and variable cost structure, and the margins and velocity required to cover them	Ways of working together to address recurrent tasks in a consistent way: training, development, guidelines, budgeting, planning, etc.

FIGURE 10.3 ◆ The Elements of a Business Model

Source: Based on Clayton M. Christensen, Thomas Bartman, and Derek van Bever, MIT Sloan Magazine, 'The Hard Truth About Business Model Innovation', Fall 2016 Issue.

new business model, with the right idea behind it, to be successful. They start with the four elements of any business model that we are familiar with, as shown in Figure 10.3.

They explain these components and how they play out over time as a model moves from 'creation' to 'efficiency'. In the main, we find this consistent with the stages we have observed in the field and the priorities needed at each stage. Along with other commentators, however, we find the term 'efficiency' to describe the last stage a little limiting. In reality, we know that, for some segments, sustainable models are more multi-dimensional than 'efficiency' implies – and we propose that this stage is better termed 'aligned'. We have also taken the liberty of overlaying the P-A-D-I logics, introduced in Chapter 2, because they allow us to extend the Christensen *et al.* model to examine the capabilities needed at each stage. Figure 10.4 captures the merging of their insights with our own observations at the various stages of the life cycle of a new business model.

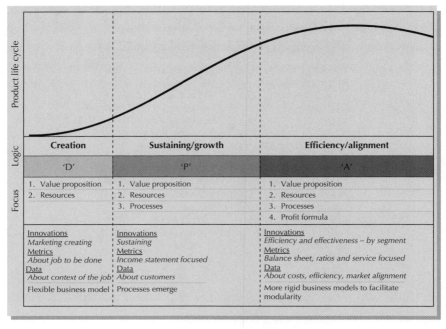

FIGURE 10.4 ◆ **The three stages of the new Business Model journey**

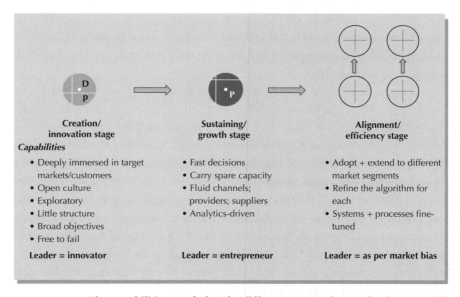

FIGURE 10.5 ◆ **The capabilities needed at the different stages of a new business model**

Thus, if we overlay our Alignment thinking, as depicted in Figure 10.5, we are able to focus in on the capabilities needed to support each stage. In the Creation (or 'D') stage, the focus is to find and understand the job to be done, and how and to whom new value can be delivered. This is followed by a sustaining and growth phase (P) and, finally, settling down to an aligned stage where the model for efficiency and effectiveness is established and extended. As we have indicated previously, we also consider that the different stages have different 'ideal' leadership style profiles.

Supply chain business model shifts

We turn our attention now more specifically to the supply chain aspects of the business model and some of the important shifts that we consider could change the rules in many industries. Common themes are 'aggregation' and 'synchronization' via data and this is consistent with the trends we saw earlier with business models emerging, framed around asset sharing and collaborative ecosystems.

Network of networks in the macro supply chain

First, let's take a broader view of the pathways to customers. In many ways, the concept of a supply 'chain' is a misnomer. The reality is that most organizations sit within, and utilize, a complex network of flows and relationships in 3D, rather than the neat, linear arrangement that 'chain' implies. Envisioning this network can bring more clarity to the supply chain task and the strategic options within it. In Chapter 5, when discussing network modeling, we used a 'Network Map' - a simple, but powerful, way to capture the key features of the physical infrastructure and relationships in an enterprise supply chain.

But taking an even broader view of the *ecosystem* and seeing our own network in the context of those with which we overlap – the competitors running parallel supply chains, other suppliers serving the same customers, the alternatives to our own assets – can point to opportunities that previously we may never have considered.

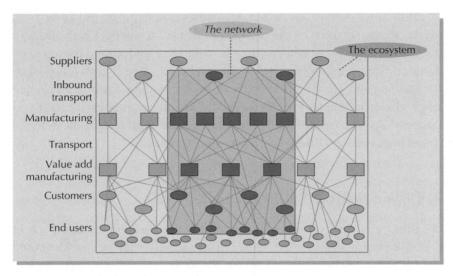

FIGURE 10.6 ◆ **The broader operating** *ecosystem*

An extended ecosystem is difficult to depict, but even the adjacencies at each level can provide insight, as illustrated in Figure 10.6.

One of the most influential global businesses in the last 30 years, Li & Fung was built on the concept of giving its clients access to large amounts of capacity beyond its own network. Li & Fung is the largest manufacturer in the world, and yet owns no manufacturing plants – instead it *orchestrates* a network of networks of manufacturing plants owned by others. Brand owners are thus essentially operating without manufacturing constraints and without the burden of long-term fixed costs associated with a particular location or process. This extended network brings enormous flexibility for growth or changes in direction; but, of course, less control than if all processes were within their own walls.

Shared supply chain assets

The notion of shared supply chains arises from this broader view of the potential operating horizon. Australia has some of the best examples of this supply chain model, perhaps because of the vast distances. The cost and scale efficiencies of shared assets are at the heart of organizations such as CBH Grain in Western Australia and the Hunter Valley Coal Chain Coordinator (HVCCC) in Newcastle.

CBH, a cooperative owned by growers, operates an extensive network of silos, ports and a rail fleet. It uses the cooperative structure to share assets and provides its grower-owners with a cost advantage over the commercial owners of such assets on the other side of the country; it is also a centralized planning and coordination capability that enables the use of those assets to be optimized, both in the long term and day-to-day. HVCCC, on the other hand, is a planning and coordinating body only. The assets (load points, trains, track, terminals and ports) are owned by different parties, but the HVCCC coordinates their activity, in the long and short term, and in doing so releases capacity all along the chain compared to the situation if the 11 coal producers were competing for capacity. The often unrecognized additional benefit of this arrangement is the flexibility that access to a larger, more diverse array of assets provides to each individual stakeholder. For a more detailed look at these shared supply chains, refer to the end of this chapter for the HVCCC case study and the end of Chapter 5 for the CBH case study.

This concept of the shared supply chain is now extending beyond bulk handling and resources to the 'Uberization' of freight and warehousing. Wherever there is under-utilized capacity, there exists the possibility of new business models emerging to leverage it – often for mutual advantage, involving what would have once been unlikely commercial partners. In both transport and warehousing of packaged products, the natural pattern that seems to be emerging is that the established format of stable, owned and third party provider contracts takes care of 'baseload', and regular requirements, while the shared platforms are used to manage unplanned surges on top.

Beyond the cost impacts, sustainability, resource frugality and city congestion are other strong drivers pointing towards the need for more efficient use of transport resources in particular. Central business district last-mile delivery consolidation hubs are an obvious solution in this vein, enabling fewer delivery vehicles and lower emissions, but they have been much slower to get off the ground than anyone would have imagined. There are a few examples emerging, mainly from Europe. In the 15th arrondissement in Paris, a 312,000 sq. ft facility receives and aggregates deliveries for much of the Paris metropolitan area. And, in the UK, an Urban Consolidation Centre (UCC) serves the last-mile deliveries for the London boroughs of Camden, Enfield and Islington. But these examples are rare.

The data 'lead box' as an enabler for shared supply chain models

One of the barriers to implementing or leveraging full value from extended networks, shared supply chains and any form of serious horizontal collaboration along the supply chain is the ability to share data.

We first wrote about this concept in Gattorna (2015)[6] when we coined the term 'lead box' to describe what we saw as a solution to the lost data opportunity. We have since seen the terms 'infomediary' and 'cleanroom' used for basically the same purpose.

But, irrespective of which term you prefer, the intended function is the same – to aggregate data from a range of otherwise confidential sources, analyze it and utilize the data to make more informed decisions. Data and selected analyses can be disseminated back to contributing stakeholders – they receive feedback on their own individual position, along with the aggregate position, but they do not see the data of their co-contributors. This maintains the strict confidentiality protocols that this type of facility relies on.

An example of this model and the associated protocols in action is the company set up by the four major trading banks in Australia to facilitate the cash supply chain across the country. Its role was to avoid, after the central bank stepped out of cash, the inefficiency of each bank filling its own ATMs and branches. Instead, a single truck visited all cash points, for all banks, in a suburb. While this was a physical supply chain, the real challenge was in the data. The company, Cash Services Australia,[7] saw all cash inflows, inventory positions and outflows. It used them to plan and manage the operation and provide the overnight holdings to the central bank; but its feedback to each of its owners (the trading banks), included only their own position and the aggregate. The competition regulator in Australia, the ACCC, defined and audited the protocols and security arrangements under which the model was approved.

To date, we have seen relatively few examples of this type of facility, but we think that situation will change rapidly in the foreseeable future as competitive intensity increases across many industries and the advantages of an extended data view and larger pie to optimize become compelling.

By way of summary, we have included a modified version of the original Figure 14.15 from *Dynamic Supply Chains* (2015) as Figure 10.7.

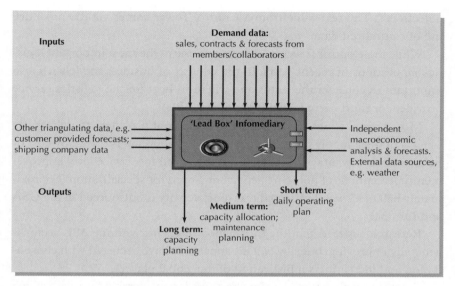

FIGURE 10.7 ◆ A new business model is needed to manage demand and capacity planning in multi-user supply chains – the 'lead box' concept

Source: Gattorna, J. (2015) *Dynamic Supply Chains*, p. 482

Supply Chain Control Towers and logistics service providers

The Supply Chain Control Tower, now adopted by some major multinational corporations, is a facility to control the flow of their products centrally and virtually, and is a step in the direction of the infomediary facility described above – aggregating data from wide sources, both internal and external. Third party logistics providers have their own version of this type of facility also because it is core to their business model and, increasingly, these are being enriched with triangulating data and supported by AI (the Kuehne + Nagel Innovation Centres in Singapore and the Netherlands are good examples).

There are many definitions of the Control Tower, but the one we prefer is that it '. . . is a central hub with the required technology, organisation, and processes to capture and use supply chain data to provide enhanced visibility for short- and long-term decision-making that is aligned with strategic objectives'[8]. The real value from a Control Tower comes via the proactive use of centralized data.

While the Control Tower is emerging as one of the most important logistics innovations in recent years, in the context of business models it's also important to consider the status and where-to-next for the logistics service provider (or third party logistics provider – 3PL).

Most organizations are dependent on external providers to deliver key aspects of their supply chain performance. Outsourcing is driven by cost or balance sheet advantages, seeking flexibility, need for service level improvements, perceptions of non-core activity or a need for specialization. Approximately half of all warehouse and transport activity is outsourced in the USA and Europe.

Research suggests that the satisfaction of clients with the 3PL sector is generally improving, but slowly. This appears to have occurred with consolidation and increasing sophistication of the global players.

But it is also clear that, despite this, there is considerable flux, with a high proportion of companies shifting between providers at contract renewal time.

On the provider side, logistics continues to be a difficult business, with margins well below those in many other industries. And Amazon and other non-traditional players are causing further disruption and uncertainty. There are numerous studies to indicate that 'successful' outcomes from client-provider arrangements derive from inputs typically associated with collaborative relationships, i.e. open and regular communications; information sharing; longer-term commitments; development of personal relationships; and shared continuous improvement.

To maximize benefit via this route, however, requires each party to have a genuinely *collaborative* culture or at least a relationship-style subculture. It also needs a relatively stable operating environment. But this is not always possible. Innovation is the most commonly identified gap in client expectations of logistics service providers. Innovation needs to be targeted towards what different clients value, for example:

◆ focused on reducing cost for those that will always be cost-driven;

◆ focused on enhancing flexibility where the client's needs are unpredictable.

The client's end customer/market often will provide the insights needed to generate innovative offerings or more effective processes. As clients, we need to be able to use 3PLs in a more nuanced way to help us align with different parts of our patchwork market.

As providers, we need to show we are capable of a range of solutions and be able to lead sophisticated conversations around alignment, logistics innovation and underpinning business models! And, to benefit both sides, we need requests for proposals (RFPs) and contracts that get below the averages and totals – and give potential partners a true insight into the demand patterns and the business essentials present in any given situation.

Closed-loop supply chains

Given the re-emergence of interest by large corporates in sustainability, we are likely to see a lot more focus on 'closed-loop' supply chain designs. In this respect, Apple, the Gartner-rated #1 supply chain in the world, is leading the way.

In Apple's 2018 progress report, they state that '. . . while we transition to this new supply chain model, we are committed to maintain our initiatives that ensure the materials we use in our products are sourced responsibly – through strict standards and programs that drive positive change'.[9]

A typical 'closed-loop' supply chain is depicted in Figure 10.8.

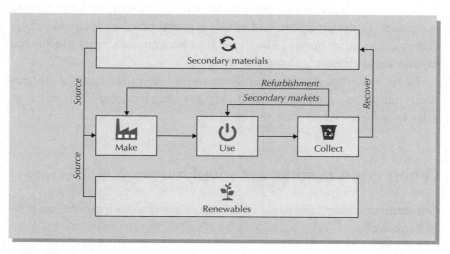

FIGURE 10.8 ◆ A closed-loop supply chain

Apple's principles for managing their version of the 'closed loop' are set out below.

Source:	Use recycled or renewable materials that are responsibly sourced.
Make efficiently:	Design and manufacture products to minimize the use of materials.
Use for a long time:	Design products to be durable, so they can have long lives.
Contribute:	Replenish market supply with an amount of recycled, reclaimed or renewable material at least equal to the amount used to make the product.

Apple is adamant that, through the right processes, they can '. . . transition to recycled or renewable materials without compromising the final product'.[10] Let's hope they can achieve their goals and that this initiative rubs off on other major corporations and governments.

Interface, a global modular flooring and carpet company, has had sustainability as a primary objective for 20 years. In April 2018, it announced that all of its products were now 100 per cent carbon neutral across the whole of the product life cycle, which it had achieved by gradually reducing its own product's carbon footprint by 60 per cent, closing the loop through recycle and re-use programs, and investing in carbon offset programs where there was no other option. They now lead programs to bring customers, suppliers and architects along with them.

In the meantime, Unilever continues to lead on a wide range of sustainability initiatives, including closed-loop plastic packaging – its goal is to halve its environmental footprint by 2030.

When governments get involved

Governments around the world have been slow to run with genuine sustainability policies.

It is clear to us, though, working across countries and supply chains, that industry has much higher awareness of the need for building sustainable and responsible supply chains than it did 10 years ago. But it is also clear that the political operating environment is not supporting this shift in mindset. The signals and incentives coming from many governments are short term and inconsistent. We see government assets sold with conditions that undermine their optimal use or the best overall outcome for the greater state or region; and road and rail infrastructure decisions made in isolation of each other, and without factoring in the environmental trade-offs that ideally should be made between them.

Platforms

One of the most significant new business models of the digital age has been the multi-sided platform. It creates value by facilitating exchanges between inter-dependent groups. Where these groups are suppliers and buyers, this facilitation can dramatically change the supply chains, and the possibilities, within an industry. For a start, it reduces the search costs of finding alternative suppliers and new products and, beyond that, provides easy engagement for collaboration and further innovation. The following three platforms, at different levels of maturity, illustrate the impact of the platform models.

Alibaba

Alibaba started life in 1999 as an e-commerce business designed to help small Chinese manufacturers and entrepreneurs to sell globally. While very successful, it was the decision its management team took to build the platform into a complete ecosystem and its focus on 'smart business' that turned it into a global juggernaut. Ming Zeng, the director of strategic planning, explains:

> Alibaba today is not just an online commerce company. It is what you get if you take all functions associated with retail and coordinate them online into a sprawling, data-driven network of sellers, marketers, service providers, logistics companies, and manufacturers. [11]

When he explains 'smart business', Zeng essentially describes the AI and data-driven business model that Alibaba and Tencent in China, and Amazon, Google and Facebook in the USA, are built on and why it is so dangerous for traditional business if they don't keep up:

> This tech-enabled model, in which most operational decisions are made by machines, allows companies to adapt dynamically and rapidly to changing market conditions and customer preferences, gaining tremendous competitive advantage over traditional businesses.[12]

Haier

Haier is a China-based, white goods and consumer durables manufacturer. Its products include air conditioners, mobile phones, televisions, refrigerators and washing machines for a global market. From 1995 to 2012, its focus has been building a brand and expanding internationally. In 2012, this strategy was replaced with what the CEO calls its 'Networking Strategy'. This aims to position Haier as an internet and platform business.

It has built an internet-based incubation platform for innovation and entrepreneurship called COSMOPlat. This is also its vehicle for mass customization. The company presented it at the Hannover Fair in 2018. The eventual output aims to be customer co-created products:

> Through interaction with the platform, customers can create personalized orders for products such as washing machines or refrigerators, embedding their individual preferences. During the manufacturing stage, an open network of online factories was created to make the process visual and transparent for every consumer. With various devices and human activities embedded with sensors, robotics and AI are inter-connected to enable a smart and flexible production process. Just as orders are directly sent by customers to the factory, finished products are directly delivered to clients from the factory, removing the traditional storage and distribution processes.[13]

But the platform is also envisaged as a way to connect suppliers to Haier and to a wider audience. It suits small and new businesses to become part of the platform, as it gives them instant access to a huge market. Haier's knowledge and contacts are opened up to them. Haier is understood to currently have 60,000 suppliers on its platform.[14]

QualityTrade ISO certified marketplace[15]

And, on a slightly smaller scale, we look at an emerging platform solving a two-sided problem.

QualityTrade Pty Ltd, an Australian start-up company, has developed the world's first trade marketplace for companies who hold valid ISO accredited certifications. There are over 1,650,000 companies around the globe who hold such certifications. QualityTrade also has the contract to build, operate and own the global register for the global governing body, the International Accreditation Forum (IAF).

At present, it is difficult for buyers to find new suppliers around the world whom they can trust, beyond their current network. Buyers searching for suppliers online are often directed to low-quality or fraudulent companies. There is also no way of easily reviewing companies against ethical standards and, thus, buyers can be unknowingly exposed to low workplace standards, child labor and poor environmental practices.

By aggregating certified companies together, it is easier for buyers to find and trade with businesses they can trust. Therefore, they receive better trading experiences and develop higher quality and more compliant supply chains.

For the supplier, the value proposition is trade leads. Suppliers invest a huge amount to become certified and maintain their certification. However, they are restricted in the value they get beyond their current customers. QualityTrade gives them access to government tenders from around the world, procure-to-pay buyers looking for suppliers or buyers using general digital channels such as search.

QualityTrade is aiming to create a trustworthy trade marketplace by serving as a gateway to legitimate certified companies from across the world. This will ensure companies have access to products and services that are safe, reliable and of good quality, from companies who do the right thing by their customers, employees and the environment at large.

Synchronization

As we draw together the threads of this exploration on future business models, it's apparent that the next stage of supply chain development is going to require the ability to synchronize technology, resources and extended networks in tight accord with a shifting market. Figure 10.9 captures some of the key elements that we believe will feature in this evolution.

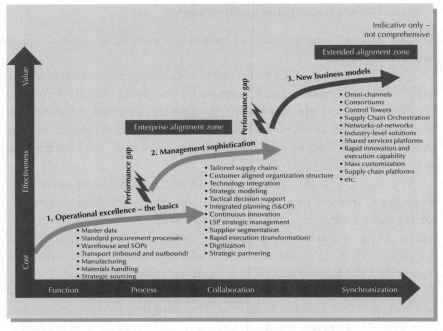

FIGURE 10.9 ◆ **New business models and synchronized supply chains**

CASE STUDY: The Hunter Valley Coal Chain Coordinator (HVCCC)

A unique collaborative planning model

Situation

Currently, 11 producers, operating 40 mines, sell US$10 billion of coal a year through one port, located 150 km north of Sydney. The Port of Newcastle is the largest export coal port in the world. Some of these producers are among the world's largest mining companies.

The coal is sourced from a region extending up to 450 km from the port. The geography and history of this region have resulted in a restricted and complex supply chain 'funnel' to the port. At the core of this is a common rail track system and three shared ship loading terminals. But it's the number of parties involved that is at the heart of this story!

Competing priorities on a common network

Much of the supply chain infrastructure that the 40 mines rely on is common. Track, ship loading terminals and port operations had historically serviced each of the mining companies that usually had independent commercial arrangements.

But, as the number of mines and the tonnages increased in the late 1990s, the competition for track and terminal capacity was intense. Capacity was being lost as decisions were made in isolation, and because of the number of parties involved it was difficult to agree the terms for expanding the capacity of the key common assets. Long vessel queues were the result; queues peaked above 80 by 2007.

It became apparent that this was a complex, interdependent supply chain and that decisions made by one logistics provider or one producer had flow-on effects to all others using the same infrastructure.

A new format supply chain solution

A collaborative supply chain planning body was formed in 2003 and the concept of planning the use of the assets centrally was tested. By 2009, it was clear that this body was essential to the efficient operation of shared assets, and it was incorporated and became known as the HVCCC.

HVCCC is an independent, member-owned company operating under a 'not for profit' model. Its role is to plan the cooperative operation and alignment of the coal chain in order to maximize throughput, minimize cost and satisfy the agreed collective needs of its members. All 11 mining companies and nine service providers (covering port operations, track, rail haulage and terminals) in the Hunter Valley are members of HVCCC. Any single movement of coal from mine to vessel involves at least six of these parties. The parties still have independent commercial arrangements, but they rely on HVCCC to plan the movements from load point to terminal.

Results

By managing the coal chain as an end-to-end 'system', HVCCC is widely recognized for significantly increasing coal throughput while keeping the cost down for producers.

Maintenance is coordinated, so that track, ship loading terminals and load points align the timing of their shutdowns; train paths are planned to optimize track usage; constraints are managed; and the overall capacity is monitored and planned with a focus on identifying where in the chain the next level of improvement projects are needed to maximize capacity.

HVCCC has been a data-driven organization from day one and, over time, increasingly sophisticated decision support tools have been applied to the task of optimizing both the day-to-day planning and the strategic planning of the coal chain.

The centralized oversight and planning effectively allows more sales with asset efficiency in mind; thus minimizing the cost per tonne and increasing the value from existing assets.

What can we learn?

Important and widely applicable lessons emerge from the Hunter Valley Coal Chain:

- There is potential for using shared supply chains to reduce the cost to serve and more fully utilize assets and minimize environmental impact.

- Companies can still compete in the market and differentiate on the front end of their business, while coordinating their supply chain activity for efficiency at the back end.

- The HVCCC has become skilled at identifying and focusing on the key system constraints – there are many operations in resources, and beyond, where this tight focus could lift performance.

- The optimal 'system' result is invariably superior to the sum of the best 'subsystem' results. While we operate in silos, and lose sight of the overall system, we sacrifice efficiency.

Points of view

1 Understanding the target customer intimately and shaping the killer *customer value proposition* are key to developing winning new business models.

2 Current new models are typically emerging where technology trends and shifting market needs intersect.

3 'Networks-of-networks' (of all varieties) and sharing assets in an orderly way for mutual benefit can create step-change scale and cost efficiencies.

4 Are our strategic opportunities inhibited by thinking only within the constraints of our current network? The digitized era opens up a plethora of new opportunities outside its constraints.

5   Are there assets in the business that are under-utilized? Are there new business model options beyond our own four walls that can be leveraged?

6   The management of sensitive data within the protocols of a 'lead box' can open the door to shared supply chains, hubs and much wider visibility for forecasting and planning.

7   Closed-loop supply chains will increase in number as major corporations pursue a sustainable future in the vacuum left by governments around the world.

8   Life is easier, and relationships are more sustainable, if client and logistics providers are generally aligned. And RFPs and contracts need to reflect the real dynamics of the business. Get below the averages!

9   3PLs will always under-deliver on innovation if they are being measured and rewarded only on cost and reliability. Give them a chance to prove they can deliver innovative value-adding methods to the business, for mutual benefit. And don't underestimate what a 3PL can tell you about your own business!

Kick-start your thinking

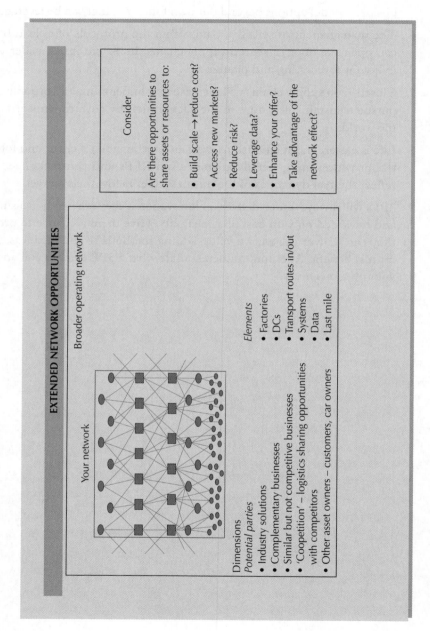

EXTENDED NETWORK OPPORTUNITIES

Your network

Broader operating network

Dimensions
Potential parties
- Industry solutions
- Complementary businesses
- Similar but not competitive businesses
- 'Coopetition' – logistics sharing opportunities with competitors
- Other asset owners – customers, car owners

Elements
- Factories
- DCs
- Transport routes in/out
- Systems
- Data
- Last mile

Consider

Are there opportunities to share assets or resources to:

- Build scale → reduce cost?
- Access new markets?
- Reduce risk?
- Leverage data?
- Enhance your offer?
- Take advantage of the network effect?

CHAPTER 11

Transformation delivered

With all its moving parts: one step back; two steps forward

It's not the strongest that survive, it's not the smartest that survive, it's the most adaptive that survive . . . We are in the middle of a giant adaptation challenge.

—Thomas Friedman, July 2018[1]

The forces driving change

The necessity to keep pace with changes in the operating environment has never been greater. And the supply chains running through our businesses are at the forefront.

In the markets they serve, customer expectations have been reset. The leaders in e-commerce and omni-channel retail are breaking through the barriers of the last-mile delivery challenge: lead times are faster, more predictable and order progress is more visible. The bar has been raised and the higher expectations are passing along the chain to suppliers and diffusing to other industries.

Channel relationships are also changing. Where intermediaries could add value by positioning product closer to the customer and create scale and choice through range and aggregations, these benefits can now often be achieved digitally through buying platforms and large online retailers. Wholesale and distribution business models are increasingly being disintermediated. Customers, whether consumer or industrial, are becoming more comfortable with direct relationships with suppliers.

Expectations around sustainability and ethical procurement have been building and spreading wider across demographic segments, business partners and government buyers. And manufacturers are increasingly under pressure to take responsibility for the full life cycle of their products, including disposal or recycling at the end.

And, after food quality and substitution scandals in China and food safety issues across the world, risk mitigation and provenance assurances have risen in importance. And the interaction between business, consumers and communities is called into question more often – with the social licence to operate at risk when business practices and community standards fail to align.

For those planning the supply chain, the geographic shifts in both demand and supply have been significant in recent years. Asian consumption is growing faster than other regions and less disparity in supply economics (along with the occasional trade war) is pulling manufacturing closer to the market for many categories.

These trends sit over the top of some others that we now take for granted. Globalization, while going through a difficult period, is basically assumed as the trading model. And the by-product of it, commoditization – the driving down of the cost and prices of key essentials over time (the Walmart effect) – is similarly assumed.

And, of course, the digital revolution is impacting all aspects of business, both directly and indirectly.

Indirectly, the availability and low cost of accessing software and computing power have lowered the barriers to entry in many industries. Smaller businesses are able to compete and start-ups can have an impact in industries that were once inaccessible without scale. Essentially, there are now more competitors than ever before and they are often more nimble – being unencumbered by legacy organization structures and mindsets. Some have called this influx of new influences the 'democratization' of the supply chain.

On the inside of established enterprises, we are becoming aware, in this context, of the need to develop new capabilities faster than ever before to keep abreast.

We have discussed many of the digital capabilities in previous chapters, but we'll list them in one place below. Essentially, these tools and capabilities are shifting us closer and closer to operating the supply chain in real time.

Digital capabilities impacting the supply chain include:

- analytics and optimization-based decision making;
- artificial intelligence (AI) and machine learning;
- IoT driven, end-to-end visibility;
- robotics and automation;
- 3D-printing and customized manufacturing;
- blockchain-based efficiency, security, traceability;
- extended and integrated data networks;
- real-time mobile communication tools;
- and – the next generation of tools.

It is clear that none of the market trends discussed above, or the digital trends listed here, operates in isolation. They are interdependent and the combined effect is an amplification of impact.

This is the background to what has become a pressing need to transform our businesses and institutions in line with the expected demands in the third decade of the 21st century.

One thing we do know from experience is that the type and scale of change needed will not be easy. And, in some cases, it will be necessary to take a backward step, clear the decks and then move forward with purpose. This path will not be embraced easily by enterprises with timid leadership and an eye only to the stock market.

Transformation in two parts

So, where do we start?

For established enterprises, there is an incumbent business model and a supply chain arrangement that has served us well in the past, and may still be doing so. It is built on known markets, established products and recognized ways of arranging resources to serve customers and compete. While we are looking to take advantage of new digital capabilities and to respond to changing expectations of the customers within those markets, we must also be careful to protect, and to continue to leverage, what is working.

The approach here is what could be called 'incremental transformation'. We are refining the supply chain in the context of the current business model and making it fit for the future. As we saw in the last chapter, the risk here comes from new business models that do a better job of delivering value to our customers than we do. And hence the early chapters of this book are clearly focusing on breaking up our current customers into manageable segments based on common evaluations of value and then focusing intently on defining strategies and internal capabilities that line up with each segment's underlying needs.

Within the context of rising expectations, especially around speed and ease, this is likely to look different than it would have 10 years ago. And this means that it is also likely that there will be new digital tools needed to meet those expectations. But all that we have learnt suggests that the most dangerous position to take is the 'one-size-fits-all' approach; because this will leave all of the customers who do not fit the universal value proposition exposed to better offers!

And this cannot be a one-off exercise. As the environment changes, strategies and resources will need to be refined and recalibrated to keep 'current business' in synch with the market.

Beyond the current business model, however, there also needs to be a parallel focus on more radical options for the future. The shifting operating environment throws up breakthrough opportunities as well as disruptive risks. And both need to be continually scanned to ensure that the enterprise survives and thrives. This is the world of supplier-led innovation: better solutions to customer problems; new markets or channels; and new business models. What is common to the incremental transformation position, though, is that more radical options still require the same intense focus on creating customer value; and strategies and internal capabilities will need to be carefully aligned to be able to deliver that value.

These two versions of transformation are depicted in Figure 11.1. We consider that this dual focus is the way to achieve a more adaptive, and thus sustainable, set of supply chains and business models.

Allocating resources to transformation efforts

Many of the organizations we encounter are in some stage of transformation; or at least have a team focused on innovation. One of the difficulties they face is how to allocate resources and how to define the scope

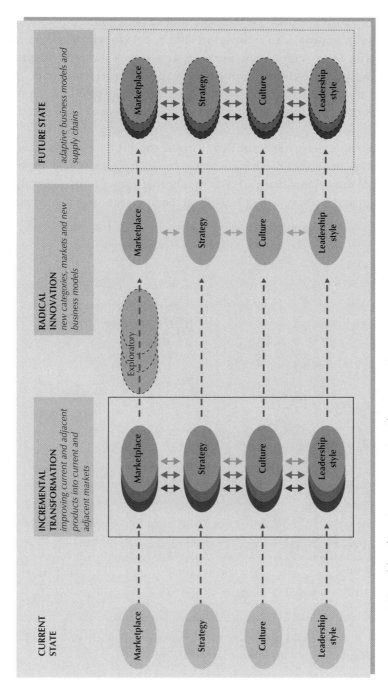

FIGURE 11.1 ◆ Transiting from 'current state' to 'future state'

and focus of those resources. A valuable tool to help guide this thinking is the portfolio approach to innovation shown below, which adapts the Ansoff Matrix for a slightly new purpose. It assumes the type of transformation approach outlined above and requires leaders to decide the proportion of their innovation/transformation team to focus on the various aspects of future-building activity.[2] This portfolio approach is depicted in Figure 11.2.

An important perspective on how a team should be configured and guided to work in each of these focus zones comes from the *design thinking* movement discussed in Chapter 2. The insight that comes through strongly is that design and innovation rely heavily on the intersection of two types of

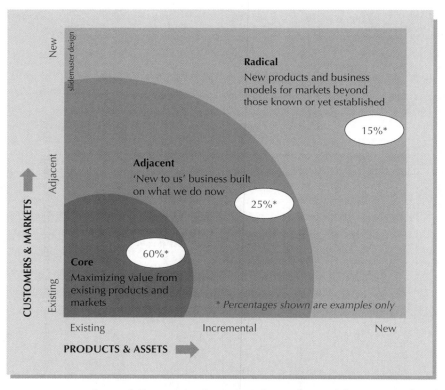

FIGURE 11.2 ◆ A portfolio approach to transformation (with an example of resources allocated across the innovation portfolio)

Source: Based on Managing your innovations portfolio, *Harvard Business Review* p. 69, May 2012

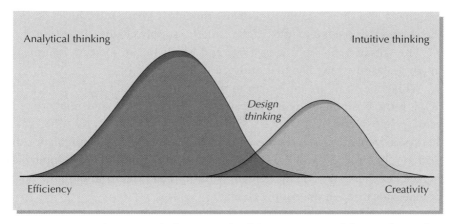

Analytical thinking

Intuitive thinking

Design thinking

Efficiency

Creativity

FIGURE 11.3 ◆ The two mindsets required in any successful transformation program

Source: Based on *The Design of Business* by Roger Martin (Harvard Business Press, 2009). Figure 2.1, p. 54

thinking: analytical thinking drawing on logic and analysis of the past; and intuitive thinking, drawing on creativity and seeing patterns. Roger Martin transferred this concept to business more generally, reminding us that analytical thinking helps us manage and improve the current 'algorithm' or method of operating, but that both mindsets were needed in order to identify and craft the next business 'heuristic'. The illustration above captures this important message, see Figure 11.3. The problem is that in most mature organizations the mindset on the left dominates.

This has important implications for the selection of people to work on new directions, the way they are measured and the ability of the organization to continue to adapt over time. Successful transformation and successful business in an era of ongoing change requires more than an operational mindset – it requires a mix of both analytical and intuitive thinking inside the enterprise.

Visualizing the supply chains of the future

We have explored in general terms the drivers for change and how leaders might structure their thinking and their resources to respond. Inevitably, this has been broader than the supply chain, but we now want to get a little more pragmatic and draw together the many threads we have introduced across the chapters to paint a picture of the *adaptive* supply chains of the future.

The components, and a possible end result for an *industrial business*, might look something like that outlined in Figure 11.4.

While new tools are important to the picture, it is only in the context of helping the business to deliver an array of differentiated and finely tuned value propositions to customers. On the supply-side, similarly differentiated procurement strategies are used to maximize the value suppliers can bring to the business and the next generation of digital tools are employed to facilitate fast and easy engagement with suppliers and to smooth the flow of materials through the supply chain.

Two barriers to successful transformation

As we have intimated in earlier chapters of this book, the real enablers or barriers to successful transition to a desired future state come from within the enterprise itself – we call it organizational culture. Indeed, it is our experience that up to 60 per cent of *intended strategy*, as written down in business plans, is never delivered because of internal organizational resistance to change. The most important message we hope to bring to the table in this regard is that building subcultures that are aligned to the desired end result significantly improves the chances of success. So, to drive the radical part of the transformation agenda, we need to build an innovation (D) subculture. To take advantage of a fast-growing, fast-changing segment of the market, we need a dynamic (P) subculture. And to build and protect relationships with our long-standing, loyal customers, we need a collaborative subculture (I).

The second major barrier to supply chain transformation is, on the surface of it, very mundane! But this is the most significant practical barrier we see standing in the way of serious adoption of digitally driven, supply chain developments for very many organizations. It is Master Data!

In all our years of consulting and working inside organizations, we have seen many, many large operations that are not on top of their Master Data. Indeed, many of them cannot even provide the basics, as listed in Figure 11.5, in an otherwise consistent and repeatable format. This is the underpinning definitional data that makes it clear if product 'A' made in the

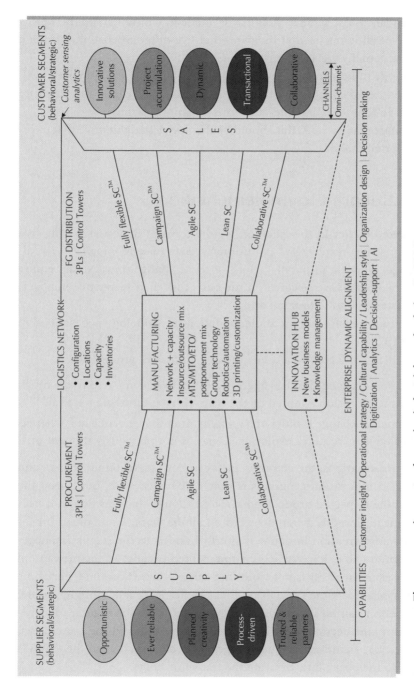

FIGURE 11.4 ◆ **The many moving parts of superior industrial supply chains (to 2030)**

German plant is the same as product 'B' made in China; carries the weight and cube of all items; or that indicates that five different customer trading names are actually the same customer.

This type of information is core to getting full value from analytics, AI, automated decision support and network modeling. It is also the structure on which IoT, automation and customized manufacturing rely.

In many organizations, this should be the first digital initiative that paves the way for all others!

From blueprint to implementation

As indicated earlier in this chapter, we see transformation as having two dimensions, i.e. *incremental* evolutionary change; and *supplier-led* radical change, working in parallel. Both of these change dimensions require focused teams that are selected on the basis that their respective mindsets are consistent with the task in hand.

This dual transformation implementation methodology is described in Figure 11.6.

Clearly the differences between the two 'mindsets' are as follows:

1 Incremental change has less aggressive objectives compared to the much more radical vision adopted by the team driving futuristic renewal.

2 Incremental change is more of a refinement of the current state, whereas radical change requires exploring scenarios not previously thought of.

In large organizations, the common factor in both incremental change and supplier-led innovation programs is that, to be successful, both need the buy-in of the impacted group. We have seen though that this does not necessarily mean that this group needs to do all the work. If the blueprint for a major transformation initiative is simply handed to the regular management team, it will risk never being implemented because of the pressure of 'business as usual'. This is not work that can be carried out on a part-time basis. It needs full-time specialized focus to get it up and running, to the point where it can be successfully migrated across to the regular management team and become core business. We have reached the conclusion, therefore, that significant change programs need a version of the 'SWAT' team to do the heavy lifting during the transition stage.

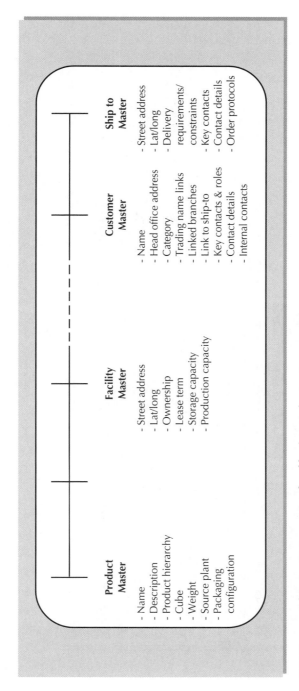

Product Master

- Name
- Description
- Product hierarchy
- Cube
- Weight
- Source plant
- Packaging configuration

Facility Master

- Street address
- Lat/long
- Ownership
- Lease term
- Storage capacity
- Production capacity

Customer Master

- Name
- Head office address
- Category
- Trading name links
- Linked branches
- Link to ship-to
- Key contacts & roles
- Contact details
- Internal contacts

Ship to Master

- Street address
- Lat/long
- Delivery requirements/ constraints
- Key contacts
- Contact details
- Order protocols

FIGURE 11.5 ◆ **Master Data – example of basic requirements**

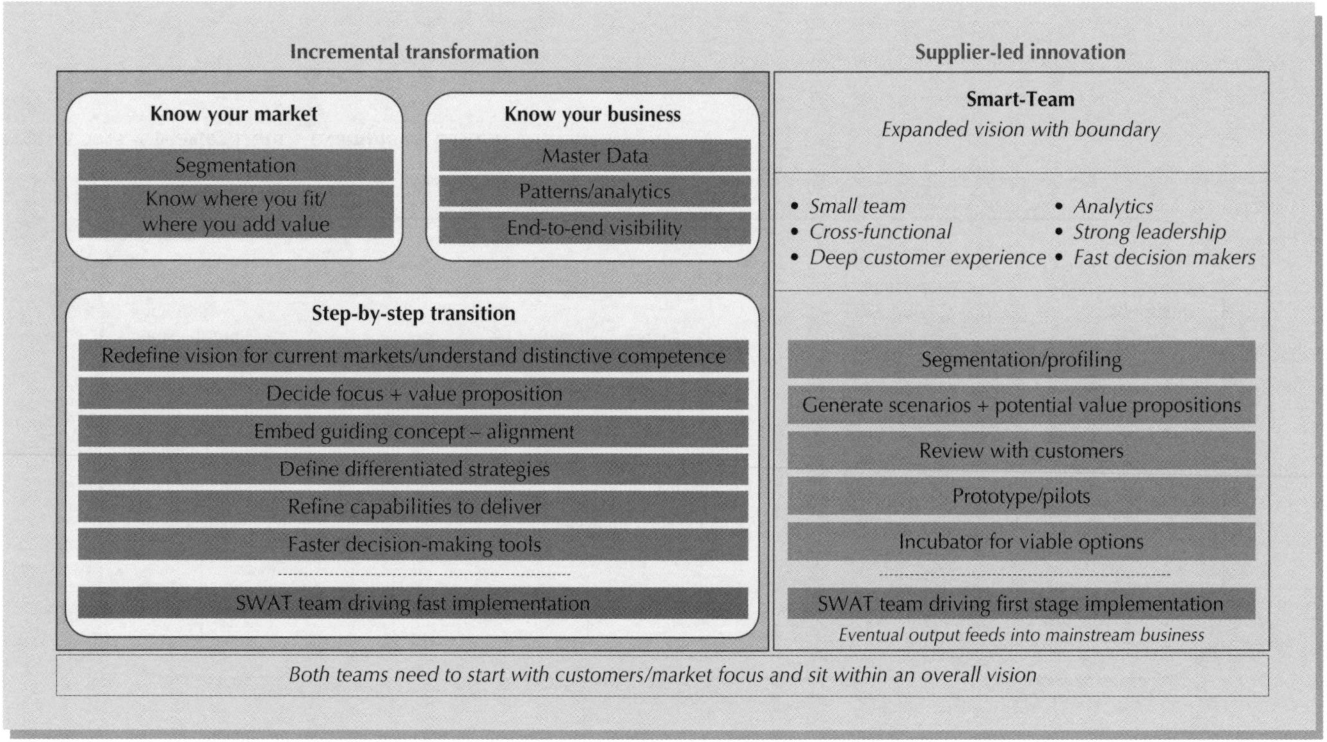

Incremental transformation

Know your market

Segmentation

Know where you fit/
where you add value

Know your business

Master Data

Patterns/analytics

End-to-end visibility

Step-by-step transition

Redefine vision for current markets/understand distinctive competence

Decide focus + value proposition

Embed guiding concept – alignment

Define differentiated strategies

Refine capabilities to deliver

Faster decision-making tools

SWAT team driving fast implementation

Supplier-led innovation

Smart-Team

Expanded vision with boundary

- Small team
- Cross-functional
- Deep customer experience
- Analytics
- Strong leadership
- Fast decision makers

Segmentation/profiling

Generate scenarios + potential value propositions

Review with customers

Prototype/pilots

Incubator for viable options

SWAT team driving first stage implementation

Eventual output feeds into mainstream business

Both teams need to start with customers/market focus and sit within an overall vision

FIGURE 11.6 ◆ **Multiple-team approach to successful transformation**

But this additional resource should not, and cannot, replace the 'buy-in' of the teams that will eventually manage and run new operations. Our own experience points to the early involvement of affected managers in developing new strategies and the change roadmap as important components of buy-in. This is supported by our colleague Ivana Crestani's research,[3] who highlights the role of 'feeling valued' in change programs. She shows that change that is seemingly imposed is what most staff object to; and that involvement in new directions, if handled well, can be very energizing. Once again, it is the 'people' part of the equation that is the key!

Bringing it all together

You should now be able to see our methodology in full light – we have taken you, the reader, through a journey using a number of critical frameworks and filters, as summarized in Figure 11.7. What we are hoping is that you will be able to view your own business through these lenses and that they will help you derive a customized solution that is appropriate for your particular situation and market positioning. We are confident if you embrace this 'outside-in' formula you won't be too far off the mark, which is *delivering sustained performance in volatile markets.*

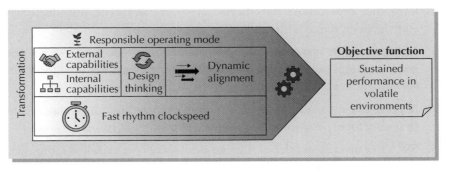

FIGURE 11.7 ◆ **Frameworks – the new supply chain imperative**

A final word

The two pivotal ingredients of success we see for supply chains of tomorrow are:

1 *Precision* in the way each supply chain is configured to best align with a particular customer segment, thereby ensuring optimal use of resources for the impact achieved in the marketplace; and

2 Fast *rhythms* (clockspeed) across the entire enterprise in order to satisfy customers' increased expectations and to out-decision competitors.

And as we indicated right at the start of this book, it will come down to one key area of focus: the critical interface between the way we think about our customers, and how we translate that into action albeit with the assistance of all the digital tools available to us.

Think customer: act digital

Points of view

1. Future supply chains need to be dynamic and adaptive; versus static and steadfast, to cope with a more volatile and fast changing operating environment.

2. Customer expectations have been reset by e-commerce, but this influence is spreading to wider industry.

3. Multiple supply chains provide built-in flexibility - meaning we do not need to change our complete supply chain structure every time the market shifts, i.e. achieving *flex* without the usual cost penalty.

4. A portfolio approach to transformation creates boundary and corresponding focus, and forces a conscious allocation of resources.

5. SWAT teams can accelerate change across large organizations, but they need to also manage the transition to the local team.

6. And finally, have we reached a stage where transformation is now every senior supply chain leader's 'day job'?

Kick-start your thinking

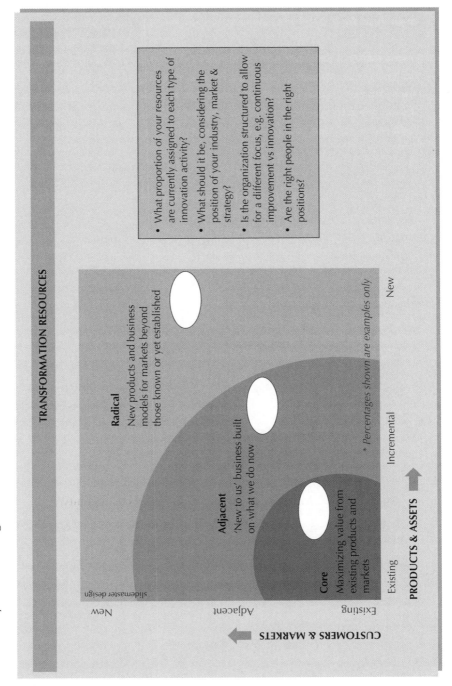

TRANSFORMATION RESOURCES

- What proportion of your resources are currently assigned to each type of innovation activity?
- What should it be, considering the position of your industry, market & strategy?
- Is the organization structured to allow for a different focus, e.g. continuous improvement vs innovation?
- Are the right people in the right positions?

Radical
New products and business models for markets beyond those known or yet established

Adjacent
'New to us' business built on what we do now

Core
Maximizing value from existing products and markets

* Percentages shown are examples only

Existing   Incremental   New

PRODUCTS & ASSETS

CUSTOMERS & MARKETS

New   Adjacent   Existing

slidemaster design

Endnotes

A word about the title

1 Gattorna, J. (2015) *Dynamic Supply Chains,* 3rd edn. Harlow: FT Publishing.

Preface

1 Christopher, M. and Holweg, M. (2017) 'Supply chain 2.0 revisited: a framework for managing volatility-induced risk in the supply chain', *International Journal of Physical Distribution & Logistics Management,* Vol. 47, No. 1, pp. 2–17.

Chapter 1

1 Taken from his album of the same name (1993).
2 Ibid.
3 This is a major theme in a new book under preparation by Steve O'Sullivan, with the working title: *Aligning Business Strategy and Supply Chain Tactics: Responding Faster to Supply Chain Disruption,* due to be published by Kogan Page, London, in 2019.
4 'How the US-led Trade Wars Imperil the Global Economy', Knowledge@Wharton, 10 July 2018.
5 Brown, R. (2018) 'Trade Wars Will Disrupt Supply Chains, Slow Global Growth', Forbes.com, 19 July.
6 Giles, C. (2017) 'UK-EU supply chains begin to break amid Brexit trade fears', Bloomberg, 5 November.
7 Ibid.
8 Lewis, M., *The Fifth Risk.* New York: W.W. Norton & Co., p. 75.
9 Ibid. p. 76.
10 Foroohar, R. (2018) 'Corporate elites overlook deglobalisation', *Australian Financial Review,* 16 October p. 31.
11 Ibid.
12 'The Effects of Climate Change on Cargill's Supply Chain', HBS Rules, posted 4 November 2017.
13 Molin, A. (2018) 'Ikea sets new climate goals to tackle unsustainable consumption', Bloomberg.com, 7 June.
14 Toor, A. (2017) 'Apple, Google, Microsoft, and Amazon will continue to fight climate change despite Trump's order', The Verge, 31 March.
15 Kell, J. (2016) 'Here's how Adidas plans to drastically cut down on waste', Fortune.com, 14 April.

16 Eccles, R., Ioannou, I. and Serafeim, G. (2012) 'Is sustainability now the key to corporate success?' The Guardian.com, 7 January.

17 Friedman, T.L. (2016) in conversation with Edward Teller, in *Thank You For Being Late*. London: Allen Lane-Penguin Random House.

18 Friedman draws on Edward Teller for this assessment.

19 Ashby, W.R. (1956) *An Introduction to Cybernetics*. London: Chapman & Hall; and by the same author, *Design for a Brain*, 2nd edn. New York, NY: John Wiley.

20 Ganapathy, V. 'Case Study: The Uberisation of Supply Chain', *SAMVAD: SIBM Pune Research Journal*, Vol. X, June 2016, pp. 26–31.

21 Ryder, G. speaking at the Fortune TIME Global Forum, Rome, 2 December 2016.

22 Ibid.

23 Bozeman, D. in a panel discussion at the CSCMP Edge Conference, Nashville, 1 October 2018.

24 Quesenberry, K.A. (2016) 'Social Media is too Important to be Left to the Marketing Department', *Harvard Business Review*, April.

25 Christopher, M. and Holweg, M. (2017) 'Supply chain 2.0 revisited: a framework for managing volatility-induced risk in the supply chain', *International Journal of Physical Distribution & Logistics Management*, Vol. 47, No. 1, pp. 2–17.

26 Christopher, M. and Holweg, M. (2011) 'Supply Chain 2.0: managing supply chains in the era of turbulence', *International Journal of Physical Distribution & Logistics Management*, Vol. 41, No. 1, p. 65.

27 Op. cit. p. 11.

28 Op. cit. p. 13.

29 Op. cit. p. 15.

30 Michelman, P. editor in chief, (2018) *MIT Sloan Management Review*, in his editorial 'The high cost of actions we don't take', Vol. 60, No. 1, Fall.

31 'How Zipline is using emerging technology to save lives', *Supply Chain Quarterly*, 2 October 2018. See post dated 5 October 2018. Available at: https://www.supplychainquarterly.com/news/20181002-how-zipline-is-using-emerging-technology-to-save-lives/-using-emerging-technology-to-save-lives/?utm_medium=email&utm_campaign.

32 Ibid.

33 Ibid.

34 Samit, J. (2018) '5 ways augmented reality is disrupting the supply chain', Fortune.com, 1 March.

35 Op. cit. p. 2.

Chapter 2

1 Martin, R. (2009) *The Design of Business: Why Design Thinking is the Next Competitive Advantage*. Boston, MA: Harvard Business Press.

2 Norman Chorn was a partner in the Gattorna Strategy consulting business from 1989, with particular expertise in cultural capability.

3 Chorn, N.H., Myres, K.L. and Gattorna, J.L. (1990) 'Bridging Strategy Formulation and Implementation', unpublished paper presented to the 10th Annual International Conference of the Strategic Management Society, Stockholm.

4 See Adler, G., Fordham, M. and Read, H. (eds) (1971) *The Collected Works of CG Jung Volume 6: Psychological Types* (translated by R.F.C. Hull). Ewing, NJ: Bollingen Series 20, Princeton University Press.

5   Adizes, I. (1979) *How to Solve the Mismanagement Crisis,* 1st printing. Dow-Jones-Irwin; (1985) 5th printing. Santa Monica, CA: Adizes Institute.
6   Faust, G.W., president, Faust Management Corporation, Poway, CA (previously president of the Adizes Institute).
7   Op. cit., Adizes, I. (1979).
8   Cameron, K. and Quinn, R. (2011) *Diagnosing and Changing Organizational Culture: Based on the Competing Values Framework.* San Francisco: John Wiley and Sons. By Cameron, K.S. and Quinn, R.E.
9   Mandela, N. (1995) *Long Walk to Freedom.* Boston: Back Bay Books. The autobiography of Nelson Mandela, p. 94.
10 Op. cit., Martin, I. (2009).
11 Each chapter will have some challenging questions for the readers to answer and apply to their own organization, immediately.

Chapter 3

1   Neuschel, R.P. (1967) 'Physical distribution – forgotten frontier', *Harvard Business Review,* March–April, Vol. 45, No. 2, pp. 125–34.
2   Stolle, J.F. (1967) 'How to manage physical distribution', *Harvard Business Review,* July–August, Vol. 45, No. 4, pp. 93–100.
3   The Coefficient of Variation (CoV) is a measure of relative variability. It is the ratio of the standard deviation to the mean.
4   Fisher, M.L. (1997) 'What is the right supply chain for your product?', *Harvard Business Review,* Vol. 75, No. 2, March–April, pp. 105–16.
5   Lee, H.L. (2002) 'Aligning supply chain strategies with product uncertainties', *California Management Review,* Vol. 44, No. 3, Spring, pp. 105–19.
6   In their book, Knut Alicke *et al.* continually refer to 'supply chain segmentation' and, at other times, use the phrase 'supply chain differentiation'; this is confusing because they are very different. See Alicke, K. and Forsting, M. in Protopappa-Sieke, M. and Thonemann, U.W. (eds) (2017) *Supply Chain Segmentation.* Springer International Publishing AG, Ch. 2.
7   This case drew on the following primary sources:
    Whiting, S.M. (2006) unpublished MSc thesis, Cranfield School of Management, Cranfield University; and Coltman, T., Gattorna, J. and Whiting, S. (2010) 'Realigning Service Operations Strategy at DHL Express', *Interfaces,* Vol. 40, No. 3, May–June, pp. 175–83.
8   For a full description of this coding system, please refer to Figures 2.2 and 2.3 and associated narrative in Chapter 2.
9   Kraljic, P. (1983) 'Purchasing must become supply management', *Harvard Business Review,* Sep–Oct, pp. 109–17.
10 Bueler, D. (2006) 'Supplier segmentation – the tool for differentiation and results', a paper presented at the 91st Annual International Supply Chain Management Conference, Minneapolis, MN, 7–10 May 2006.
11 *Sources:* 1. Gattorna, J. (2015) *Dynamic Supply Chains.* 3rd edn. Harlow: FT Publishing, pp. 384–5; 2. Case study: *JBS-traceability and collaboration to secure deforestation-free supply,* CDP Report on JBS, 1 January 2010; refer also to: https://www.cdp.net/en/articles/forests/case-study-jbs.

Chapter 4

1   This term was coined by Annette Clayton, CSCO, Schneider Electric, in 2012.
2   Sometimes called Project Supply Chains.

3 Latham, Sir Michael (1994) 'Constructing the Team: Final Report of the Government/Industry Review of Procurement and Contractual Arrangements in the UK Construction Industry'. London: HMSO. Department of Trade and Industry (1998) 'Rethinking Construction: The Report of the Construction Task Force' (known as the Egan Report). London: HMSO.
4 Wolstenholme, A., *et al.* (2009) 'Never waste a good crisis: a review of progress since Rethinking Construction and thoughts for our future'. London: Constructing Excellence.
5 Schneider Electric started this review in its Pacific Region in about 2015 when the shift from products to projects became very evident.

Chapter 5

1 Minto, B. (1987) *The Pyramid Principle: Logic in Writing and Thinking*. Pitman Publishing.
2 Vaughan, J., senior news writer (2015) 'The Weather Co. buy boosts IBM big data analytics push'. Available at: https://searchdatamanagement.techtarget.com/opinion/The-Weather-Co-buy-boosts-IBM-big-data-analytics-push/.
3 Lewis, M. (2018) *The Fifth Risk*. New York: W.W. Norton & Company, p. 156.
4 Ibid. p. 158.
5 Ibid. p. 163.
6 Snowden, D. and Boone, M. (2007) 'The Leaders Framework', *Harvard Business Review*, November (categorizing decisions).
7 Kahneman, D. (2011) *Thinking Fast and Slow*. London: Penguin.
8 See, for example, Tversky, A. and Kahneman, D. (1981) 'The framing of decisions and the psychology of choice', *Science*, 211, No. 4481, pp. 453–58.
9 By Gattorna Alignment Pty Ltd and Solvoyo.

Chapter 6

1 Christopher, M. (2016) *Logistics and Supply Chain Management*. 5th edn. Pearson, p. 58.
2 A quote during discussion with John Morschel, CEO LLC, when acquiring MLC in the mid-1980s.
3 See: https://www.statista.com/statistics/379046/worldwide-retail-e-commerce-sales. Accessed: 19 October 2018.
4 FY 2017–8, Sainsbury's Annual Report.
5 This case study draws on the excellent article by SupplyChainBrain and their video interview with Phil Hull, distribution director of Sainsbury's Argos: SupplyChainBrain, 'How Argos Transformed its Store Network for the Omnichannel', 19 December 2017. Available at: https://www.supplychainbrain.com/articles/27350-how-argos-transformed-its-store-network-for-the-omnichannel.
6 Ibid.
7 Argos and LLamasoft received the 2016 European Supply Chain Excellence Awards in the category of Supply Chain Strategy Design and Innovation and were runners up in the CSCMP's 2017 Supply Chain Innovation Award.

Chapter 7

1 Schein, E.H. (1988) *Organizational Culture and Leadership*. Jossey-Bass Publishers, p. 9.

2 Brooks, J.S. and Jean-Marie Gaetane (2007) 'Black Leadership, White Leadership: Race and Race Relations in an Urban High School', *Journal of Educational Administration,* Vol. 45, No. 6, p. 758.

3 Ibid.

4 Ibid. pp. 758–9.

5 Hofstede, G. and Hofstede, G.J. (2005) *Cultures and Organisations: Software of the Mind.* 2nd edn. New York, NY: McGraw Hill.

6 Charan, R. (2013) 'You Can't be a Wimp; make the tough calls', an interview in *Harvard Business Review,* November, pp. 73–8.

7 Ibid. p. 74.

8 The Myers–Briggs Type Indicator (MBTI™) is the original and best known instrument for measuring leadership style. Like our Dynamic Alignment™ model, it is based on Jungian psychology.

9 Avolio, B.J. and Wernsing, T.S. (2008) 'Practicing Authentic Leadership', *Pursuing Human Flourishing,* Chapter 9, p. 148. Praeger.

10 The All Blacks Rugby Union team is the national rugby team for New Zealand; they are the current World Champions in Rugby Union and widely regarded as the best team of any code in the world.

11 In Kerr, J. (2013) *Legacy.* London: Constable, p. 123.

12 George, B. (2007) *True North: Discover your Authentic Leadership.* Jossey Bass, p. x.

13 De Crespigny, R. (2018) *FLY!: Life Lessons from the Cockpit of QF32.* Australia: Viking Books.

14 Ibid. pp. 1–2.

15 Ibid. p. 94.

16 Ibid. p. 195.

17 Ibid.

18 Benton, D.A. and Wright-Ford, K. (2017) *The Leadership Mind Switch.* New York, NY: McGraw Hill Education, p. 2.

19 Kerr, J. (2013) *LEGACY: What the All Blacks Can Teach Us About the Business of Life.* UK: Constable, p. vii.

20 Ibid. p. 10.

21 Ibid. p. 13.

22 Ibid. p. 24.

23 Ibid. p. 29.

Chapter 8

1 Westerman, G. (2016) 'Why Digital Transformation Needs a Heart', *MIT Sloan Management Review.* Reprint #58130. Available at: http://mitsmr.com/2cmzay6.

2 Vincent, J. (2018) 'Welcome to the Automated Warehouse of the Future', The Verge, 8 May. Available at: https://www.theverge.com/2018/5/8/17331250/automated-warehouses-jobs-ocado-andover-amazon.

3 'Woolworths to take wraps off automated warehouse', *Australian Financial Review,* 23 April 2018. Available at: https://www.afr.com/business/retail/woolworths-to-take-wraps-off-automated-warehouse-20180423-h0z452.

4 Moore, A.W. (2016) 'Predicting a Future Where the Future is Routinely Predicted', *MIT Sloan Management Review.* Reprint #58108. Available at: http://mitsmr.com/2czxOSY.

5 McKinsey Global Institute (2017) 'Artificial Intelligence: The Next Digital Frontier', discussion paper, June. Available at: https://www.mckinsey.com/~/media/McKinsey/Industries/

Advanced%20Electronics/Our%20Insights/How%20artificial%20intelligence%20can%20 deliver%20real%20value%20to%20companies/MGI-Artificial-Intelligence-Discussion-paper.ashx.

6 Ibid.

7 Ibid.

8 The Ptolemy Project, UC Berkeley. Available at: https://ptolemy.berkeley.edu/projects/cps/.

9 See: https://www.trackster.tech/.

10 Birdoo is a digital application specifically designed for the poultry industry, worldwide. The team, led by Dr Mahender Singh, consists of 20 senior leaders, management graduates and engineers from top institutes in India, such as IIT, NIT, BITS, DTU and SIOM. The team has diverse experience across sectors such as livestock, IT services, e-commerce, manufacturing, logistics, retail, pharma and FMCG.

11 Taken from KNEX Prospectus, dated 21 November 2018.

12 Aglive and TBSx3 have collaborated on developing this application.

13 Bloomberg Technology (Olga Kharif) (2016) 'Wal-Mart Tackles Food Safety with Trial of Blockchain', 18 November. Available at: https://www.bloomberg.com/news/articles/ 2016-11-18/wal-mart-tackles-food-safety-with-test-of-blockchain-technology.

14 Eric Schmidt, executive chairman, Google, USA, at World Economic Forum Davos, 2015.

15 Data extracted from Walmart's 2018 Annual Report.

16 CEO Letter, 2018 Walmart Annual Report, p. 1.

17 Nash, K.S. (2018) 'Walmart-led blockchain effort seeks farm-to-grocery-aisle view of food supply chain', CIO, *Wall St Journal*, 25 June, p. 1.

18 O'Keefe, B. (2017) 'What's driving Walmart's Digital focus? Paranoia, top exec says', *Fortune magazine*, 7 December, p. 2.

19 Capgemini Consulting, 'Walmart: Where Digital Meets Physical', 3 August 2015. Available at: https://www.capgemini.com/resources/walmart-where-digital-meets-physical/.

Chapter 9

1 Friedman, T. (2016) *Thank You For Being Late*. UK: Allen Lane – Penguin Random House, p. 36.

2 Adapted from Fine, C.H. (1998) *Clockspeed: Winning Industry Control in the Age of Temporary Advantage*. Cambridge, MA: Basic Books, p. 146.

3 Op. cit.

4 Khan, O. (2019) *Product Design and the Supply Chain: Competing Through Design*. Great Britain: Kogan Page, p. 31.

5 Blackburn, J.D., Guide, D.R. Jr., Souza, G.C. and Van Wassenhove, L.N. (2004) 'Reverse Supply Chains for Commercial Returns', *California Management Review, Berkeley*, 46.2, pp. 6–22.

6 Conducted by Gattorna Alignment, in partnership with the client's modeling team and Solvoyo.

7 Op. cit, p. 71.

8 Rigby, D.K., Sutherland, J. and Noble, A. (2018) 'Agile Scale: how to go from a few teams to hundreds', *Harvard Business Review*, May–June, pp. 88–96.

9 Ibid. p. 90.

10 Press release, Siemens AG website, 1 August 2018.

11 Sourced from Gattorna (2015), pp. 426–31, following an earlier site visit to Inditex in La Coruña.

12 Bleeke, J.A. 'Peak Strategies' in *McKinsey Quarterly*, Spring 1989.

Chapter 10

1 Eyring, M., Johnson, M.W. and Nair, H. (2011) 'New Business Models in Emerging Markets', *Harvard Business Review,* January–February, p. 4.
2 Kavadias, S., Ladas, K. and Loch, C. (2016) 'The Transformative Business Model: How to tell if you have one', *Harvard Business Review,* October.
3 Ibid.
4 Osterwalder, A. and Pigneur, Y. (2010) *Business Model Generation.* Wiley.
5 Christensen, C.M., Bartman, T. and van Bever, D. (2016) 'The Hard Truth About Business Model Innovation', *MIT Sloan Magazine,* Fall Issue.
6 Gattorna, J. (2015) *Dynamic Supply Chains.* 3rd edn. Harlow: FT Publishing, pp. 477–82.
7 CSA was bought in 2017 by the global security company Prosegur, which operates under similar protocols.
8 Capgemini Consulting (2013) 'Global Supply Chain Towers'. Available at: https://www .capgemini.com/wp-content/uploads/2017/07/Global_Supply_Chain_Control_Towers.pdf.
9 Apple Inc, 'Environmental Responsibility Report', 2018 Progress Report, covering FY 2017, p. 20.
10 Ibid. p. 21.
11 Zeng, M. (2018) 'Alibaba and the Future of Business', *Harvard Business Review,* September–October.
12 Ibid.
13 Haier press release, 25 April 2018.
14 Presentation by Xiande Zhao, professor of operations and supply chain management at the China Europe International Business School (CEIBS), MGSM Lighthouse Lecture Series, Sydney, 10 October 2018.
15 Details of this new marketplace made available by permission of the owner, Nigel Johnson.

Chapter 11

1 Thomas Friedman, speaking at Fortune's Brainstorm Conference, July 2018. Available at: http://fortune.com/2018/07/18/thomas-friedman-climate-change-fortune-brainstorm-tech/.
2 Nagji, B. and Tuff, G. (2012) 'Managing your Innovation Portfolio', *Harvard Business Review* May.
3 Crestani, I. (2018) *Feeling Valued: The role of communication in preparing employees for change.* Unpublished PhD Thesis, Charles Stuart University, Australia.

Selected bibliography

Abrahamson, E. and Freedman, D.H. (2006) *A Perfect Mess: The Hidden Benefits of Disorder.* New York: Little, Brown and Company.

Belfiore, M. (2009) *The Department of Mad Scientists.* New York, NY: Harper.

Benton, D.A. and Wright-Ford, K. (2017) *The Leadership Mind Switch.* New York, NY: McGraw Hill Education.

Christopher, M. (2016) *Logistics and Supply Chain Management.* 5th edn. Pearson.

Chung, P. and Bowie, R. (2018) *DHL: From Start-up to Global Upstart.* Boston/Berlin: Walter de Gruyter Inc.

De Crespigny, R. (2018) *FLY! Life Lessons From the Cockpit of QF32.* Viking Australia.

Dobelli, R. (2014) *The Art of Thinking Clearly.* Sceptre.

Fine, C.H. (1998) *Clockspeed: Winning Industry Control in the Age of Temporary Advantage.* Cambridge, MA: Basic Books.

Friedman, T.L. (2017) *Thank You for Being Late: An Optimist's Guide to Thriving in the Age of Accelerations.* UK: Penguin Random House.

Hoffman, B.G. (2017) *RED Teaming: Transform Your Business by Thinking Like the Enemy.* UK: Piatkus.

Kahneman, D. (2011) *Thinking, Fast and Slow.* London: Penguin Books.

Khan, O. (2019) *Product Design and the Supply Chain: Competing Through Design.* London: Kogan Page.

Kerr, J. (2013) *Legacy: What the All Blacks Can Teach Us About the Business of Life.* London: Constable.

Lewis, M. (2017) *The Undoing Project.* New York: W.W. Norton & Company.

Lewis, M. (2018) *The Fifth Risk.* New York: W.W. Norton & Company.

Lynn, B.C. (2005) *End of the Line: The Rise and Coming Fall of the Global Corporation.* New York: Currency Doubleday.

Martin, R. (2009) 'The Design of Business: Why design thinking is the next competitive advantage', Boston, MA: Harvard Business Press.

McQueen, M. (2016) *Momentum: How to Build It, Keep It, or Get It Back.* Melbourne: John Wiley & Sons.

Protopappa-Sieke, M. and Thonemann, U.W. (eds) (2017) *Supply Chain Segmentation Best in Class Cases, Practical Insights and Foundations.* Switzerland: Springer International Publishing AG.

Rein, S. (2014) *The End of Cheap China.* New Jersey: John Wiley & Sons.

Sheffi, Y. with Blanco, E. (2018) *Balancing Green: When to Embrace Sustainability in a Business (and when not to).* Cambridge, MA: The MIT Press.

Simchi-Levi, D. (2010) *Operations Rules.* MIT Press.

Sundararajan, A. *The Sharing Economy, The End of Employment and the Rise of Crowd-Based Capitalism.* Cambridge, MA: The MIT Press.

Tao, T., de Cremer, D. and Wu, C. (2017) *Huawei: Leadership, Culture, and Connectivity.* New Delhi: Sage Publications India Pvt Ltd.

Tett, G. (2015) *The Silo Effect: Why Putting Everything in its Place Isn't Such a Bright Idea.* Great Britain: Little Brown.

Wolff, M. (2018) *Fire and Fury: Inside the Trump White House.* UK: Little, Brown.

Index